Franz Joseph and
Elisabeth

Franz Joseph and Elisabeth

The Last Great Monarchs of Austria-Hungary

KAREN OWENS

McFarland & Company, Inc., Publishers
Jefferson, North Carolina, and London

LIBRARY OF CONGRESS CATALOGUING-IN-PUBLICATION DATA

Owens, Karen (Karen B.)
    Franz Joseph and Elisabeth : the last great monarchs of Austria-Hungary / Karen Owens.
    p.   cm.
    Includes bibliographical references and index.

    ISBN 978-0-7864-7674-9
    softcover : acid free paper ∞

    1. Franz Joseph I, Emperor of Austria, 1830–1916. 2. Elisabeth, Empress, consort of Franz Joseph I, Emperor of Austria, 1837–1898. 3. Austria—Kings and rulers—Biography. 4. Empresses—Austria—Biography. 5. Austria—History—Franz Joseph I, 1848–1916. I. Title.
    DB87.O94 2014
    943.6'0440922—dc23
    [B]   2013041240

BRITISH LIBRARY CATALOGUING DATA ARE AVAILABLE

© 2014 Karen Owens. All rights reserved

No part of this book may be reproduced or transmitted in any form or by any means, electronic or mechanical, including photocopying or recording, or by any information storage and retrieval system, without permission in writing from the publisher.

On the cover: Emperor Franz Joseph I of Austria, detail of a print for the Vienna world's fair, 1873 (Library of Congress); Empress Elisabeth of Austria, ca. 1910–1915 (Library of Congress); Habsburg coat of arms

Manufactured in the United States of America

McFarland & Company, Inc., Publishers
  Box 611, Jefferson, North Carolina 28640
  www.mcfarlandpub.com

To the Owens family:

Eric Christopher Owens
Gordon Owens
Meade Owens
Caitlin Meade Owens
Karen Parker Owens

With special thanks to
Karen Parker's parents,
Gordon and Meade,
for the wonderful namesake honor

Contents

Preface 1

ONE. The New Emperor and Old Vienna 5
TWO. Revolutions 21
THREE. Franz Joseph 39
FOUR. Sisi 56
FIVE. The Newlyweds 68
SIX. The Royal Children 82
SEVEN. The Royal Mistress 99
EIGHT. Hungary 116
NINE. *Repräsentazions-pflicht:* "The duty of
    keeping up a fine front" 129
TEN. The Fates 141
ELEVEN. The Aging Emperor 155
TWELVE. Into History 166

Appendix A 175
Appendix B 177
Notes 178
References 186
Index 191

Preface

The reign of Franz Joseph represents an age of imperialism, liberalism and nationalism. Franz Joseph used his sovereignty as emperor of the most powerful country, Austria, and the most commanding dynasty, the Habsburg, to control or influence less powerful countries. Imperialism has been a common practice throughout the history of this world and his rule characterizes a time when monarchs extended their power and dominion through direct territorial acquisition or through politically astute marriages and by uniting the separate governments of the autonomous regions within their borders for the purpose of securing a single state. Over the course of Franz Joseph's reign, imperialism fueled liberal thinking and nationalist fervor. Italy and Germany, both of which were heterogeneous patchworks of independent states and principalities, and the Habsburg lands, such as Hungary and Bohemia, all had a desire to exert their greatness on the European global scene. Liberal ideas and nationalism led to the struggles of these Habsburg satellite nations searching for freedom and of Habsburg policies made to preserve the dynasty. When liberal ideas emerged, revolution, or at least an attempt at revolution, was inevitable and the Habsburg dynasty could not escape this trajectory.

Using these seditious times as a backdrop for this work, I explore the equally provocative lives of Franz Joseph and Elisabeth. What follows, then, is a biography: portraits of two people, both holding absolute convictions — one for the Habsburg dynasty and Austria and one for individual recognition and self-realization. Franz Joseph ruled for nearly 68 years, but there is more to Franz Joseph than the longevity of serving as the monarch of the powerful Habsburg dynasty. Myriad images reflect Emperor Franz. Some historians have labeled him an "imperialist tyrant" who denied freedom to the nations of his empire — one who maintained the German hegemony at the expense of the Slavs. He was seen as shy and inhibited, one who felt more comfortable when surrounded by paperwork than when surrounded by society at large. Even as a young boy, Franz was already "old-fashioned" and later in life deigned modernity in personal preferences and in the government he ran. Throughout his reign, Franz Joseph stuck with what he knew best: the sacredness of divine rulers, great-power politics, military pomp and parades. His motto was Viribus Unitis (with united strength) and that imperial motto helped Franz Joseph save the Habsburg dynasty during the revolutions that rocked the dynasty to its core.

Empress Elisabeth also has many images but one seems to be paramount: her never-ending attempts to receive recognition. Her first attempt was to be outstandingly beautiful, and, while nature endowed her with spectacular beauty, she would spend endless hours in perfecting that beauty. She tried to obtain recognition as a sportswoman and spent untold hours training to become a woman of unparalleled equestrian skills. Elisabeth tried to find posthumous fame in her poetry using Heinrich Heine as her revered model. Each of these pursuits, however, would elude the recognition she sought or would wane as time passed. Elisabeth was blessed with Helen of Troy looks and cursed with a Cassandra complex. Her life at court was one of rejection, for her blood was deemed by the proper court to be an improper hue of blue. She abhorred ceremony and excoriated the excesses of aristocratic systems — just like the unfortunate Queen Marie Antoinette.

What follows is history, an overview of the events that immediately preceded, and those that occurred during, the reign of Franz Joseph (1848–1916). Franz, along with the heads of other European countries and dynasties, was not attuned to the growing wave of discontent. Subsequently the history of the mid–1800 and early 1900s is a history of the upheavals that occurred throughout all of Central Europe as the laboring classes fought against their imperial occupiers. It is a history of Austria's dominating prime minister — Metternich — and of Austria's conquerors — Napoleon and Bismarck — and of revolutions and compromises and the war "to end all wars."

What follows is the story of the Habsburgs. Franz Joseph and Elisabeth presided over the most strict and pompous court in all of Europe and reigned over a society with strong caste hierarchies — the "haves" and the "have nots." Imperialism here refers to the subjugation of the "proletariat class." In the ninth century, for example, under the first Habsburg emperor, Charlemagne, the Slavs were worked to death in his mines. So frequent and prolonged was the enslavement of Eastern Europeans that "Slav" became synonymous with servitude. Indeed, the word "slave" derives from "Slav." Thus, a major thread woven within the cultural fabric of the 1800s was the imperialistic belief that monarchs, kings, and emperors were superior to the masses. They gave themselves deity-like status and saw themselves as rulers "by divine right." For centuries the masses believed in the inherent sacredness of sovereign power. Their rule was absolute over their subjects, who were deemed incapable of ruling themselves. Franz believed, was conditioned to believe, that all men were created *un*equal. It never occurred to him that he should try to be more "accommodating" to his subjects and to listen to their needs. Nor did he ever do anything to attract their affection. Franz did not crave popularity from the "common people." Most monarchs simply thought it undignified or beneath them to curry favor with the masses. Franz Joseph's wife, the Empress Elisabeth, learned to think in similar ways and led a self-serving life that placed her above those of lesser status. Those with royal, aristocratic blood were above "common man" and common man was not among their concerns. This thinking proved disastrous.

What follows is Vienna. When one speaks of 1800 Vienna, it's hard not to conjure pictures of royalty in their imperial finery, castles with gold-leaf embellishments, melodic waltzes, all capturing the romanticism of a glittery bygone era. Vienna speaks of famous names—Empress Maria Theresa, Emperor Franz Joseph, Empress Elisabeth, Mozart, Hayden, King Ludwig II—of breathtaking structures—Schönbrunn, Hofburg Palace, St. Stephen's Cathedral and castles with nearly unpronounceable names on barely accessible mountain heights—Hohenschwangau, Herrenchiemsee, Neuschwanstein—of majestic music, with Strauss' *Blue Danube* personifying the beauty of this city.

It is a time of powerful dynasties—Romanov, Hohenzollern, Ottoman, and Habsburg. The House of Habsburg was the principle sovereign dynasty of Europe, ruling from the 15th to the 20th century. The dominant monarchs of the Habsburg dynasty continue to be Maria Theresa and Franz Joseph; each match the widespread appeal of Queen Victoria within the United Kingdom. It is a time long gone and yet the names have not been erased and present a picture of intrigue and fascination. Franz Joseph played all the roles assigned to him as emperor. Elisabeth played none as a wife, mother, or empress. Yet, many factors played a part in her "abdication" from Austria and the city of Vienna. Similarly, many factors played a role in the decisions Franz Joseph made during his reign, none more enigmatic than the Peace Emperor's (a self-proclaimed sobriquet) final act of declaring the mobilization of Austria-Hungary's armies to detonate a war that cost the lives of sixteen million people from one hundred countries.

I have been a professor for thirty years teaching psychology, and have continually enjoyed doing research, which has culminated in writing two college textbooks, a scholarly book on self-esteem, and a handbook on critical thinking. But, as a research hobby outside my field, my secondary passion, if you will, falls to history and biographies. Jean-Louis-Ernest Meissonier (1815–1891), painter extraordinaire, once commented, "If I had not been a painter, I should have liked to be a historian. I don't think any other subject could be so interesting as history." Substituting psychologist for painter summarizes my sentiments as well. My interests have focused on the 1800s and Central Europe, the Habsburgs, and Emperor Franz Joseph and Empress Elisabeth. My interest in this period began a few decades ago with my first visits to the former lands of the Habsburg dynasty. The last ten years have been spent consolidating disparate elements of my research and reading, culminating in the work that follows.

CHAPTER ONE

The New Emperor and Old Vienna

Franz Joseph was born in the first half of the 1800s, a captivating time in history when sweeping changes would occur throughout Central Europe as borders were redrawn, states reorganized, and territories either ceded or annexed. At the onset of the 19th century, the seeds of change were planted and slowly took root, culminating in revolutions, compromises, and wars. Franz Joseph would become the last significant ruler of the Habsburg Dynasty, which began with the crowning of Charlemagne in 800 C.E.

Like his predecessors, Franz Joseph, even as a young child, was dignified, noble, handsome, and self-assured. Honor, loyalty and an obsessive sense of duty to the Habsburg dynasty and to Austria would also become part of his defining personality traits. He ruled, as did all emperors, with an almost deity status and the people, who were deemed incapable of ruling themselves, willingly worshipped their protectorate father figure. No other titular head has exercised complete sovereignty for so long. The court over which he ruled was, since time immemorial, the center of the greatest realm in Europe. So comprehensive were the range of countries and peoples over whom he reigned; so long was the period of his governance; so strong was his influence on national and international events that, indeed, Franz Joseph was, and will likely remain, chief among European monarchs.

When Franz was born, Austria was the most politically and culturally powerful country in all of Europe with the exception of Russia. As its subsequent ruler, early socialization practices focused on preparing Franz for his role as the head of the House of Habsburg and its vast dominions. Archduchess Sophie, his mother, a woman of strong wills, brought him up and educated him as heir to the throne. Sophie, controlling and dictatorial, along with Franz's tutors, often engaged in brutal teaching techniques and believed that Franz must learn to deny his feelings and to never show weakness.

The lack of Franz Joseph's emotionality toward others is candidly given to us from an inscription in the diary of Princess Melanie Metternich, daughter of Austrian diplomat Prince Klemens von Metternich. Her passage reads, "I remember Archduchess Sophia saying to me, several years ago, in Nice, that one never ought to regard individuality as having any importance; that she, the Archduchess, has always seen that one man can be replaced by another without its making the smallest difference."[1] The Archduchess' views appeared to have been internalized by Franz Joseph, becoming an enduring part of his personality throughout his whole life. People were perceived as "functional creatures." Franz Joseph would rarely be close to others; he barricaded himself behind a wall of isolationism and only a limited few were able to chisel their way through, and then only for a brief time.

One of those few was Count Karl Grunne, who became the emperor's aide-de-camp and head of the imperial armies. Grunne's political philosophy boiled down to a belief in using military discipline to eradicate society's subversive impulses and his belief served only to encourage the young emperor's innate militaristic leanings. Franz's mother, Sophie, appointed Grunne chamberlain to her son, thus putting him in a position to act as imperial mentor to the young man. Grunne received this position because of his uncompromising opposition to all liberal ideas, which certainly won Sophie's favor. Grunne had the strongest influence on the young monarch. To some, however, Grunne was an incarnation of all that was evil in the Viennese Court.[2]

Descriptions of Grunne's character show him as dull, narrow-minded, ignorant, old-fashioned, and brutal.[3] As the emperor's adjutant general and chief of the military chancery, Grunne would become one of the mightiest men in the empire in the first decade of Franz Joseph's reign. A confidential personal relation grew up between the young emperor and the aristocratic officer who was more than twice his age. Grunne soon became indispensable. Insofar as Franz Joseph had a private life, Grunne was his counselor and helper. This mentor's influence determined the views, the decisions, and the actions of his young master more and more as the months passed, in political as well as personal matters. In 1852, when with fifteen-year-old Elisabeth, Franz Joseph was able, briefly, to escape from the emotionless iron cloak worn from early childhood. Franz, whose personality mirrored the strict Viennese Court decorum, was drawn to Sisi's (a nickname from her early childhood) spirited and carefree ways. Their lives together would unfold amidst the volatile era of countries seeking power through the expansion of their territories as well as through the unification of independent states within their borders. Great dynasties were the means by which this could be done.

Dynasties have always shaped the historical framework of Europe. Each dynastic ruler sought to increase their family's prestige, wealth, and influence. In the United Kingdom, Henry II founded the Plantagenet line, a more significant dynasty than the Tudors, so many historians claim. Henry II was one of fifteen Plantagenet monarchs ruling England from 1154 to 1485. The Tudors of England, who formed the Church of England, began their dynasty with the reign of Henry VII in 1485 and ended with the death of Queen Elizabeth I in 1603. When Elizabeth took power, England was a poor, second-rate nation. Her death brought an end to the Tudor dynasty, but England had become prosperous and was second to none on the power grid of nations.

Preeminent Central European and Asian dynasties reached the zenith of their influence in the 1800s. The Rothschild family, beginning with Mayer Amschel Rothschild, was a financial and international banking dynasty of German Jews. Five lines of the Austrian branch of the Rothschild family were given hereditary baronies of the Habsburg Empire by Emperor Francis I in 1816. The Ottoman dynasty was founded by Osman I in 1299 and is known in modern Turkish as *Osmanlı Hanedanı*, meaning "House of Osman." The Ottoman Empire was centered in present-day Turkey and extended its influence into southeastern Europe as well as the Middle East. The Turkish dynasty ruled the Ottoman Empire from the 13th century to its dissolution after World War I.

The dynasty of the kings and emperors of Prussia, Germany and Romania formed the House of Hohenzollern, the ruling house of Brandenburg-Prussia (1415–1918) and of imperial Germany (1871–1918). Its founder was Burgrave Frederick I of Nuremberg; its final sovereign was Emperor Wilhelm II. The Romanov dynasty, rulers of Russia, elected Czar Michael Romanov to rule at age sixteen. He began the Romanov dynasty, which would rule for more than three centuries, from 1613 to the Russian Revolution of February 1917. The Habsburg dynasty, however, had perhaps the most phenomenal career of all the ruling houses.

No other royal dynasty on the continent lasted so long or left its mark on so many centuries and so many countries as the Habsburgs. The dynasty had just one constant aim, to maintain and enhance the power and prestige of itself. The Habsburgs *were* the history of Central Europe. Countless territories and alliances were formed; statesmen and ideas were changed and often changed in tune with the whim and fancy of the reigning Habsburg monarch. Historian and author Alan Sked has noted that the Habsburgs "provided rulers for empires, kingdoms, duchies and principalities in Germany, Austria, Spain, Italy, Belgium, Holland, Czechoslovakia, Yugoslavia, Romania, Poland, and Hungary."[4] In short, the Habsburgs were the greatest dynasty of modern history, supplying the continent with a nearly uninterrupted stream of rulers for more than six hundred years. While political fates ebbed and flowed and as holdings expanded or contracted, their cultural leadership role remained a constant force. In 1848, Franz Joseph would join this long line of rulers.

Emerging from playing war games with his tin soldiers within the confines of his warm nursery and then from his more austere school classroom, Franz Joseph metamorphosed into the leader of the mighty Habsburgs. Emperor Ferdinand I stroked the young man's hair and lifting him to his feet, proclaimed, "God bless you! Be good and God will protect. I have done this willingly."[5] With a solemn nod to those present and an inaudible sigh, Franz Joseph[6] became emperor of Austria — one of his many fanciful sounding titles including King of Hungary and Bohemia, King of Lombardy and Venetia, Grand Duke of Tuscany and Krakow, Grand Duke of Transylvania, and Margrave of Moravia. His ambitious mother, Sophie of Bavaria, played a large role in securing the emperorship for her son, pouring into him all the hopes for the future greatness of Austria but also hoping to share in the great power she could never realize for herself. Franz Joseph was just eighteen years old in 1848. His reign began during the closing months of one of Europe's greatest upheavals, the Revolutions of 1848.

Within hours of his coronation, Franz Joseph's first political action was a manifesto to his people: "Convinced, on our own motion, of the need and value of free institutions expressive of the spirit of the age, we enter with due confidence, on the path leading to a salutary transformation and rejuvenation of the monarchy as a whole. On the basis of genuine liberty, on the basis of equality of all the nations of the realm and the equality before the law of all its citizens in legislation, our Fatherland may enjoy a resurrection to its old greatness and a new force. Determined to maintain the splendor of the crown undimmed and the monarchy as a

One. The New Emperor and Old Vienna

whole undiminished, but ready to share our rights with the representative of our peoples, we count on succeeding with the blessing of God and in understanding with our peoples, in uniting all the regions and races of the monarchy in one great state."[7] Franz Joseph entered his reign with what he must have known to be a lie.

The second political action of the newly crowned emperor was to have his official state photograph taken, an equally important step for several reasons. The reason of most importance was to send out the message to all his subjects that he was powerful and omnipresent. He was their father figure, albeit young, protectively watching over his dominions. Thus he began his "paternalistic autocracy," which he would carry through until his eighties. It assured the subjects that the monarchy would continue to exist. Replicas of Franz Joseph's image would soon be hung everywhere, from palaces to town halls to museums and theatres to individual homes. The portrait's place of prominence would be in the gallery among the previous members of the Habsburg family, which had exclusively held the emperor title of the Holy Roman Empire, an alliance of German and Italian states, for nearly four centuries. His portrait reflected his lithe frame; his handsome face was as orderly as his life.

The newly crowned emperor then entered one of the royal court's equipages, which was sumptuously painted with the Austrian double eagle and driven by a liveried coachman sitting tall and holding his whip as a scepter as though *he* were the emperor. Slowly the coach-and-six with its magnificently matched Lipizzaner grays moved from the center gate at Schönbrunn. Mounted escorts, footmen, trumpeters, and standard-bearers did not surround his coach. The streets were not crowded with people; no flags were waving from prominent buildings; no church bells were ringing to salute the new emperor.[8]

The Austrian Empire was engulfed in revolutions and the Habsburg rule was dangerously close to extinction. The year 1848 was a year of proletariat unrest fueled by needs for sustenance, a situation caused by harvest failures and yearnings for freedom and greater representation in government, the latter brought on by nationalistic enthusiasm. In previous years, many of the proletariat demands had not been met but were simply quashed by their rulers, adding more fuel to the already burning fires in the bellies of the masses. These frustrations culminated in the Revolutions of 1848, a period of Europe-wide unrest leading to a number of uprisings in Austria, which the Habsburg dynasty did not escape. The idea of "nationalism" or "liberalism" was so abhorrent to Archduchess Sophie that she claimed that she could more easily have borne the loss of one of her children than she could submit to the ignominy of submitting to a mass of proletariats. Her thoughts mirror the hatred she felt for the revolution. Emperor Ferdinand was so befuddled by his subjects' angry cries and actions, he simply asked, "Yes, but are they allowed to?"

Prior to Franz Joseph's coronation, in the early stormy months of 1848, the former and most inept Emperor Franz Ferdinand had compromised the dynasty by giving in to all the insurgents' demands. Now a way had to be found to get out of Ferdinand's hastily given constitutional promises: "The sham rule of Ferdinand must be ended and the scepter must be handed to the strong youth. This was the only way that the Revolution could be beaten and the Empire saved."[9] The newly installed monarch would not be duty bound by his predecessor's commitments. The "emperor switch" was presented to the people as a fait accompli. Ferdinand was incompetent but was also kindly and loved by his subjects.[10] It was feared that a pre-coronation announcement of a new emperor would most certainly have added fuel to this most volatile situation. The Habsburgs — shrewd and powerful — lived to rule another day, indeed, another several decades, taking their place among the many prominent dynasties.

The Habsburg name came from the castle of Habichtsburg, meaning "Hawk's Castle," which was built during the early 11th century in Aargau, Switzerland, and their dynasty began with Count Werner I (?–1096). But, the first member of the family of real substance was Rudolph I, who was elected king of Germany and the Holy Roman Empire in 1273. In 1276 Rudolph became sovereign ruler of Austria and began initiating an important phase of building on the Church of St. Stephen, raising it to the status of a cathedral. He founded the University of Vienna, which became the second university of the German-speaking world. His sons Albrecht and Rudolf presided over Austria and Styria, thus assuring the Habsburg rule in Austria from then until 1918. Austria was the firm foundation of Habsburg power and the family came to be known as the House of Austria. The ambitious, astute, and far-sighted Habsburgs reigned over an ever-expanding territory that grew from a small section of Austria along the Danube to a parcel of land stretching across Europe into Africa, Mexico and Peru.

Some royal dynasties have fought a succession of wars to gain supremacy; others have intrigued their way up the empire-building ladder. The Habsburgs avoided both these strategies. War was limited to defensive struggles to keep other rulers from taking over distant possessions. The Habsburg motto could have been "Make love not war!" as they married their way to dynastic power and turned their attention from martial to marital conquests. They had an uncanny talent for choosing the right spouses from the right royal houses to make just the right alliances and, subsequently, inherited the right properties. Thus, most of their vast holdings were accomplished through marriages entered into solely for the furtherance of various political schemes. In this way, properties ranging from the Netherlands, Burgundy, the duchy of Milan, Sicily and finally Spain became a part of the Habsburg's dominions. Within a relatively short time, the family territories expanded and, with the reign of Charles V (1500–1558), one could say that the sun never set on the lands of the House of Habsburg.

The Habsburgs chose Vienna as their place of residence. Franz Joseph ruled over an empire that included much of today's Austria, Hungary, Romania, Albania, Serbia and Croatia. As such, the Habsburg Empire was not bound by geography or by a homogenous people. The population within its dynastic borders was about 37½ million. Germans, Slavs, Italians, Magyars (Hungarians), Romanians, Jews, and gypsies called the Habsburg Empire home. In the Habsburg dynasty there was no racial, national, or language predominance.

Despite the continued grumblings of the masses, Franz Joseph's reign was mirrored by the splendor of royal Viennese pomp. Beaming with motherly pride, Sophie took center stage over the incessant balls that epitomized Vienna. The imperial fetes, however, always followed the appropriate decorum and ceremonial protocol. The Viennese Court of Franz Joseph was particularly conservative and most conscious of tradition, as noted by Lady Mary Wortley Montagu. Lady Mary was well known throughout polite society for her wit and poetic verse; she was also a prominent authority on Vienna court etiquette. The following is a paraphrase from her book, *Selected Letters*: The centre of the Vienna Court was the Emperor, who was inapproachable and far above the banalities of everyday life. The Emperor was exalted in a mystical, almost religious manner. When the Emperor appeared in person or even if his name was uttered at public ceremonies, he was due the highest reverence — courtiers would show their submission by making a deep bow on bended knee. To flout this rule was tantamount to questioning the omnipotence of the great Emperor. All acts of state as well as dynastic celebrations such as baptisms, weddings and funerals followed very strict rules: each step and gesture had to be imbued with solemn dignity. Individuality and spontaneity were undesirable.[11]

Franz Joseph was, as were all Habsburgs, a staunch supporter of the pope and the Holy Roman Catholic Church. His mother's strong faith had a profound effect on Franz Joseph. Unlike today, during Franz's time, a commoner's beliefs were not a private matter. While religion played a large role in the private life of each citizen, the church also influenced and shaped society. In the eyes of Franz Joseph, Catholicism was the only true faith. Those who disagreed or those who had other beliefs were persecuted or, at best, marginalized. While the Habsburgs ruled, the primacy of the Roman Catholic Church was never called into question.

A powerful ceremony that strengthened the bond between the Habsburgs and the Catholic Church was the most solemn ceremony — the Corpus Christi Procession. The name "Corpus Christi" is a Latin phrase that refers to the body of Christ. The emperor and noble men donned all their magnificent finery and displayed their power and wealth to all the commoners eager to view their reverent extravagance. It all began with Franz Joseph taking the state coach to St. Stephen's Cathedral, one of the most significant buildings of the late Gothic period. It is a striking emblem of Vienna with its steep and gigantic roof of ornate patterns of colored tiles, and the tall, slender tower (about 450 feet). Franz Joseph, in ceremonial dress, led the progression, followed by the cathedral's clergy and then by the Archbishop of Vienna walking beneath a canopy and carrying the consecrated Eucharistic host in an adorned vessel called a "monstrance."

The Hofburg Palace was the winter residence of the Austrian sovereigns and on 6 May 1849, the emperor made it his home and remained there for the next seventy years. Over the course of the centuries it developed into one of the most important centers of European history. Dating from the 13th century, originally it was a fortified castle located inside Vienna's medieval walls. Each emperor extended the Hofburg so that eventually it came to resemble a city within a city. A complex of 17 buildings from 17 different eras and architectural styles, it housed the Imperial Library, consisting of some 300,000 volumes; thousands of rare manuscripts from the 14th century were lodged in a separate large room. It was from here that the Habsburgs reigned from the 13th century, first as rulers of their Austrian inherited lands and then from 1440 to 1806 as emperors of the Holy Roman Empire (with one exception: 1742–45 when a non–Habsburg Charles VII Albert, a member of the Wittelsbach family, was elected), and finally as emperors of Austria from 1806 until the end of the monarchy in 1918.

The Hofburg Palace in its magnificent splendor hosted many balls replete with the equal splendor of the royal court — men in full dress uniform and women in sumptuous gowns and jewels, gliding along its finely polished marble floors and swirling under crystal chandeliers lit by over ten thousand candles. Unquestionably the epitome of glamour and decadence, these balls were the most-awaited calendar events. Certainly the coveted and grandest was the *Hofball*, which took place in February. In the largest room, the *Redoutensaal*, in the Hofburg Palace, archdukes and archduchesses and their retinues would eagerly await Franz Joseph's prompt arrival at 8:30 P.M., marking the commencement of the ball.

As usual, Johann Strauss, conducting with his violin bow, would lead his orchestra. The waltz stemmed from the *Landler*, an Austro-German dance in three-quarter time. It was sometime around 1780 that it first appeared and almost spontaneously ignited the craze not just in Vienna but in most of Europe, although Vienna was its headquarters. Vienna was the important center of musical innovation. Eighteenth and nineteenth century composers were drawn to the city due to the patronage of the Habsburgs and made Vienna the European capital of classical music.

A French journalist noted that the waltz was quite popular by all classes of the Viennese people and stated, in 1852 that in every house and on every piano in Vienna lay Strauss waltzes.[12] Louis Hector Berlioz, a French composer, visited Vienna in 1845 and in his *Memoirs* devoted a long paragraph to his observations of the waltz while attending a great ball at the Redoutensaal. He marveled at the "comparable waltzers whirling around in great clouds, and in admiring the choreographic precision of the quadrilles — two hundred people at a time, drawn up in two long lines — and the vivid character dances, which for originality and polished execution I have not seen surpassed anywhere except in Hungary."[13] And there stood Strauss directing his orchestra. Sometimes, when one of the new waltzes he wrote for every society ball made a special hit, the dancers would stop to applaud and the ladies would go over to his rostrum and throw him their bouquets.

Pre-Lenten carnival was the most wildly exciting time of balls and merrymaking, known as *Fasching*. During Fasching, as many as fifty balls might be held on a single evening. It was the one time in socially stratified Vienna that lower classes wore masks and were allowed to mingle and mimic the royals and even clergy with impunity. It was the one time that the Viennese relaxed their rigid class structure and just enjoyed the democratizing influence of the waltz. Franz Joseph would make his customary appearance at these balls. But as soon as he had stayed the proper amount of time, he left for the solitude of his rooms at the Hofburg Palace if it were winter or Schönbrunn Palace during the summer months.

If *The Blue Danube* represents the lyrical symbol of Vienna, Schönbrunn would arguably be the lavish Baroque concrete and mortar that personifies Vienna. Franz Joseph always had special ties with his summer residence; it was his birthplace and it would be here that he would die. When his uncle Emperor Ferdinand I bequeathed his power to Franz Joseph, the new emperor took over Schönbrunn, with its magnificent Rococo furnishings. Throughout the palace the reception rooms are decorated with the color scheme of white and red and are accented with gold leaf. Franz Joseph's apartments lacked the vivid splendor seen in reception areas and were almost Spartan in design. His suite of rooms seemed to reflect the staid form of government most favored by the new emperor.

Schönbrunn literally means "beautiful fountain" and was named after an artesian well with exceptionally clear and pure water. Franz Joseph would serve the water to his guests on special occasions. The land had been in the possession of the Habsburgs since 1569, when the wife of Emperor Ferdinand II had a summer residence built there in 1642. It was designed to be a palatial hunting lodge for the heir to the throne. Half a century later Schönbrunn Palace was to become the magnificent focus of court life. Empress Maria Theresa, eldest daughter of Holy Roman Emperor Charles VI and Elizabeth of Brunswick-Wolfenbuttel, would rebuild and redesign Schönbrunn to resemble its present-day glory. In 1743, Empress Maria Theresa renovated and extended the house to over 1400 rooms and added a chapel and a theatre and painted it her favorite shade of yellow, known to this day as "Maria Theresa yellow."

Maria Theresa was the first and only woman ruler in the Habsburg dynasty and one of the most successful. She strengthened Austria's resources by initiating financial and educational reforms, promoting commerce and the development of agriculture, and reorganizing the army. She also enlarged her country to the size of an empire, mostly due to a very wise political course of marriages and not wars. Maria gave birth to sixteen children, and, despite all her court activities, was considered by her many biographers to be a good and caring mother. She reigned for over forty years; in 1765, she ruled jointly with her son Joseph II.

Six-year-old Mozart, who played his first concert in the Mirror Room, entertained the dual monarchs in 1772. His father, Leopold, was beside himself with joy at the initial success of his son and daughter's concerts. He noted that all of Vienna, it seemed, were anxiously awaiting the arrival of the prodigies from Salzburg. "We are already being talked of everywhere," Leopold reported to Lorenz Hagenauer, his friend and landlord back home. "Everyone is amazed, especially at the boy, and everyone whom I have heard says that his genius is incomprehensible." The children's appearance at Schönbrunn Palace on 13 October was judged by Leopold to be an astonishing success. He wrote, "Their Majesties received us with such extraordinary graciousness that, when I shall tell of it, people will declare that I have made it up. Suffice it to say that Wolferl jumped up on the Empress' lap, put his arms round her neck and kissed her heartily."[14]

Most royal houses receive their name via the male line; for this reason there were a series of replacements of extinct lines of the Habsburg dynasty. In 1521, the family split into the Austrian and the Spanish Habsburgs. The hereditary lands of the Austrian line ruled over the kingdoms of Bohemia and Hungary; the Spanish Habsburgs ruled over Spain, the Netherlands, and Portugal. Upon the death of Charles II in 1700 the Spanish branch became extinct. The heiress of the last Austrian Habsburgs, Maria Theresa, married Francis Stephan, Duke of Lorraine. When Empress Maria Theresa died, the Austrian branch became extinct and was replaced by the Vaudemont branch of the House of Lorraine when her son Joseph II succeeded his mother to the throne. Their descendants carried the dynastic name Habsburg-Lorraine. The new line was called the House of Habsburg-Lorraine, so technically the House of Habsburg is known as the House of Habsburg-Lorraine (*Lothringen* in German).

Joseph II unleashed an array of radical reforms that furthered the modernity of Austria. He carried little doubt about the character of his empire: it was to be a German state. In his words, "I am Emperor of the German *Reich*; therefore all other states which I possess are provinces of it."[15] Under his rule, secular thought gained momentum; many monasteries were torn down and the church no longer held it prestigious power. Protestants and Jews, however, were greatly liberated. In the cultural sphere, Joseph II relaxed censorship of the press (at least until it became too critical of his reform systems). He also abolished serfdom, a state in which serfs were simply chattels on the land.

The exterior of Maria Theresa's Schönbrunn is as breathtaking as its interior. At the top of the pyramid columns framing the gateway of Schönbrunn are the gilded French eagles mounted there on Napoleon's orders. Since eagles were proud symbols of both France and Austria, they continue to this day to overlook the palace courtyard, despite the fact that the French eagle boasts only one head while the Habsburg species boasts two, holding the majestic sword and imperial orb. Napoleon Bonaparte lived here for a short period of time — not, however, as an invited guest but as conqueror of Austria. Napoleon claimed that he did not intend to fight any but the English, until the Austrian General Mack "provoked him." He suddenly and rapidly marched to the Rhine; one hundred and eighty thousand troops entered Austria. On a battlefield near Elm, 27,000 Austrians surrendered to Napoleon. He accomplished his objective and destroyed the Austrian army by "simply marching." Austria was obliged to open its capital. It was deemed futile to resist this "man of destiny." In little over a decade Napoleon had risen from an unemployed artillery officer, without friends or family influence, to subdue in turn all the monarchies of Europe, with the exception of Russia and England. Nothing in history approaches the facts of his amazing career.

For most of his conquering life, no matter how negative the situation was or how many tactical mistakes he made, Napoleon spoke of military campaign errors of judgment as deliberate mistakes that lured his opponents to their destruction. He always behaved like a winner — whether he was winning or not. Unlike many new men in the military, Napoleon acted as though he were a starred general, with an ego and confidence to match. In short, he behaved like the political and military genius that many of his subordinates believed him to be. Success often begins with a positive belief system. Of course, this must be accompanied by successful actions and, for the time being, Napoleon delivered. One of these successful actions was conquering Austria and Vienna in the Battle of Austerlitz.

His optimism and egocentrism soared the night before the battle, further enhanced by his troops shouting, *"Vive l'empereur!"* On 2 December 1805, caught up in this momentous event, Napoleon told an aide that this would be the finest evening of his life. And it was. He had won a great victory. Happy with his soldiers he said, "I am pleased with you.... You have decorated your eagles with an immortal glory.... You will be greeted with joy, and it will be enough for you to say, 'I was at the battle of Austerlitz,' for people to reply, 'There goes a brave man.'"[16] Following his victory at Austerlitz, Napoleon quartered himself and his army at Schönbrunn.

Austerlitz crippled Austria, but the Habsburg dynasty prevailed even though Ferdinand was now considered a second-rate emperor. The humiliating and crushing defeat at Austerlitz in 1805 only confirmed Austria's belief that something needed to be done to defeat Napoleon. This was their impetus for being the aggressor in 1809. The Austrians thought that Russia would remain neutral and that Prussia would probably join the

Austrians in defeating Napoleon. Their assumptions were wrong. Prussia remained neutral in the Austro-French war, declaring that it was not rich enough to use up its strength in wars that did not earn them anything. Subsequently, the war almost completely obliterated Austria.

If there is a positive side, the Habsburg dynasty was preserved and in the end Napoleon sought more modest goals in return for promises of Franco-Austrian peace and friendship. Austria lost lands containing over three million subjects, about one-fifth of her total population. The Treaty of Vienna was signed between France and Austria at the Schönbrunn Palace of Vienna on 14 October 1809. To the Viennese it was an intense relief when Napoleon left Schönbrunn, but for generations the shock of French occupation dominated the thoughts of Viennese society. (Napoleon's fall was as clear a destiny as his rise, and he eventually suffered unexampled and bitter humiliation. France — a country, his country, which he had raised to an esteemed greatness — repudiated him; he was dethroned and imprisoned at Elba; and subsequently he was confined to the rock of St. Helena until his death.)

While at Schönbrunn, Napoleon, a fine equestrian, made frequent visits to the Spanish Riding School, which housed some of the most beautiful horses in the world. Franz Joseph, like Napoleon, also became a fine equestrian and an admirer of the Spanish horses that formed one of the bases of the Lipizzaner breed, which were exclusively used at the Spanish Riding School (the only institution in the world that has practiced for over 460 years). In 1729 Emperor Charles VI commissioned the architect Josef Emanuel Fischer von Erlach to build the magnificent Winter Riding School in the Hofburg Palace, and it was completed in 1735.

In addition to riding, Franz Joseph also had an interest in art; in fact, as a young boy he had a natural talent for drawing. This was something he did not pursue as an adult but he was drawn to the work of great artists, such as Gustav Klimt. In 1888, Klimt was awarded the Golden Order of Merit from Emperor Franz Joseph. Klimt is particularly known for his "Golden Phase," marked by his extensive use of gold leaf. An outstanding example of this detail is found in *The Kiss*, which depicts a couple embracing and totally entwined in decorative gold robes — a stunning example of Art Nouveau style.

Franz was also a patron of Hans Makart, who maintained a powerful artistic influence on the academic art and high culture of Vienna and was acknowledged by many to be the leader of artistic life. He was both an artist and an arbiter of interior design for the Viennese upper class. His style dictated the use of carved and inlaid furniture and heavy velvet window coverings, which completely reflected the style of this era. Makart was also fascinated with historical costumes and designed many that were worn by the ladies of elegance to the various fetes of Vienna. But his obvious appeal was his huge artistic compositions, rich in Rubenistic color that made him a giant among his contemporaries.

One condition favoring the artistic and creative climate of Vienna was the influence, the patronage, and the wealth of the Habsburgs and the princes who were key courtiers and advisors who attracted the talented and the gifted among architects, composers, musicians, painters, sculptors, and scholars. Another condition was the public, who were there to appreciate fine art. And these audiences were not confined to a limited societal class; most Viennese enjoyed the cultural life of old Vienna.

Old Vienna was enclosed on three sides by a moat and a city wall; on its eastern side ran the mighty Danube. The outskirts of the city, known as the "Glacis," was a broad expanse of grassy land almost always filled with soldiers engaged in marching maneuvers, along with market stalls, coffee traders and various artisans selling their wares. A relatively small number of inhabitants, about fifty thousand, lived within these city walls. But these enclosures — in terms of brick and mortar and in broader terms of hegemony by the dominant powers — would not last for long. Nationalism and liberalism would define the mid–1800s, not just for Vienna but for all of Central Europe. These ideologies would begin with the French Revolution, which would spark nationalism throughout Europe. Fighting broke out all over Europe as nationalists tried to force the creation of new states. Only two great powers escaped the turmoil: Great Britain, which already had liberalism and nationalism along with a constitution and a middle class, and Russia, sans all the above.

Revolutions particularly defined Vienna in 1848 when liberal ideas began to infiltrate the populace of the Habsburg imperial lands. When liberal ideas emerge, revolution, or at least an attempt at revolution, is inevitable. Among the non–German peoples in the empire, Italy was strongly seized by the revolution and the struggle for freedom. Italy was once more approaching the boiling point. Nationalist sentiment was growing in the Austrian Kingdom of Lombardy-Venetia and the elites there looked for support from the kingdom of Piedmont-Sardinia. Hungary was also vying for its freedom from the Austrian Habsburg Empire. The Magyar princes of Hungary for centuries have fought against the Habsburg nobles for their autonomy and independence. Cries of "liberalism" filled the air as Franz Joseph ascended to the throne, but a liberal constitutional state was not part of Franz's plan. What were his thoughts? Only absolute power could break the will of this newly emerging middle class.

But these issues of European nationalism were not easily dismissed and had a way of quickly spilling over into the rest of the world. The United States was brewing over slavery issues. Henry Clay opened the great debate on slavery and warned the South against succession. Harriet Beecher Stowe galvanized public opinion against slavery and stiffened its defenders in the South by writing *Uncle Tom's Cabin,* depicting the slave Tom as the protagonist, with his moral verve, and Simon Legree as the antagonist, symbolizing greed. Nathaniel Hawthorne published *The Scarlet Letter,* depicting American life under Puritan rule during colonial times. Herman Melville published *White Jacket,* describing abuses in the navy, including an emphasis on flogging.

It was also a time of inventions: refrigeration, photography, the electric motor, the steam-powered locomotive, and elevators (with brakes). It was a time of discoveries. European populations expanded as a result of advances in understanding the human body and disease prevention. As a result, during the 19th century, the population of Vienna swelled to seven times its original number, making it the fourth largest city in the world. Louis Pasteur, best known for inventing a method to stop milk and wine from causing sickness, published his findings about a process that came to be called pasteurization. Gregor Mendel published his book on pea plants, which would be later known as Mendel's laws. Charles Darwin published *The Origin of Species,* putting forward the theory of evolution by natural selection.

It was an age also fascinated by the past. The novelist Gustave Flaubert regarded this keen sense of history as a completely new phenomenon, as yet another of the century's many bold inventions. "The historical sense dates from only yesterday," he wrote in 1860, "and it is perhaps one of the nineteenth century's finest achievements."[17] It was an entrepreneurial time — one of expansion and renovating — and an "out with the old and in with the new" type of spirit prevailed. In 1850 England had over four thousand factories. In Paris, Baron Georges Haussman, the prefect of the Seine, began the reconstruction of the 85 miles of the streets of Paris. Long, narrow, winding roads were made into straight, broad boulevards using macadam and asphalt instead of cobblestones, not strictly for aesthetic reasons, as wider streets would make it more difficult for the ever-revolutionist Parisians to construct barricades.

Emperor Franz Joseph assumed the throne of the Austrian Empire, *Kaisertum Österreich*, as the Habsburg empire or monarchy was officially called in the 1800s, and remained for no less than 68 years (until his death in 1916). Though his death belongs to a now distant past, the almost eight decades since then have not erased knowledge of him and his extraordinary life. To clearly understand Franz Joseph's life and reign, it is necessary to see the close connection with the political transformation of Europe and the seismic shift in world power that went on between the Congress of Vienna (1814–1815) and the signing of the Treaty of Versailles on 19 June 1919.

CHAPTER TWO

Revolutions

When Strauss the younger wrote "The Beautiful Blue Danube" waltz it was the nostalgic representation of *Alt-Wien*. However, "old Vienna" would go through a political transformation along with all of Central Europe. A progressive shift in world power occurs as we progress through the mid- to late 1800s. These changes unfold slowly and begin before Emperor Ferdinand I abdicated and Franz Joseph ascended to the throne.

In November 1806, Emperor Francis II stood on the balcony of the Church of the Nine Choirs of Angels in Vienna. For almost four centuries his Habsburg forebears had held the title of Holy Roman Emperor. In 1792 Emperor Francis II had been duly crowned in Frankfurt as the 54th successor to Charlemagne. Perhaps it could be said that the French Revolution and the European war that broke out as a result in 1792 ultimately led to the destruction of the Holy Roman Empire. The armies of Napoleon Bonaparte had overrun much of the continent and in November 1805 had entered Vienna itself. Francis II was under no illusions; he needed a more precisely defined authority. The Holy Roman Empire, once Europe's greatest state, was now a mere shadow of its former glory — just a curious relic of a system of feudal obligations.

To guarantee the family's continued imperial status, in 1806, addressing the crowd gathered beneath the church balcony, Francis II announced the dissolution of Charlemagne's thousand-year-old *sacrum Romanum imperium nationis Germanicae* — the Holy Roman Empire of the German nation. The revolutionary upheaval in France and Napoleon's subsequent imperial aspirations, and Austria's momentous defeat at Austerlitz, made Francis II seek a new title, one that would assert his sovereignty over all Habsburg lands. He had no way of ensuring victory on the battlefield to foil Napoleon but he found a simple way of frustrating the ambitious plans of his ubiquitous French rival. Francis II laid down the scepter of the old empire and the nation of Austria was born. He adopted a new hereditary title and would now be known as Francis I, "Emperor of Austria," a powerful kingdom of more than 360 distinct entities differing widely in size, rank, and power.

Napoleon, however, took advantage of Austria's weakened state and a new confederation was formed. This was the Confederation of the Rhine, formed in July 1806. The very appearance of it precipitated the demise of the Holy Roman Empire. The confederation was initially composed of just sixteen minor German-state members, along with the newly created kingdoms of Bavaria and Wurttemberg, who decided to disavow their allegiances to the Holy Roman Empire and throw their nations' futures in with Napoleon and France. All of the confederacy's German states had agreed to take sides with France against the two outcast German nations of Austria and Prussia. It further enlarged to thirty states in 1808, making up almost all of the German states. Napoleon had no desire to unify Germany, but he wished to have several independent states, or groups of states, which he could conveniently bring under his control.[1] In a message given to Austria and Prussia, Napoleon informed them that the new Confederation of the Rhine, of which he was to be protector, would be incompatible with the continued existence of the venerable Holy Roman Empire.

The final chapter of the Napoleonic Confederation of the Rhine occurred in 1813 as a result of Napoleon's decisive defeat at Leipzig, signifying his loss of power and control over the German states. The Confederation of the Rhine would eventually be replaced by a new union, the German Confederation — a union of thirty-nine small German states with Austria in permanent control of the presidency — created by the Congress of Vienna in 1815. Its purpose was to guarantee external peace in that its members would provide mutual defense against attacking nations, along with internal peace, which guaranteed independence of its member states. The German Confederation lasted until 1866, when Prussia founded the North German Confederation, which sowed the seeds of nascent nationalism and became a forerunner of the German empire. The German Confederation united the German-speaking territories outside of Austria and Switzerland under Prussian leadership in 1871. This later served as the predecessor-state of modern Germany.

Vienna's wish to rid the world of Napoleon finally was realized when the Battle of Waterloo on 18 June 1815 put an end to Napoleon's dream of resurrection. Following the downfall of Napoleon, Metternich was given the job of state chancellor. Count (later Prince) Klemens von Metternich was a complex individual who embodied the principles of 19th century conservatism; he personified Austria with his pliant diplomacy and his ingenious treaties. He became foreign minister in 1809. Metternich was born in the western European Rhineland and was proud of his German ancestry. Asserting his German character, he, and subsequently Austria, accepted Prussia as the second "Great Power" to Austria. Both of these powers had been shaken by the Napoleonic wars and each had a common fear of France that camouflaged their rivalry and individual quests for power, at least for the time being. Like his French nemesis Napoleon, Metternich was egotistic and believed in his own Divine Providence.[2] He was quick, superficially clever and had great experience of the world. From the old school, he held the belief that the monarchs of the time were sacrosanct.

He was a student at the University of Strasburg when the revolutionary cannons exploded in France in 1789 and the Bastille literally crumbled under proletariat hands. He and his fellow students heard tales of the sufferings of the upper-class nobles, lords, and clergy. Coming from a privileged background, his impressionistic mind greatly sympathized with the terror and bloodshed of the aristocratic French, to say nothing about those supporting the monarchy who were being guillotined by the hundreds.[3] These early experiences would leave their indelible mark on Metternich's future philosophy of government. Between the years of 1803 and 1815, when the Napoleonic Wars conquered much of Europe, Metternich's self-aggrandizements may have been warranted. Because of his diplomatic skill, he was able to carry Austria through these most dangerous years.

Napoleon retreated to Fontainebleau, where he abdicated on 6 April 1814. The Treaty of Paris was signed 30 May 1814, the terms of which were incredibly lenient. The art treasures that Napoleon's troops had looted from other European nations would remain in Paris. There would be no demands for reparation payments. France was reduced to its frontiers of 1792, and Louis XVIII, brother of the decapitated Louis XVI, was placed on the French throne. Louis XVIII was neither a great kin nor a great man; his long exile of twenty years and his travels to many countries in Europe had liberalized his thinking and helped him to possess great social and conversational powers. The treaty more or less restored Central Europe to its Ancient Regime. The leniency shown by the Allies was purely political, as imposing a harsh settlement upon France would only weaken Louis' position and lead to a possible revival of Bonapartist sentiment.

The Allies did what was necessary to prevent further hostilities with France, a nation whose welfare was subservient to Napoleon's own glory and his diabolical egotism and arrogance.

On 10 March 1815 Napoleon escaped from Elba and attempted to resurrect his power. His defeat resulted in a new Treaty of Paris. This second treaty was more harsh: France would have to return all the art treasures that Napoleon had claimed as spoils of victory. She would also be required to pay 700 million francs as a settlement fee, support the occupying Allied troops for five years, and reduce the French army to 150 thousand men. The treaty also stipulated that a congress would be held in Vienna to decide the fate of the recovered territories. All the important decisions made — in particular, how to divide among the conquerors the spoils taken from the vanquished — at the congress would be made by the four conquering great powers: England, Austria, Prussia and Russia. The other nations were not allowed to partake in these secret dispositions. Metternich, who had become the chief minister of the Emperor Francis I, was also the acting president of the congress, representing Austria. It was one of the grandest gatherings of princes and statesmen seen since the Diet of Worms in 1521. The Russians sent Alexander I, the Emperor of Russia. The main delegate from Prussia was Prince Karl August von Hardenberg. Lord Castlereagh, and later Arthur Wellesley, the first duke of Wellington, represented Great Britain. Disagreement between Russia and Prussia on the one hand and Britain and Austria on the other about boundary provisions in Eastern Europe led to a threat of renewed hostilities. The British enlisted the new French government, under the restored Bourbon dynasty in the person of King Louis XVIII, as an ally.

As a result, France was invited to send a representative to the Congress of Vienna, and was, thereafter, involved as the fifth great power of the Grand Alliance. Charles Maurice de Talleyrand, appointed foreign minister to Louis XVIII, would represent France at the Congress of Vienna. With the return of France on the diplomatic scene, the Allies tried to boost Louis XVIII's prestige and prove that they were not making war against France but against Napoleon. Talleyrand was successful in allowing France to have an equal voice in the negotiations and due to his wonderful skill as a diplomat soon made his power felt. His vote often became the deciding vote in many of the decisions.

Charles Maurice de Talleyrand-Perigord lived through the reign of Louis XVI, Napoleon I, Louis XVIII, Charles X, and Louis Philippe, spanning the years of his birth in 1754 to his death in Paris on 17 May 1838.

Talleyrand managed to survive the reign of Louis XVI, the last Bourbon king of France, who, after a number of governing missteps, was found guilty of high treason and executed by guillotine in 1793. (His wife, Marie Antoinette, received the same execution sentence nine months later.) Talleyrand thus survived the French Revolution and the reign of terror. During Napoleon's reign, he was named foreign minister. His long political life began with the Age of Enlightenment, a way of looking at the world based on reason, evidence and proof and not religious beliefs. He became its perfect representative even to the end of his life when the liberal industrial bourgeoisie was triumphantly flexing its muscles before he died in Paris. His power came not through tyranny and violence — Napoleon's modus operandi — but through his diplomatic skills (and luck).

Talleyrand came from an aristocratic family. His father held a high rank in the French Royal army; his mother was Alexandrine (née) de Damas Antigny. Both parents descended from ancient and powerful families. Because of his social class, Talleyrand would, like his father, most likely have chosen a career in the military. However, because of a congenital disorder called Marfan syndrome, a symptom of which is clubfoot, the military was not an option. Throughout his life, he blamed his nurse for his "dislocated foot." He insisted that his malformed foot was caused by a fall and asserted that his nurse delayed telling his parents about the fall until its consequences could not be remedied.[4]

A physical disability during this time placed severe limitations not only on his future career, but also on his future, period. Talleyrand's parents formally deprived him of some of his titles and properties; his brother became the recipient of what should have been Talleyrand's birthright. A physical disability, however, did not bar one from the clergy. As such, the only course of action open to him led him to Saint-Sulpice College. After his graduation in 1779, he was ordained a priest. In 1780, he was appointed agent-general of the French clergy and in 1789 he was appointed the bishop of Autun.

On 4 June 1806, after Napoleon's fall, King Louis XVIII was in power and ennobled Talleyrand with the title of Prince de Talleyrand and the further title "Peer of France." Talleyrand's aristocratic and courtly manners, and his irrepressible wit, his extraordinary abilities enabled him to be received in the highest social and political societies of Paris. At the Congress of Vienna, the newly created Prince de Talleyrand was able to elevate his position of power; he also improved France's position from one of defeat and subservience to power so great it became one of Europe's historic major nations. Metternich described Talleyrand as a "sharp edged instrument, with which it is dangerous to play."⁵ The prince gave rise to the saying throughout France of *il est un Talleyrand*— a phrase used to denote a statesman of great resource and skill. At the congress he contrived to bring France back again into political importance and to restore her rank among the great political powers.

As the opening days of the Congress of Vienna unfolded, true to its Austrian cultural heritage, a series of glittery balls and lavish entertainment took place. After all, the princes and diplomats needed to have some joie de vivre. The government allowed 10,000 pounds a day for the expense of entertainment, equal in that country and at that time to 50,000 pounds in London. So, along with deciding the fate of Central Europe, the attendees could enjoy concerts, balls, and numerous other festivities, with the greatest actors, singers, and dancers each and every evening. Beethoven, at the height of his fame, was also there. No wonder Eugene, Prince de Ligne, uttered his famous line: *"Le congres ne marche pas, il danse."*⁶ By day, the arduous work of drawing up a plan to alter Europe politically and territorially began.

What was foremost in the minds of the four powers was to prevent the extensive expansion of any one great power, such as Napoleon had brought about. Subsequently, many territorial decisions had to be made. Succinctly, the conference was to create a balance of power that would preserve the peace and reinstate conservative regimes, illustrate the altruistic attitude of the national representatives present and support the overall purpose of preventing future widespread conflict. The delegates at the Congress of Vienna were motivated to a surprisingly large degree by the desire to benefit Europe as a whole, and this is reflected in their purpose in calling the congress together and the settlement they reached. National interest was modified for the sake of the general interest of Europe.⁷

The delegates to the congress made decisive changes to the political map of Europe. The model of diplomatic spheres of influence resulting from the Congress of Vienna in 1814-15 after the Napoleonic Wars endorsed Austrian dominance in Central Europe. Thus, the Congress of Vienna established Habsburg leadership of the new German Confederation, and reaffirmed the dynasty's control over the Austrian Empire's great multinational realm. The provisions of the Congress of Vienna confirmed Austria as one of the dominant European powers. The members of the congress did not see, however, the growing strength of Prussia and subsequently did not foresee that it would challenge Austria for dominance within the

German states. But, for now, the monarchy emerged from the Napoleonic Wars victorious and the congress gave the Habsburg dynasty the leadership of Italy and Germany. Metternich played a decisive role in the settlement that left the Dynasty more territorially consolidated and produced a security against future threats from France.

As a logical consequence of the Congress of Vienna, this new era was epitomized by the Holy Alliance formed in 1815, which essentially was an agreement to preserve the old social order among Friedrich Wilhelm III, the Protestant king of Prussia; Alexander I, the Orthodox czar of Russia; and Franz Joseph, the Catholic emperor of Austria. The sovereigns joined hands "in the name of the holy and indivisible Trinity," the prime slogan of Europe's conservative Christian monarchs when they created the Holy Alliance on 26 September 1815. The goal of this coalition was to make the Christian religion the foundation of politics and to maintain the territorial claims of the respective dynasties. The designation of the alliance as "holy" reflects the fact that the monarchs regarded their legitimacy as deriving from God, seeing themselves as rulers "by divine right." For the Habsburgs, the religious emphasis was nothing unusual. A marked piety is considered to have been a family characteristic of the Habsburg dynasty generally, and indeed of other Christian dynasties of this time.[8] Because it was merely an agreement that the sovereigns would conduct themselves in ways consonant with Christian principles, the alliance accomplished very little.

When the Congress of Vienna was brought to a close, several goals had been accomplished:

- France was deprived of all territory conquered by Napoleon.
- Norway and Sweden were joined under a single ruler.
- Switzerland was declared neutral.
- Russia got Finland and effective control over the new kingdom of Poland.
- Prussia was given much of Saxony and important parts of Westphalia and the Rhine Province.
- Austria was given back most of the territory it had lost and was also given land in Germany and Italy (Lombardy and Venice).
- Britain got several strategic colonial territories, and they also gained control of the seas.
- The Netherlands and Holland were united in one kingdom.
- The petty independent states of Germany (some 300) were united into a confederation of thirty-seven called the German Confederacy: Austria

and Prussia were to have two votes each in the Diet, while Bavaria, Wurtemberg, and Hanover were to have one vote each.

For thirty years Metternich's hand was felt, if not seen, in all the political affairs of Europe, and judgments of him have been mixed. For the democratic liberals, Metternich is viewed as one with an obsession to repress revolution, one who believed in the power of the monarchy and thus suppressed the establishment of reforming regimes in Central Europe. Other historians have been kind to Metternich, particularly for his skills as an amazing negotiator and arbitrator who was able to balance the needs of the prima donna conquering nations.[9]

After Napoleon's demise, Metternich, in regard to foreign powers, had seen enough of war, which had brought Germany to the verge of political ruin. His efforts as chancellor were always focused on preservation of peace and the balance of power among nations. During peace would be the time to help Germany, which was poor, to develop the material resources of the empire. The preservation of the status quo was Metternich's desire—without change. His policy, then, was against all expansion and all progress. While men might carry on in their pubs to smoke and drink beer, any serious discussions on politics or in forming clubs for any political intent, or even reading agitating tracts or books, was forbidden. Further, Metternich thought that people should be content to remain in the economic sphere into which they were born. Similarly, he had no great love for universities in which liberal ideas could be fomented, for these ideas would disturb the order of things. For forty years his advice had been to put down popular movements and uphold absolutism at any cost.

The delegates' system of appeasement at the congress and the lack of harsh reprisals toward France was historically praiseworthy. Talleyrand was treated as an in-group partner. Even though others may not have revered Metternich in the 19th century (even though he revered himself and considered himself to be infallible),[10] he was a leader whose attributes have stood the test of time and whose abilities have received praise from historical scholars. However, Metternich was wrong when he thought he had redrawn the European map "for eternity." He ignored—just as Napoleon did—"the strong national aspirations of many people (Polish, Italians, Belgians, Germans, and Spaniards among others) that led to the fall of Napoleon's Empire."[11]

Francis I died and his son Ferdinand I became emperor of Austria and associated dominions in 1835. Prior to his death, Emperor Francis I had willed, and Prince Metternich had agreed, despite all Ferdinand's flaws that he was deemed fit to rule, or, more precisely, fit to be ruled and that was no doubt Metternich's aim. Moreover, Dr. Stifft, imperial physician, announced that there were no medical reasons why Ferdinand should not marry. This news was so unexpected that Archduchess Sophie was sorely dismayed, for if Ferdinand had a son it would be most unlikely that either her husband or her son would ever become emperor. Dr. Stifft, however, mollified her anxiety, for he was most positive that Ferdinand would never "make any attempt to assert his marital rights."[12] Dr. Stifft's prophecy was correct; the couple had no heirs.

Ferdinand was married to Maria Anna of Savoy and as usual, the archduchess had no choice in this betrothal matter. Unfortunately for her, Ferdinand was a most undesirable future partner. Historians claim that Ferdinand was basically an idiot with a hydrocephalic head and "thick tongue that could not squeeze out two connected sentences."[13] State chancellor Prince Klemens von Metternich characterized him as a "lump of putty." Metternich, shrewd and powerful, became the real ruler of the Habsburg monarchy. Things progressed rather smoothly until 1848 when a number of uprisings occurred throughout Europe, all of which were met with violent, iron-handed suppression. The proletariat demands were not met but were simply quashed by their rulers. These conflicts culminated in the Revolutions of 1848. The discharge of tensions began in France but soon spread throughout many locations in Europe. The revolution in the Habsburg empire flared up in some places, then quieted down only to move to other provinces. There was no continuity in these revolutionary events, unlike those of the 1789 French Revolution. As such, the Habsburg revolutions had neither unity of action nor unity of problems and attempted solutions.

While today insurgents may blame the leaders of the country for their plights, even the most radical Viennese were unswerving in their loyalty to the Habsburg ruler. The emperor was still considered sacred. Not the emperor but the bureaucracy was held responsible for the malfeasances of government. To the liberals, Emperor Ferdinand I remained the good-hearted, beloved father of the Austrian people whose every command was to be obeyed.[14] In old Vienna the king was the law and was never to be questioned. The emperor was the keeper of the absolute traditions. The Viennese still believed in the divinity of kings.

In almost every corner of the Habsburg empire, Austrian Germans, Hungarians, Slovenes, Poles, Czechs, Croats, Slovakians, Ukrainians, and

Italians attempted in the course of the revolution to achieve autonomy, independence, or even hegemony over other nationalities. The first revolutionary outbreak came in Hungary in early February. The Magyar nationalists demanded an autonomous government. On 3 March, revolutionaries in Buda Pest[15] had set up a constitutional government for Hungary. By August they were pressing for autonomy for their country, if not outright independence, defying the claims of imperial authority. Vienna was victorious and for now Hungary was subdued. But, she was pacified only on the surface. Beneath that surface the Hungarian people continued to agitate with revolutionary and nationalistic ideas.

In Vienna on 13 March 1848, large sectors of the population of Vienna rose up against the bureaucracy. Petitions of a liberal character were promoted by professional men and students and were circulated between March 6 and 12. The petitions cited demands for "freedom of the press, jury trials, civil rights, abolition of religious discrimination, academic freedom, full emancipation of the peasants, and above all a constitutional representative government. Most of these requests expressed the interests of the urban education middle class."[16] Prior to Franz Joseph's reign, Viennese students joined the citizens' organization in petitioning the government. Ferdinand (i.e., Metternich) persisted in his authoritarian style of ruling. Now, an increasingly brave group of liberals were demanding written legislation that would set limits on the ruler's rights. "*Constitution!*" became the watchword of the 1848 movement. Vienna experienced an escalation of this volatile atmosphere, which had already led to unrest in France and Germany as well as Hungary. When enraged students and citizens demonstrated on their way to the imperial palace, the military was ordered to disperse the gathering in the Herrengasse. Archduke Albrecht, the military commander of Vienna, rode through the crowded street and was hit by a piece of wood. The soldiers responded by opening fire, causing the first fatal casualties.

Fifty or so people were killed, leading to barricades being thrown up and the burning of factories. Ferdinand I was ill equipped to counter demands for change in his empire and was content to leave everything to Metternich.[17] But before the day ended, Metternich had been driven from office and from Vienna. The imperial family insisted that he be sacrificed to save them as they fled to Innsbruck. The crown permitted the establishment of a national guard of the citizenry, and freedom of the press, and a liberal constitution was promised for the near future.

On 6 May 1848, the revolution began in Italy. Sophie had sent Franz

Joseph there, not so much to show his military prowess as to remove him from the dangers in revolutionary Vienna, of being implicated in government affairs and of later being held responsible for promises made or acts committed by Emperor Ferdinand I and the government. At the Battle of Santa Lucia, Franz Joseph was given a chance to prove himself worthy of wearing the Austrian uniform. On the day of the battle, he wrote his mother that "he was overjoyed when he heard the cannon balls whistling around him for the first time."[18] Now that he had gone through his baptism in warfare, his mother called him home. Soon Franz Joseph would be initiated into the secret plans for his succession to the throne. On 24 and 25 May 1848, Austrian field marshal Radetzky defeated the Piedmontese army of Charles Albert and restored rule in northern Italy. King Charles abdicated his Italian throne. On 17 June the Czech revolt in Prague was suppressed. The Habsburgs and the old order were once again in total control.

In the wings, Archduchess Sophie was already lining up her son Franz Joseph to become the successor to the incompetent Ferdinand. Archduke Franz Karl, Ferdinand's brother and Sophie's husband, should have been the next in line but was completely overlooked (twice). Sophie absolutely despised Metternich for the accession of the weak-minded Ferdinand.[19] Her husband should have been chosen emperor over Ferdinand, but Franz Karl was weak and unambitious — easy to overlook. Franz Karl may have been ambitionless; Sophie was not. Ever-plotting Sophie, however, let bygones be bygones. She relinquished her thoughts of being future empress of Austria, sacrificed her husband's chances of emperorship, and chose her firstborn son, Franz Joseph, to be the next in line for the throne. Franz Joseph could be dominated, which would essentially make her the empress in all but name. She was easily able to convince her husband of the sacrifice he needed to make, as handing the scepter to the strong and youthful Franz Joseph was the right choice. Franz Joseph, she argued, could fuse all the peoples of the Austrian Empire into a comprehensive whole.

On 2 December 1848 Emperor Ferdinand read out a prepared statement on behalf of himself and his wife, the Empress Maria Anna. "Important reasons," he began, "have led us to the irrevocable decision to lay down Our Crown in favor of Our beloved nephew, Archduke Franz Joseph."[20] (For good measure, Franz had added Joseph to his name, partly with the view of molding opinion that he, too, like Emperor Joseph II, the Reformer, would be the one to give the Austrians what they wanted — a constitution — and partly to distinguish himself from Franz Ferdinand.)

The crowds, upon seeing Franz Joseph, would shout, "Long live the Constitutional Emperor Franz Joseph!"[21] Even though he was just a lad, he must have known he was living a lie, for Franz Joseph believed only in the power of absolutism; he lived in a world of aristocracy and autocracy. He preferred centralism to federalism because only the former could guarantee him the power and control he needed to fulfill his role in the Habsburg dynasty. He remained a believer in autocracy all his life.

Both Franz Joseph and Metternich believed in absolutism — monarchy as the only proper system of government, a true monarchy, not the constitutional variety. Absolutism relied on power, a power system designed to create more power for the Habsburg dynasty, and its ruler Franz Joseph. In Metternich's opinion, the government should first of all consist of a council that would advise the emperor, but in a purely consultive role. The advice presented by the council could be accepted or rejected by the monarch. Further, the council would only advise the emperor on issues that he presented to the council. The masses, however, had a different version of the type of government they wanted.

Subsequently, almost immediately into his reign, Franz Joseph inherited the rebellious uprisings that had started under Ferdinand's reign. It was a most precarious time for the Habsburg empire. More than any other time, even for most of World War I, the Habsburg dynasty came closest to dissolution in 1848 and 1849. From March 1848 through July 1849 the Habsburg Austrian Empire was threatened by revolutionary movements that often had a nationalistic character.

On 14 April 1849 the Hungarian parliament proclaimed Hungary a republic, under Regent-President Lajos Kossuth, and declared Franz Joseph dispossessed. Kossuth was a young, fiery provincial lawyer from the Slovakian region. He was striving for the full emancipation of the Hungarian peasants, the rights of any man to own property and to hold any public office, and the recognition of Magyar as the national language throughout Hungary. He sought taxation of the nobles and an end to economic monopolies and special privileges and believed in universal education and an end to censorship.

Franz Joseph decided to go on the offensive. Just a month after he became emperor, his army drove the Hungarian rebel forces out of Budapest. As Austrian troops fought the rebels across Hungary during the summer of 1849, Franz Joseph could not resist in joining the fight. However, when a shell exploded just a few feet away from the emperor, his generals persuaded him to leave the military campaign to them. As long as Austria was involved in the Hungarian war of independence, and during the following months of pacification, Prussia would gain the upper hand.

Franz Joseph officially requested military aid from Nicholas I of Russia "to prevent," as he put it, "the Hungarian insurrection developing into a European calamity."[22] As it happened, the Hungarians were defeated before the Russians could make any significant contribution to the fighting; the Habsburg armies would probably have been able to put down the Hungarian insurrection without Russian intervention. Yet it was to the Russian commander, Paskievicz, that the Hungarians, under Gorgei, surrendered at Vilagos on 13 August 1849. For their insurrections, 114 Hungarians would be shot or hanged, 13 of them senior officers from Hungarian regiments. The executions of 1849 reflected the character of the men around Franz Joseph at that time, most of them generals. Men like Schwarzenberg and Grunne believed in terror because violence was the principle tenet of their lives.[23] Once his Prime Minister Schwarzenberg proposed his policy of "a little hanging first," Franz Joseph quickly followed his orders. But Franz Joseph was now the absolute, autocratic monarch. The victory was symbolized by the triumphal return of Metternich. For Franz Joseph there was little triumph. Rather than beginning his emperorship in the spirit of conciliation and holding an olive branch, the young emperor was forced to make his way to power over the scaffold and bloodbath of Hungarians.

It was during the revolutionary uprisings, in the first crucial years of his reign, that Prince Felix of Schwarzenberg rose to power and played a pivotal role in restoring the Habsburg empire following the revolutions. Franz Joseph remained the obedient pupil that he had been before his accession, but now his teacher was neither Bombelles nor Metternich, but the new prime minister, Schwarzenberg. He was a "determined man, ruthless, willing to use any means to gain his ends, and without moral scruples."[24] He had an undistinguished career up until the revolutions.

Prince Felix was the second son of a rich and powerful family from Bohemia and was born 2 October 1800. Franz Joseph immediately took to the elderly prince as his mentor. What may have won young Franz Joseph to quickly elevate Felix to prime minister was that, in his boyish mind, Felix became a father figure — an ideal father figure. His own father was insipid, indifferent, and lacked motivation for just about anything; Felix was strong, had an unbending pride, and believed in the great power of Austria. Similarly Franz Joseph and Schwarzenberg were great believers in force and did not believe in parliaments and constitutions.[25]

Although Franz Joseph had barely reached his majority, Felix considered Franz Joseph's opinions with respect. Within a matter of months, Franz Joseph listened to Felix as he did no one else with the exception of another close advisor, Karl Grunne. Most historians write that Felix was responsible for the practical side of the emperor's education. Franz Joseph called Felix "the greatest minister I ever had at my side."[26] Metternich on one occasion called him "a pupil of my diplomatic school. A man of firm character, genuine courage and clear vision."[27]

Schwarzenberg noted that "facing the truth was a lauded quality of Franz Joseph." He continued by saying that "Franz Joseph had the ability to face the truth, even the bitterest."[28] That may have been a true assessment at one point in time, but things changed after 1850. As trusted and skilled as Felix and Karl were, they both established a system of secrecy and concealment. Anything unpleasant was hidden from the young emperor as long as possible. Perhaps this was not solely their fault, for Franz Joseph was rather mulish about disagreeable things. Hearing unpleasant news made the patient emperor impatient, and contrary to his calm demeanor he became rather brusque, to the point of positive discourtesy.

Domestic political problems continued to confront the new emperor. The most pressing of these was delivering on Ferdinand's promise of a written constitution. In March 1849, after declaring his readiness to "share our right with the representatives of our peoples," Franz Joseph announced the completion of this much-anticipated Viennese document. The document made no reference at all to popular rule, reaffirmed the monarch as the primary institution in the Austrian political system, and, rather than establishing a more federal system, upheld the empire as a unitary state with a centralized government in Vienna.

Two years later, in Prussia in 1851, King Frederick Wilhelm IV appointed Otto von Bismarck as Prussian representative to the German Confederation. Bismarck then served as ambassador to Russia and France. In 1862, at the age of 47, he returned to Prussia and was appointed Prussian prime minister and imperial chancellor by Wilhelm I, the new head of the Hollenzollern family and king of Prussia.

Otto von Bismarck, born on 1 April 1815, was the fourth son of Ferdinand von Bismarck and his wife, Wilhelmine Mencken. Otto had a strained relationship with his father, whom he saw as "kindly incompetent, weak and ineffectual."[29] His relationship with his mother was worse, for he never captured her love or admiration. She blatantly conveyed her disappointment in her son by saying she had hoped he would "penetrate deep into the world of the intellect more than I as a woman could do."[30] But her hopes of that dream had simply faded away, in her words, "for ever." Bismarck's need for nurturing and love was never fulfilled. His mother was cold, intelligent, ambitious, and unloving and was never "there" for him. It is speculated that his misogynistic tendencies stemmed from his relationship, or lack thereof, with his mother, which would be reflected in his personal and professional life.[31] His relationship with his parents was reflected in Bismarck's ruthless, often brutal behavior with others; consequently, he made very few friends. Thus, he earned labels from various historians — neurotic, vindictive, insensitive. At times, however, the true diplomat emerged and he was warm, charming and very charismatic.

On the subject of women, Bismarck, on 10 September 1843, wrote to a friend: "I love contact with women but marriage is a dubious proposition and my experiences have made me think twice. I feel partly comfortable, partly bored and very chilled in spirits, and as long as I can hold out, I will."[32] Eventually, however, Bismarck did marry a Prussian noblewoman, Johanna Friederike Charlotte Dorothea Eleonore von Puttkamer. The union produced two sons, Herbert and Wilhelm von Bismarck.

Bismarck was always subject to some physical or mental disorder. Although he had a strong constitution, he suffered his whole life from anxiety disorders, sleeplessness, hypochondria, paranoia, and stomach problems. At one point in his life, Bismarck was on the verge of collapse from complete sleeplessness. His doctor wrapped him in a warm body roll and gave him a few drops of a sleeping medication (medications had not worked before). Then the doctor sat by his bedside and held his hand — as a mother might do for her restless child — and Bismarck slept.

Professionally, Bismarck was under the rule of a weak and complaisant King Wilhelm I, and his domineering queen, Augusta, whom Bismarck hated because she incessantly interfered with his relationship with the king. His hatred was so intense that he could not even be in the same room as Queen Augusta; at one point, he dropped out of attending a state dinner minutes before it commenced when he found out he was to be seated next to her. He was, however, to obey and tolerate her, as once was the case with his parents years before.

Bismarck's passion was politics. He was an ultraconservative champion of the Prussian landed aristocracy (Junkers). His first address to parliament was to request an increase in the size of the army. His words to the assembled representatives were the oft-quoted blood and iron speech: "The great questions of the day will not be settled by speeches and majority decisions but by blood and iron."[33] Bismarck relied on William's weakness and subsequently was able to govern and outmaneuver all the generals and sovereign princes of the German states. Bismarck's program of Prussian consolidation succeeded, in part, by his exploiting the wave of Prussian nationalism among its people, through strategic wars that he often instigated, his defensive alliances and his military genius.

One of Bismarck's earliest moves as chancellor was to champion the liberties of the Germans in Schleswig and Holstein, who were being drawn more tightly into the Danish state. When Prussia declared war on Denmark, Austria joined in the revolt, for it could not let Prussia be the sole champion of German liberties. The subsequent Danish War of 1864 would entangle both these powers in the joint occupation of Schleswig and Holstein. Disputes between Prussia and Austria over the administration of these principalities led to the 1866 Austro-Prussian War.

Austria was completely defeated in this war and its position as the leading state of Germany ended forever. The remaining German minor states were soon absorbed into the German Empire created by Prussia. Historians note that this war was deliberately provoked by Bismarck, over the objections of his king.[34] The purpose of the war was to expel Austria from the German Confederation, thus furthering Bismarck's efforts for the unification of Germany under Prussian dominance. On 26 July, Austria signed a preliminary peace agreement with Prussia, which established that Austria would withdraw entirely from the association of the German states. In addition, Austria was to recognize the formation of a federation of the North German states under Prussian leadership. Finally, Austria was to pay 40 million thaler (a former German silver coin worth about three shillings sterling, or about 73 cents, around 1900) for war damages.

The scale of Bismarck's triumph cannot be exaggerated: "He alone had brought about a complete transformation of the European international order…. He achieved this incredible feat without commanding an army, and without the ability to give an order to the humblest common soldier, without control of a large party, without public support, indeed, in the face of almost universal hostility, without a majority in parliament, without control of his cabinet and without a loyal following in the bureaucracy."[35]

In a matter of hours, Bismarck became the "genius-statesman." Pictures and busts of Bismarck would sell by the thousands. He was now a public idol. He was the "Iron Chancellor," his silver helmet topped by an eagle, which, at this juncture in his life, would become symbolic of German greatness. His image would be stamped on souvenirs conveying the notion of "blood and iron," contributing to the "cult of German militarism." The grateful king ordered a "donation," on 7 June 1867 and royal monies were given to Bismarck, a sum large enough for him to purchase an estate in Pomerania.

Bismarck knew that he was a servant who could always be dismissed at will by his sovereign, but from 1862 to 1890 Wilhelm I always seemed to succumb to Bismarck's power and give his confidence to Bismarck unconditionally. Bismarck, a master of manipulation, would often engage in histrionic temper tantrums, tears, and hysterical outbursts peppered with frequent threats of resignation to get his way. It is no wonder then that the king sighed that "it is was hard to be king under Bismarck."[36]

Bismarck knew he could not live without the power extracted from Wilhelm I. The crowning of Wilhelm II brought the end to Bismarck's political career. In Wilhelm II's letter to Bismarck, the reasons for his dismissal related to the "lust for power that had taken a demonic hold on this noble, great man."[37] Bismarck died at the age of 83 at Friedrichsruh on 28 July 1898. On his tomb he requested the following inscription: "A true German servant of the Emperor Wilhelm I." To many, Bismarck was *the* greatest diplomat, whose greatest achievement was the unification of Germany. Like Franz Joseph, Bismarck was a committed monarchist; each could never see the effectiveness of a constitution giving power to the people and checking the power of the reigning ruler.

In the wake of Austria's defeat by Prussia, there were renewed calls in Hungary for complete separation from Austria. To lose Hungary was unthinkable. To avoid this, Emperor Franz Joseph I of Austria and his court floated the suggestion of a dual monarchy. The decision to compromise, *Ausgleich* of 1867, created a dual monarchy known as Austria-Hungary, or the Austro-Hungarian Empire. Borders remained the same, but now Hungary and the rest of Austria became two separate states ruled by a common Habsburg monarch. The 1867 compromise with Hungary was one of the last major reorganizations of the lands ruled by the Habsburgs and it became the main preoccupation of Franz Joseph's reign to successfully maintain this dualistic monarchy. This role was, to the end of his days, his most difficult and his most important task.

Each country would view the outcomes of the revolutions of the 1800s through the perception of its own myopic lens. To the French, the revolutions may have been seen as a step toward *liberté, égalité, fraternité*. Those loyal to Marx would most probably denounce 1848, viewing it as a betrayal by the bourgeoisie to the ideals of the working class. To the Prussians, the revolutions were most likely considered to be a giant step towards their becoming the most powerful country in Central Europe. To the Austrians, the jury has vacillated: some trumpet the revolutions as a harbinger of hope; some view the revolutions as an albatross that delayed further progress. However, the national achievements of the revolution were extremely meager and "if balanced against the degree of illusions destroyed and resentment created far more negative than positive. Yet the impetus given to the development of national political life, even through so short a period as the revolutionary one, was not in vain. It left its indelible traces. The political developments after 1867 would have been inconceivable without the vivid memories of 1848."[38]

CHAPTER THREE

Franz Joseph

With the exception of the habitual grumbling of the masses over heavy taxation, in 1830 Vienna, indeed all of Austria, was relishing a wonderful time of peace. And, in this tranquil period, a long-awaited event occurred. On 18 August the stillness of the day was broken by the loud clamoring of bells throughout all the Catholic churches of the town. Thunderous roars erupted twenty-one times from the imperial cannons. People flocked to the courtyard of Schönbrunn, with most jubilant faces, where it was announced "on the 18th of August at a quarter past nine o'clock in the morning, Her Imperial Highness, the Most Illustrious Archduchess Sophie, consort of His Imperial Highness, the Most Illustrious Archduke Franz Karl, was happily delivered of an Archduke in the Imperial-Royal Palace of Schönbrunn...."[1]

Archduchess Sophie had just given birth to her firstborn — a son — the most probable heir apparent (at least by Sophie's calculations). With national flags waving, the celebrants were not necessarily saluting Sophie, for with her arrogant and pious ways, she wasn't a crowd favorite.[2] But, with this wonderful birth, there would be cause for celebrations in Vienna's public parks — Auergarten and Prater — and that, plus a newborn son breathing life into the Habsburg dynasty, was something to cheer about.

The journey leading to this moment had been rather long and arduous, but after six years of marriage and several miscarriages, the Archduchess Sophie gave birth to Franz Joseph. Sophie was twenty-five and a most solicitous mother. In addition to his wife's overseeing eyes, the Archduke had his own household, a whole battalion of others: a nurse, cook, chamber woman, a general-purpose maid, a scullery maid, all eagerly attending one small infant. Also included were a coachman and a footman attending the coach-and-six, which was used to take the infant Franz Joseph for periodic drives so he could breathe the country's fresh air. From his first few weeks in the nursery, a pattern of regimentation and orderliness shaped his daily schedule, which would later reflect his daily adult schedule.

Franz Joseph's proud mother, Sophie Friederike Dorothea von Wittelsbach, was one of thirteen children born to King Maximilian I Joseph of Bavaria and his second wife, Fiederike Karoline von Baden-Hochberg. The House of Wittelsbach was a German noble family whose name was taken from the castle of Wittelsbach, formerly standing near Aichach on the Paar in Bavaria. Of prominent interest is Sophie's sister, Marie Ludovika, born three years after Sophie in 1808 and eventually married to Duke Maximilian Joseph in Bavaria. Ludovika would become the mother of Sisi, Franz Joseph's future bride.

On 4 November 1824 Sophie was married to Archduke Franz Karl von Habsburg, second son of Emperor Francis I. Marriage, at least for the upper classes and royalty, was a property transaction. Royals entered into mutually profitable alliances with others, and an arranged union sealed deals, both economic and political. So it was not surprising that the ink was barely dry on the official marriage papers when Sophie, a high-spirited girl with a love for excitement and change, discovered that her husband was the polar opposite of these, her cardinal traits.[3] She was a natural ruler and her courage and faith would dramatically alter personal and political relationships of the Habsburgs. Franz Karl was described as kind and tolerant; these traits were foreign to Sophie. Franz Joseph seemed to have had very little involvement with his father. Sophie was the domineering tyrant. In contrast to Franz Joseph's mother, his father seemed weak and ineffectual.

The arts and music could count on Sophie's patronage. She was a conventionally devout Catholic and was most respectful of her spiritual confessor, Abbot Joseph von Rauscher. Her maternal drive was boundless and her children realized this. Franz Joseph, more so than the other siblings, was always grateful to his mother for all she had done for him.[4] Throughout his life, he remained extremely close to her and, as she was confidante, he respected her opinion. Sophie would always strive to be a role model for her children. She would hold her emotions in check because it was most essential that her sons, particularly Franz Joseph, should learn to be unemotional and show an iron façade in the face of any type of adversity. Sophie succeeded, as Franz Joseph dealt with horrendous deeds of fate: the death of a child, defeat in war, the death of his brother, the murder of his wife, and the assassination of his nephew and heir-apparent.

Sophie gave her eldest child physical beauty and strength. But would he also inherit the perilous mental instability, which caused so many tragedies in the Wittelsbach house in the course of the 19th century? The Wittelsbach line was not free of hereditary taints, and there were several cases of mental illness. Duke Max's father and King Ferdinand were feebleminded and crippled. The two sons of the Bavarian king, Crown Prince Ludwig II and Prince Otto, were also mentally ill. The disease so greatly feared by the Habsburgs was epilepsy, which had entered the family by way of Maria Louisa, a princess of Bourbon Spain and the mother of Emperor Francis I. Habsburgs Archduke Karl and Archduke Rainer suffered from it.

Of Sophie's four sons, two would be deemed normal, though differing in personality from each other. Two would show the crippling characteristics of a heritage of inbreeding, from both the Habsburg side and the Wittelsbach side. Requirements for eligibility as spouses of members of the Habsburg family were these: one, the candidate had to belong to a reigning family, and two, the chosen one had to be a member of the Roman Catholic Church. This was not a difficult thing in the first several decades of the dynasty, because most families were Roman Catholic. But as reigning houses started to dwindle in number and large numbers of families became Protestant, the Habsburg family was forced to marry within the House of Habsburg. Franz Joseph would not be condemned like his predecessors; it appeared that he was normal and sturdy.

Sophie was a dutiful wife, giving birth to four more children. Two years after the birth of Franz Joseph, Ferdinand Maximilian was born. Maximilian turned out to be studious, rather intellectual, and quite sensitive. Franz Joseph and Max would become Sophie's favorites. She devoted her life to these two and, with her domineering and politically ambitious ways, it is not surprising that the former son would become an emperor and the latter son a king. Franz Joseph with his strong character would become her strength and Ferdinand Maximilian with his tender and romantic ways was her delight.

Max was particularly clever and the most curious of Sophie's children. He was appealing, gifted, funny, imaginative, and very unmilitary; he just had an engaging personality.[5] His wife, Princess Charlotte, was beautiful and ambitious and very rich. Sophie constantly talked about Charlotte's impeccable pedigree, her very blue blood and her illustrious family, so important to Sophie and to the principals of the Viennese Court. Charlotte approved of Max's accepting the imperial crown of Mexico in 1864.

Napoleon III had sent a French force to Mexico to collect and acquire a fresh dependency in the New World. He needed a Habsburg figurehead to act as the king there to legitimize his ambitions. Thus, Max was originally brought to Mexico by France as a puppet figurehead. But, he was quite independent; he would not be a tool of the French government. He sought a brighter spotlight, with himself as a liberating emperor of Mexico. French forces took Mexico City and Max proclaimed himself the imperial ruler of Mexico in June of 1863. He succeeded in ruling for about two years.

His influence, however, rapidly eroded and the Mexican people wanted one of their own to rule. The republic opposition, led by Benito Juarez, saw Max only as a puppet of their enemy country, France. In 1866, France withdrew from Mexico, saying that Maximilian could manage on his own and leaving him behind with no support. Max was unaware of the hatred of the French intervention felt by the Mexican people. With the growing reality of a return of the Juárez regime Max was able to hold out for less than one year before his troops were overrun in Querétaro. His wife pleaded with Napoleon III to help her husband but her pleas fell on deaf ears. On 19 June 1867 Ferdinand Maximilian was executed by firing squad. He was 35 years old. Sophie profoundly and continually mourned his death for the remaining five years of her life.

Karl Ludwig (1833), born one year after Maximilian, grew up to be a "half mad, religious mystic."[6] That, however, did not stop him from having three wives. He would most resemble his unambitious and somewhat witless father. A daughter, Marianne, was born in 1835 but tragically died at four years of age; a stillborn brother followed her. Ludwig Viktor (1842), twelve years younger than Franz Joseph, was Sophie's "Luzi wuzi," weak, effeminate and a homosexual. Ludwig never did a stroke of work. Emperor Franz Joseph, because of Ludwig's sexual preferences and transvestitism, finally forbade him to stay in Vienna.

Despite the number of progeny, Sophie's marriage to Archduke Franz Karl was an unhappy one. When a marriage is unhappy, one's attentions turn to other sources. For Sophie her energies turned to molding and shaping the lives of her sons, Franz and Max — from regulating the nursery to matchmaking for her sons. There is a painting of Sophie leading her son Franz Joseph up the steps to the throne blazoned with the Habsburg imperial insignia. The portrait is quite emblematic of the future of Sophie's firstborn son and her role in leading him to the throne and keeping him there.

But the emperorship was a few years hence, so, for now, Sophie's attention turned to her strong and healthy little "Franzl." A huge cause for alarm occurred just before Franz Joseph celebrated his first birthday. A cholera epidemic was raging and advancing remorselessly across Russia and Poland; it had already killed the czar's brother and his wife. Sophie was paralyzed with fear, as was each family, no matter what their social class; all feared the consequences of this epidemic. It soon crossed into the northern counties of Hungary during the year and was to claim the lives of 1 in 25 of the population. The imperial family reacted as if it were the plague. At Schönbrunn, isolation was imposed with rigor. For this reason, cholera made less impact in the city of Vienna than in London a year later.

"Vibrant," "protectively maternal," "dominating," "conservative" and "fervently religious" are some of the character labels historians have given to Sophie.[7] Metternich and Sophie were the prominent two who emerged as dominant and responsible members of the royal court, a situation earning her the dubious title of "the only man at court." Sophie was truly the most formidable figure in the family.

The first six years of Franz Joseph's life were entrusted to his *aja*, or governess, a spinster with a firm but affable temperament, Baroness Luise von Sturmfeder. She was sixteen years older than Sophie and was the sixth child in a family of eleven from the lesser Prussian nobility. Her young charge remained personally devoted to the baroness, whom he affectionately called "Amie." Luise wrote down many endearing incidents that took place under her watch.[8] Her personal reflections were published forty years after her death but while Franz Joseph was still alive. She described Franz Joseph as a sweet and sensitive child. As with any royal marked as an heir to the throne, fears become exaggerated over relatively minor mishaps. Frau Sturmfeder recalled the near panic of Franzl's entourage of caregivers when he arrived back from a walk in the park with his hands quite blue because no one had given him gloves.

We also learn from Baroness von Sturmfeder about Franzl's delight in looking down from a gallery on his first masked ball or seeing his father riding back from a hunt. Her remarks relate the joy young Franzl showed when he received tambourines and a toy drummer-girl, left as presents beneath a Christmas tree when he was still too young to verbally express his enthusiasm. Despite a few minor oversights, Franz Joseph's early care was predominantly devoted to his physical well-being. He grew up a remarkably handsome boy with good-looking features, slim and rather muscular, with impeccable manners and a faultless bearing. Even in boyhood his distinguishing trait was a self-control beyond his years.

Another well-known portrait, by Ferdinand Waldmuller, shows the future emperor at the age of two, wearing a soldier's frock and holding a toy musket in his right hand. With a child's helmet above his blond curls, his left hand firmly grasps the wooden head of a carefully carved officer doll in trim white uniform. By age of four, he was often dressed up in military uniforms, which he continued to wear all his life. "Ever since childhood," his mother wrote to Field Marshal Radetzky in 1848, "Franz has been passionately devoted to the military profession."[9] (According to his valet, Ketterl, as an adult Franz Joseph had "innumerable" uniforms, many of them magnificent foreign ones presented to curry favor with him.) His Christmas presents in 1834 included a large model of the palace guard from his grandparents and more hand-painted soldiers of other ranks in finest parade-ground order.

For his fourth birthday, Sophie gave him a fine hand-painted set of toy soldiers, which became his principal playthings. His collection was added to until every Austrian regiment was represented and he knew every button on every uniform. Not one of these toy soldiers was ever broken. In his teens he began to receive serious military training, to understand maneuvers, signals, strategies, weapons. At thirteen, he was appointed colonel of a regiment of dragoons. Henceforth he could play with live, instead of tin, soldiers. He was taught early how to play war and would come to revel in all aspects of military life, from the drilling of the imperial guards outside his window when he was very small to the lessons under his military tutor, Franz von Hauslab, when he was a teenager. The qualities of punctuality, punctiliousness, sense of duty and maintaining order, which he showed in abundance as a child, showcased his adult personality as well.

Archduke Franz seemed to idolize his grandfather "der gute" Kaiser Franz. And his grandfather seemed to be most fond of Franz Joseph as well. Franz Joseph was quite used to the presence of his imperial grandfather for the man often visited the nursery, chatting happily with the boy who would eventually succeed to his crowns. When his grandfather was struck with pneumonia and could drink only tea, Franzl, age five, decided, in a nice gesture of family solidarity, that it was his duty to drink nothing but tea as well. His grandfather was sinking fast, and Franz Joseph was taken on one last visit to the sick room. Emperor Franz died that night. The death of Francis I made an impression on the small boy of five. Franz

Joseph conjured up a picture in his mind of his grandfather as an ideal ruler — much different than the picture of Ferdinand, who was kind and gentle but a pathetic sight. "My son has still no attachment so strong as that which he bears to the memory of his grandfather,"[10] declared Sophie.

The Habsburg children experienced a happy childhood. In the spring and autumn months the family would spend their days at Schönbrunn or Laxenburg Palace. Franz Joseph and Karl Ludwig both preferred Laxenburg, where for the best part of every day they could be off shooting wild ducks and rabbits with their father. Maximilian instead preferred Schönbrunn, with its zoo full of strange animals and its conservatory with exotic tropical plants. Summer months were often spent in a little mountain resort in the Salzkammergut in Bad Ischl. Sophie believed in the restorative and therapeutic powers of Salzkammergut's saline springs. Perhaps these feelings were a result of her bathing there and becoming pregnant after several miscarriages.

Franz Karl, as with most fathers of the day, played very little role in the upbringing of their offspring. Fathers did have some responsibility in teaching their sons riding and hunting skills. Initially, Franz Joseph was rather afraid of horses and cried at the mere presence of one. But he was given horses that were so highly trained that they could almost read and write. Thus he overcame his fear and turned out to be an excellent equestrian along with developing a passion for hunting, which remained with him his whole life.

When Franz Joseph was six years old, he moved from the nursery to the schoolroom, and an all-male one replaced his female staff. Baroness Sturmfeder's influence was replaced by a more serious and "stern upbringing." Count Heinrich Bombelles, a soldier-courtier and trained diplomat, was to be Franz Joseph's "official instructor." Metternich warmly approved of Bombelles, whom Metternich felt was "one of the few men who thought as I thought, saw as I saw, and wished as I wished." Franz's curriculum followed the standard course of dancing, fencing, swimming, music, and drawing. Attempts to teach him music met with total indifference, and literature was just plain boring. On the 100th celebration of Goethe's birth in 1849 he wrote to his mother: "We would have done without his useless festival; we have better things and people to celebrate."[11]

Count Johan Coronini-Cronberg assisted Bombelles. Coronini was an excellent horseman and was a total non-national, as he saw himself as the servant of the Habsburg dynasty, not of Austria. Coronini would be responsible for the young Archduke's military training. Because of Franz's interest in soldiering, Coronini had a deep impact on his young charge. Matters of philosophy and religion were left to the archbishop of Vienna, Joseph von Rauscher. It was Bombelles who presented the archduchess with the first of several elaborate programs of study. Her eldest son would be expected to progress from eighteen hours a week spent over his books to thirty-six hours at the age of six, to forty-eight hours at the age of eight, and about fifty-five hours a week at the age of fifteen. His lessons began at 6:00 A.M. and lasted until 9:00 P.M.

As soon as he was old enough to understand, he began to be indoctrinated in the art of ruling. His teacher, summoned by Sophie, was old Metternich, who was to teach Franz the art of statecraft, diplomacy, politics, and government. But his "education" went beyond academic matters and encompassed learning traits of an emperor, namely, being courageous, self-assured, and dignified. He needed to "overcome every bodily weakness," and not fall victim to the plebeian failing of showing one's emotions. Coronini gave out some pretty strict and austere requirements: No frivolity — no laughter — no nonsense.

When he wrote letters to his mother, it almost appears that Franz Joseph was trying to maintain some modicum of his child-like emotional self, albeit with a strong German overtone. At one point in his letter-writing youth, he perfunctorily stated his love in its prescribed order — "first mother, second, but only distantly — father, then nature, God."[12] His letters tried to convey his love for his mother but seemed "contrived or perhaps coached." He wrote, recalling with joy "the happy day on which I received Holy Communion with you for the first time." Rather stilted for a boy of merely nine years. He seems to have only cultivated the outer man — dignified, detached — and neglected the personal and emotional side of the inner man. He appears to have stifled his inner self to protect his outward majesty.

Franz was a good linguist. Even before his eighth birthday he was writing letters in French to his mother that seem to have been his own work for he asked his mother to let him know if his choice of words was incorrect. Often, in midstream of his French-writing labors, would suddenly appear a German word or phrase. By spring he was already learning Magyar (Hungarian) and Czech as well as French and before the end of the year he had begun Italian. A little Latin was acquired at twelve and Greek at thirteen — all of the languages that might be of use to a future Habsburg emperor. Though his education appeared to be many-sided, it ceased when he was too young to have acquired any advanced scientific training.

Mixed in with all these instructors was the ever-present Sophie, who conscientiously supervised her son's lessons. She, along with the others, stressed duty, piety, formality, responsibility, obedience, and the respect due a monarch, all of which shaped Austria's post 1848-ruler. Sophie was proud to play the emperor-maker, conscious that her hands possessed the strength to mold the monarchy.

As with all monarchs, Franz Joseph had many gifts as well as many faults. In praising him, historians have agreed that the emperor was dignified, courteous, noble, handsome, and self-assured, and had a pronounced sense of honor and duty. His less attractive features were lack of imagination, lack of feelings, hard-heartedness, and narrow interests. His intellect was described, at best, as average; however he did master several languages and had an astonishing memory for detail. He also had a strong aversion to progressive ideas. Biographer Alan Palmer writes, "He was not the remote, cardboard cut-out figure of historical legend, a humourless bureaucrat able to endure personal tragedies because he lacked the human warmth to feel their impact deeply. Nor was his intelligence so limited as some writers insist; for, while he rejected pretentious intellectualism with brusque common-sense honesty, he took pains to master several languages and to prefect an astonishingly detailed memory."[13]

He was portrayed as a man who did not lose his temper, abuse anyone, or use "unseemly language." Like Queen Victoria, Franz Joseph was a compulsive writer of letters — to his wife, mistress, and mother. Unlike Queen Victoria, who tended to be engage in free and spontaneous prose, Franz Joseph was a chronicler and chose to give long, narrative accounts of his day to the three woman who were closest to him: his mother, Sophie; his wife, Empress Elisabeth; and his mistress, Katharina Schratt.[14]

Emperor Franz Joseph, unlike Ferdinand I, was not loved by his people — respected, yes, but not loved. A report of Police Commissioner Camerina claimed that Franz Joseph "since coming to the throne has been the protector of the military and lacks any love for his populace, which is made evident by the fact that neither his Majesty nor the Empress show themselves to the people, indeed at any such opportunity they seek to keep themselves distant. His Highness is also accused of devoting more time to the pleasures of hunting ... than to the business of government."[15]

It never occurred to Franz that he should try to be more affable to his subjects and win their affection. Indeed he never did anything to attract it. He did not crave popularity from the "common people"; he simply thought it undignified to curry favor with them. From his majestic eyes to his highly polished boots, he exuded stiffness, coldness, and a hardness that conveyed he was simply unapproachable. When he attended a performance at the Bohemian Theater in Prague, he barely noted the audience's somewhat warm reception. His popularity was further undermined when, under the pressure of revolutionary troubles, he withdrew the promise for a constitution that he once granted. That retraction had long aftereffects and led to feelings of distrust of Franz Joseph's rule.

From the time of his portrait as a two-year-old in his military uniform, Franz Joseph had some sort of contempt for civilian dress and always appeared in his military uniform — white tunic with gold; red trousers with gold lampas.[16] Perhaps that was one of the main causes for his lack of popularity with the masses, who with no great respect intended gave him the epithet "Lieutenant Red Legs." Middle class and working class people alike were incensed by the sudden appearance of this military atmosphere about the young monarch. The more he strove to become a just but severe ruler, the more pubic opinion turned against him. Subsequently, there occurred a revival of feelings for Emperor Joseph II, the "appreciator of mankind." The reserve and inapproachability of his young successor alienated the sympathy of the very best sections of the society of the capital.

Franz, unfortunately, believed, or was conditioned to believe, that all men were created unequal. He rarely spoke to any inhabitant below the rank of imperial royal major. His social relations were with royalty, the highest aristocracy, and generals. He did not strike even his contemporaries as being particularly amiable. He appeared to have had little love; he had no friends but he did have his honor, duty, and the Habsburg empire. He also had a deep affection and admiration for his mother. Later on, despite little time, he would become a family man who seemed to enjoy playing with his children but at the same time set store by their being brought up to become "worthy" members of the family. Prince Felix of Schwarzenberg described Franz Joseph as follows:

> The Emperor's mental powers are acute, his industry is admirable, especially in one so young as he. He works with great application ten hours a day, and no one knows better than I how many reports submitted to him by his ministers he has rejected after having examined them. His bearing is dignified; his demeanor toward people exceedingly polite, but somewhat dry. Sentimentalists ... say he does not have a warm heart. Of that warm but superficial good-nature of some Archdukes there is not a trace. Yet he is approachable, patient, and has the good intention to do justice to all. He has a profound abhorrence of every lie and is completely discreet.... I have never yet seen him discouraged for even one moment, in the most difficult circumstances.[17]

Franz Joseph continuously thought of how to make the city more picturesque. There was a great deal of building going on, mainly caused by the expansion of the city of Vienna. In 1857 Franz Joseph ordered the wall around the city to be razed. In the place of the wall, a beautiful wide boulevard was to ring the old city. The Ringstrasse, a magnificent boulevard of more than three miles, officially opened in 1865: "By the Imperial Rescript of 25 December 1857, the emperor ordered the demolition of the old bastions encircling the capital. Until Francis Joseph's intervention, the town proper had been separated from the suburbs by a featureless expanse of ground which was used by the regiments in the garrison for manoeuvres.... [T]he imperial administration sold the vast expanses of ground to capitalists who then built apartment blocks. The treasury received from this venture 220 million florins which was then spent on public buildings."[18] On 13 May, the anniversary of Maria Theresa's birth, there was an unveiling on Ringstrasse Boulevard of a grand monument to Maria Theresa, Franz Joseph's great-great-grandmother. It became the center attraction in the square between museums recently built to house the empire's natural history and art collections. The monument was a salute to the Habsburg empress whose courage had saved the Habsburg dynasty.

When the wall was razed, the daily newspapers were filled with cries of anguish quite like those of the terror-stricken artistic Parisians when they first saw the Eiffel Tower. It gave Vienna an entirely new feeling, one of expansiveness and breadth, a link to the modern world. Initially, it was thought that the spacious area would solve Vienna's notorious housing shortage. But instead of public housing being built along the boulevard, large and expensive mansions lined the Ring.

Today the Ringstrasse continues its magic with its magnificent buildings, palaces and theaters and blocks of elegant apartment houses. The buildings continue to be impressive, not only for their architectural excellence but also as enduring monuments to Franz Joseph and his vanished dynasty. During their last brilliant decades, the Habsburgs built as though they were going to be around for at least the next thousand years.

Franz Joseph was the watchful guardian of his realm. He worked tirelessly to make this vast machine of dualism actually work smoothly from the date of its establishment to his death. He was entirely committed to the office of emperor and by all accounts had a "fanatical sense of duty and order."

One of his chief defects was his inclination to look at the surface, short-term aspects of a situation and react with too much haste. He had a strong disinclination for idle talk and a tendency to give blunt and brief orders and make even more brief decisions. When he reached a decision, the matter was closed. He developed an extreme distaste for persons who would have liked for him to consider decisions more deeply. So he continued to see issues empirically and preferred practical, expedient solutions based on common-sense principles rather than ruminating about complex policies based on higher theoretical considerations.

Franz Joseph was a Silas Marner by nature; that is, extremely parsimonious in a prodigal court. He did, however, keep a good wine cellar and enjoyed good cigars; he gave his patronage to artists of whom he approved and he made certain that the best horses were bought for his stables and the best equipment for days when he would go stalking in the mountains. And there were occasions when he was a bit more liberal with his money. When Emperor Ferdinand I died, for example, Franz Joseph became very rich. It appears that when Ferdinand abdicated, he retained his personal funds, making him the wealthiest member of the dynasty. The residue of his funds was left to Franz Joseph, now suddenly one of the richest rulers in all of Europe. Ferdinand did not play the stock market, so the *Krach* and the subsequent depression left his money untouched. "From now on, I am a rich man," [19] Franz Joseph remarked to his military adjutant general, Crenneville; no personal financial worries need trouble him anymore. Old habits die hard, but amazingly, after forty years of cautious spending, within days of inheriting this great wealth Franz Joseph tripled the annual allowance of his close family members.

Franz Joseph was not a great speaker. He made the necessary speeches in Prague or Vienna but he knew he was a terrible orator. At times he would happily confide, "For once I spoke pretty well, without a prompter and without getting stuck."[20] Once, when he was giving a speech in honor of Wilhelm II at Wilhelm's birthday celebration, he read, "And now, ladies and gentlemen, I ask you to join me in a triple salute: 'Kaiser Wilhelm, Hurrah! Hurrah!'" This was followed by a long pause as the emperor turned the page. Then he read, "Hurrah!"[21]

He was a stickler for ceremony. On one evening the emperor was not feeling well, and he called for his personal physician at three o'clock in the morning. The doctor arrived in his dressing gown, having rushed to the emperor's bedside. Franz Joseph could hardly talk because of the pain he was experiencing but he did manage to quietly exclaim, "Full-dress suit!" to the doctor.

Despite his earlier brush with death, Franz Joseph was rather cavalier about being surrounded by protective guards. He believed that no guard could be sufficient enough to protect the life of a sovereign. And there *were* attempts on his life. When he and Elisabeth were traveling to Triest to celebrate its five hundredth year of belonging to Austria, a bomb was placed under a railway bridge over which Franz Joseph was to travel. The Czech zealots who had planted the bomb were caught and the disaster was averted.

Biedermeier is a term that is sometimes used to characterize Franz Joseph's reign. The term Biedermeier came to symbolize reliability, with lots of common sense, and in fact quite boring. *"Bieder"* is a German word meaning common-or-garden, everyday, plain *Meier* (Meyer is a common German surname, like Smith in the U.S.) After Napoleon's defeat at Waterloo in 1815, the mood of the people of Europe changed and the style of furniture was altered dramatically to match. In Napoleon's moments of power, the style of furniture was grand, of monumental proportions, with rich velvety materials covering ornately carved, dark mahogany woods. After his final defeat, a simpler style with clean, less encumbered lines was sought after. This is a rather remarkable example of how design can exemplify its historical period. This style, later known as "Biedermeier" was void of excessive carving and was gilding and more sleek in design, somewhat reminiscent of today's modern furniture design. The Biedermeier style, marked by simplicity and somewhat Spartan design, also denotes the artistic styles that flourished in the fields of literature, music, and the visual arts of the time.

Biedermeier also denotes Franz Joseph's reign. He correctly and somewhat mechanically ran the state for decades, while modernity passed him, and his monarchy by. Biedermeier has come to reflect his modest and simple lifestyle as well. Apart from the formal banquets, his meals were frugal. Because he spent his working days wearing the service uniform of an infantry lieutenant, he paid little attention to elegant civilian dress, and so the imperial wardrobe was extremely modest in scope. His palaces remained sparsely furnished. In the Hofburg, he slept on an iron bedstead with a camel-skin cover, and he used pitchers and bowls for the cold-water bath with which he began each morning. In Schönbrunn the imperial bedroom was furnished with solid jacaranda-wood twin beds and with wall coverings and curtains of blue Lyonnaise silk, hung in the year of his marriage and never replaced.

Although the palace was said to include 1441 rooms and 139 kitchens, Franz Joseph never had a bathroom installed in the imperial apartments at Schönbrunn; he frowned on these luxurious modern inventions. He distrusted telephones, trains, and automobiles (he rode in an automobile exactly twice in his life). Electric lights irritated his eyes. He steadfastly resisted technological changes.

Like Baroness Sturmfeder's daily recordings of the young Franz Joseph, his valet Eugen Ketterl gives us some insight into Franz in his later and elderly years. From 1894 when Ketterl was appointed valet de chambre, he looked after Franz Joseph every day until the time of Franz Joseph's death. Eugen claims that Franz was very "benevolent to all of us and uniquely polite. He never gave orders, he always asked for a service and expressed his thanks when, for instance, he was passed a glass of water." Ketterl's day began at 3:30 A.M., when he woke the emperor: "*Leg mich zu Füßen Eurer Majestät, guten Morgen*"[22] (I fall at your feet, Your Majesty, good morning!). Ketterl described some of Franz Joseph's weaker traits, such as smoking too many cigars and the growing isolation of the aging emperor within the family. But also he remarks on Franz Joseph's inner distance from the modern world outside the imperial court, which had become a relic of an age long past. His household effects were of the robust, utilitarian sort, the technical equipment outdated, and there were no modern facilities installed.

Franz Joseph's lifestyle reflected his absolutism policy of government. In personal terms, "this meant working all day every day, from dawn till dusk, to keep up with the administrative responsibilities in the army and bureaucracy which fall to the head of government."[23] The main characteristic of Franz's lifestyle was continuity. He maintained an ironclad routine. His day began between 3:30 and 4:00, and after bathing with cold water, he donned his modest infantry lieutenant's uniform. Settling down in his study — doing his duty as administrator of his empire — he would make a start on the pile of papers on his desk that required his immediate attention. While at work, the emperor would be served a frugal breakfast, and twice a week, between ten o'clock and lunchtime, he would have a cup of coffee, a butter roll, and perhaps a slice of ham. At around 7:30 A.M. he would put his paperwork aside and ring for his duty officer. He would then meet with the various military and cabinet officials, including his minister and foreign minister.[24]

On occasion he would join his family for lunch. More frequently, he would partake of a simple meal in his study — a bowl of soup, roast meat, vegetables, and a glass of beer. After this he would set to work receiving a report from the Vienna chief of police and a press summary from the foreign and domestic newspapers. Between five and six he would straighten his desk and leave for dinner. State dinners were eating races (even twelve-course dinners were concluded in about one hour).

Etiquette demanded that no one speak to the emperor unless he first addressed them. Dinner was brief and ended when the emperor, who ate very little and said very little, had very rapidly finished his meal. Ketterl wrote that "all the attendants, from the Lord Grand Master of the Kitchen to the last waiter, signed with relief when all had gone smoothly, for His Majesty, however intensely he may have seemed to be conversing with his guests, noticed every infraction, the slightest delay in the changing of plates, and heard ... even the faintest noise made in putting down a plate."[25]

When Franz Joseph did not have any official engagements he ate very modestly, and when staying at Bad Ischl in the summer, he is said even to have contented himself with just fermented milk and dark rye bread. However, on special occasions, the court chefs had to prepare lavish menus comprising several courses. Three times a week, so-called *Seriendiners* were held, to which approximately thirty guests were invited. On Sundays, family dinners took place, which all members of the imperial house who were present in Vienna were obliged to attend. Only illness was accepted as an excuse for not attending, and if need be, Franz Joseph even sent his own personal physician to check that he had not been deceived. However, when his closest and noblest relatives tried to avoid this obligatory appointment, it was not because of the poor quality of the food, but because royal dinners were far from idyllic.

Franz Joseph, it could be said, was a solitary survivor of the chivalrous age of knighthood. He cultivated attributes from this era — being fair, respectful of women — and was praised for his highly developed sense of noblesse oblige. What distinguished Franz Joseph was his industry, sense of duty, and integrity: "this synthesis served better as a unifying symbol of imperial rule than the greater talents of a more colorful man could ever have."[26] One cannot overlook his dignity — his *charisma*. His presence said so many of his contemporaries, was simply, to use a contemporary word, awesome. Most people were deeply impressed by his dignity — the dignity of the old Vienna. Franz Joseph simply had the old world gift of grace. He ruled with an authority of the eternal yesterday. As he told Theodore Roosevelt in 1910, "You see in me the last European monarch of the old school."[27] Franz's image and his name are inextricably part of the city Vienna and the country Austria.

After Schwarzenberg's death, the minister of the interior, Alexander Bach, became the leader in domestic affairs. Bach's general policy, as an attempt at modernization, was known as neo-Absolutism, sort of a rerun of Joseph II's policies: "The neo-Absolutist rationale was that the absolute state would make the concession of political rights unnecessary by forcibly providing a modern economy, administration and educational system for all…. It amounted to a power system designed to create more power for the Habsburg state and its ruler Franz Joseph, so that he could maintain and enhance his, the Habsburgs' dynastic position in Europe."[28] Franz Joseph's chosen role was to be a real absolutist. He believed that the only true form of government was monarchy, that monarchical government should be absolute. Imperial absolutism characterized his reign, in which his power as a ruler was unchecked and unlimited. Government, according to Franz Joseph, existed to protect the social order and suppress any manifestations of the popular will.

The absolutism of Franz Joseph differed from its Joseph II predecessor in its attitude toward the church. Franz Joseph's upbringing and his politics were deeply affected by Catholicism and he was "prepared to give up one of the Habsburgs' most traditional and powerful sources of authority."[29] The House of Habsburg defined itself as a Catholic dynasty. Franz Joseph's bond with the church culminated in the Concordat of 1855, which gave the church jurisdiction in marriage questions, censorship, and oversight of elementary and secondary education. Priests, entrusted with religious education in the schools, made sure teachings in all fields of instruction, did not conflict with the teachings of the church. Franz Joseph did not like change. "*Ich wechsle nicht gert*" was an oft-heard comment of the emperor's. Paradoxically, Franz Joseph granted concessions to the political liberals of the day. Equality before the law was constitutionally guaranteed, opening the way for Jewish intellectuals and artists.

Throughout his reign Franz Joseph would often stroll round the walls of the Hofburg of his beloved Vienna. There was nothing unusual in the emperor taking a walk; it was traditional. Joseph II had roamed the city in disguise, and Francis I had mingled with the people. On 18 February 1853, a bright day, Franz Joseph took a noonday walk accompanied only by one of his adjutants, Count Maximilian O'Donnell. They walked up to one of the high plateaus adjacent to the wall, which surrounded the inner city; it was a favorite spot of the Viennese, a sunny and pleasant promenade from which one could get a view of the city. Franz did not notice an insignificant young man sitting on a bench nearby.

Suddenly, the man jumped up and drew a knife from his coat. A woman standing a few paces away screamed, and Franz Joseph instinctively turned toward the noise. The gesture saved his life; the assassin's knife slipped and wounded the emperor in the neck. The richly brocaded collar of his uniform, however, reduced the force of the blow. Immediately the man prepared to strike again, but in the intervening second, O'Donnell had drawn his saber and flung himself on the would-be assassin, throwing him to the ground.[30] Franz Joseph was dazed but had not lost consciousness and seeing his assailant belabored by his adjutant, he stammered, "No, don't hit him." (But Franz Joseph would never forget or forgive the country of the would-be murderer.) Then the blood began to soil his uniform. Franz Joseph felt faint and O'Donnell led him away to the nearby palace of Archduke Albrecht. The doctors arrived in a few minutes.

Vienna was in turmoil and all of Europe seemed alarmed. Queen Victoria noted in her journal on 6 May 1853 that there was fear expressed by the doctors in England. They noted that because of the nature of the injury, while he may seem well, the emperor could die suddenly at any moment. In Vienna, a wide conspiracy was suspected, and the portals of the city were closed. The railroad stations were surrounded; the trains were brought to a standstill. Sophie wept. Identity of the assailant was soon established. He was a Hungarian, a tailor's apprentice by the name of Johann Libenyi, and he had acted by himself, without a conspiracy. "Eljen Kossuth!" ("Long live Kossuth," who was a leader of the Hungarian Independence Party). The young Hungarian revolutionary was determined to kill Franz Joseph, whom Libenyi believed responsible for his country's misfortunes and the suppression of the 1848 revolution. Libenyi was executed within a fortnight.

Nothing like this had ever happened before; no reigning Habsburg had ever been assailed. Could this be a visible symptom of the fact that a deep disturbance was continuing underground? When Franz Joseph recovered, there was no general rejoicing, even in Vienna, though the court staged a spectacular loyalty demonstration. Sympathy was excited, however, only by the courage shown by the young monarch and by the fact that he said immediately afterwards that his pain was mitigated by the sense that he was suffering with the poor soldiers fighting in Milan. Of course, Sophie was shocked and never let the anniversary of the stabbing pass without giving thanks in her diary for her son's preservation that Sunday. Now it was most important that Franz Joseph should produce an heir. The attack further intensified Sophie's determination to see her son married, and soon.

CHAPTER FOUR

Sisi

Both her parents, an overly ambitious mother and an overly eccentric father, welcomed the infant Elisabeth Amalie Eugenie. Born on Christmas Eve 1837 in Munich, Germany. Elisabeth was the daughter of the Duke and Duchess of Bavaria, Maximilian Joseph and Ludovika. Ludovika had been born the daughter of King Maximilian I of Bavaria and his second wife, Caroline of Baden, in 1808. The same year, her future husband and cousin, Maximilian, was born to the Duke Pius August of Bavaria and Princess Amelie Louise of Arenberg. Princess Ludovika of Bavaria did not marry into a royal family, but into a branch of the house of Wittelsbach. Ludovika did not love Max nor was Max enamored of Ludovika. Their elders bound them in wedlock before either of them knew enough to raise a protest.[1] Her husband, like Sophie's, showed no sign of dynastic ambitions. That her husband was granted the title Duke of Bavaria was only a minor consolation for the disappointed Ludovika.

Her sisters married quite well: Maria Anna was the twin sister of Princess Sophie of Bavaria, mother of Emperor Franz Joseph I of Austria. On 24 April 1833 in Dresden, Maria Anna married Crown Prince Frederick of Saxony, who in 1836 succeeded his uncle, Anthony, as king, thus making Maria Anna a queen. Amalie Auguste became the queen of Saxony when on 22 November 1822 she married Prince John of Saxony. Amalie Auguste was the identical twin sister of Elizabeth Louise, later queen of Prussia as wife of Frederick William IV of Prussia. Ludovika was surrounded by royalty, yet, unfortunately, in 1828, she married below her station. She did not keep her unhappiness to herself but constantly complained of her woeful marriage to her children. Elisabeth had grown up hearing her mother's complaints and how she spent her wedding night "in tears" and her wedding anniversaries "weeping." Though Ludovika had renounced love, she did "her duty," even in tears.

Historians have packaged Maximilian Joseph as a freedom loving, unreliable, altogether charming and most popular member of the House of Wittelsbach. He had an "absent-minded air about him with a far-away look in his eyes that characterize poets and sleepwalkers."[2] Duke Maximilian looked upon life with a Don Quixote air of whimsical detachment. He was amiable, unpretentious, kind, and eccentric — rather like Squire Allworthy in Henry Fielding's *Tom Jones*. He was frequently away from home and hearth, as though he needed to run away from something[3] (wife? ambition? reality?), or perhaps he was in search of something. Subsequently, he spent a lot of time traveling, scaling the Dolomites or camping on the classic plains of Asia Minor. Often in his travels he was accompanied by some willing lady or, at times, he would meet peasant girls along the way with the inevitable consequence of leaving illegitimate children sprinkled in Greece, Turkey and even Nubia.[4] The duke loved women far too much and too often. On returning to the family he would relate his adventures in flamboyant word pictures, carrying away his children, notably Sisi, on a wave of "romantic descriptions of far-away, exotic places."

On attaining his majority, Maximilian Joseph took his seat as a member of the council in accordance with the provisions of the Bavarian constitution. He had no taste for statesmanship; neither did he care to strive for distinction as a soldier. However, from the age of thirty he was a cavalry general, so now and then he donned his uniform and led his regiment in a parade. The uniform would be temporarily put back in retirement, for Max preferred to wear the alpine Tyrolean costume of loden and lederhosen. He lived on an annual grant of 250,000 guldens (about $200,000 in today's market value).

Max had intense passions of the non-libido variety as well; he loved science, literature, art and most intensely, music. During his adolescence, he learned to play the "mountain zither," a long-time companion instrument to Bavaria's national songs. Max was doing quite well with his self-taught skills when he encountered a rather renowned player of the zither, Johann Petzmachaer. Petzmacher was at once appointed director of chamber music at the little court, and remained with his art-loving benefactor until Max's death. Max composed several pieces for the zither, which were later published. His success as a zither player was unmatched by his poetry and prose endeavors, written under the pseudonym of "Phantasus," which revealed a less than extraordinary skill level — charming but with little meaning. Horses were another of Max's passions. He had a circus built behind his castle in the Ludwigstrasse in Munich. The duke himself appeared as director, often with ladies and gentlemen of the court and later his daughter Elisabeth performing.

Some historians have noted that on her wedding night Marie Ludovika locked her bridegroom in the closet.[5] But evidently he was released from time to time from his "imprisonment," at least long enough to father ten children. Ludwig Wilhelm was the firstborn, in 1831; another son, Wilhelm Karl, followed but died at birth. The apple of Ludovika's eye was Helene (Néné), who from a very early age was groomed to marry royalty, as her matchmaking mother most ardently desired. Helene, dark and slender with admirable manners and grace, took up most of Ludovika's time and energy.

Sophie's reverent hope that Néné would marry Franz Joseph did not occur; five summers after the ill-fated meeting with Franz Joseph at Bad Ischl, Helene would meet and marry the Bavarian prince Maximillian of Thurn and Taxis. She was surrounded by immense wealth and glitter. Néné, out of all Elisabeth's Wittelsbach sisters, was considered to have had the only happy marriage[6] but unfortunately it did not last long. The young prince died and Helene was a widower for more than twenty years. Her final years were marked by melancholy and depression, her last words being, "Ah yes, but life is a sorrow and a misery."[7]

Elisabeth was the second daughter born. Three of the other Wittelsbach children were also given nicknames, as was Karl Theodor, born in 1839 and called "Gackl" because of the peculiar cackling sound he made as a baby. (Gackl is the Bavarian peasant vernacular for barnyard fowl.) Karl Theodor studied to become an ophthalmologist. The Franco-Prussian War, in which he served as a colonel of the 3rd Bavarian Light Brigade, interrupted his studies. In 1880 he opened an eye clinic in his castle at Tegernsee and in 1895 he founded the *Augenklinik Herzog Karl Theodor* (Duke Charles Theodor Eye Clinic) in Munich, which to this day remains one of the most respected eye clinics in Bavaria.

Nothing appeared to be able to stop Ludovika's talent in arranging advantageous alliances. Her daughter Marie Sophie was married to the Duke of Calabria, the heir to the kingdom of Naples. Thus, she became the queen of the Two Sicilies. Maria, born in 1841, escaped being labeled. But the delicate Mathilde Ludovika, born in 1843, seemed to call for a descriptive effort; she was named "Spatz" for sparrow. Maximilian, Duke in Bavaria, was born in 1845, followed two years later by Sophie Charlotte.[8]

Sophie Charlotte, the Duchess of Alencon, who at one point was betrothed to Ludwig II of Bavaria, died under harrowing circumstances. At a charity bazaar in Paris the duchess had agreed to take charge of an embroidery booth. A moving picture magic lantern, the newest wonder of the age, was being demonstrated in an adjacent booth. There was a short circuit in the electrical wiring; the celluloid film caught fire and exploded; draperies were aflame; the smoke laden dark enclosure teemed with a frenzied mass of humanity. Panic and pandemonium prevailed, culminating in a mad stampede. In a matter of minutes, 113 persons were trampled and burned beyond recognition, Sophie among them. The final child, Maximilian Emanuel, was born in 1849. He lost his royal-sounding name and was called by the slightly nonsensical "Mapperl" (nobody knew what it meant).

To keep his family happy, Duke Maximilian Joseph bought a summer castle just eighteen miles from Munich, overlooking the Wetterstein Mountains. It was called Possenhofen, and by all accounts it was an ugly, square uninspiring building with four squat towers flanked by stables and outbuildings. Possi, as the family members fondly called it, redeemed itself for the beauty of the land that surrounded it — wooded slopes, fields of wild flowers, the mountains in the background, and the banks of Lake Starnberg close by. Largely due to a certain informality that pervaded the parental establishment, the children ran free to explore Possi's natural treasures.

Ludovika spent much of her time polishing the finishing touches to Helene's royal-character building, while Helene's younger sister, Sisi, became the consummate "outdoor girl." Eclipsed by her sister's apparently superior gifts and without the least interest in understanding anything about court life or court etiquette, Sisi grew up for a time almost unobserved.[9] She always felt herself in closer companionship with her father and brother Theodor than with her mother and sisters.

Duke Max insisted on bodily exercise for all his children — hiking in the mountains, riding, fishing, and walking in the woods — a rather idyllic lifestyle, particularly for Sisi: "I am never tired of walking, and I thank my father for it. He was an ardent sportsman, and expected my sisters and myself to skip and spring about like chamois."[10] She also had a particular passion for riding and when not at Possehofen, she could constantly be found at her father's large riding school in Munich where she rode the most unmanageable, restive horses that were there. Elisabeth's passion was horses but, in fact, she loved all animals, as her eccentric father had. She had a wide menagerie that traveled with her from the family's Munich castle to Possenhofen — rabbits, guinea pigs, canaries, dogs, hamsters, and lambs and many more.

Max thought a bookish education was rather unnecessary for pretty girls. But, in later life, Sisi studied Shakespeare in English and began to learn ancient and modern Greek. Her teacher was Konstatin Christomanos — exceedingly bright, exceedingly ugly. He was a small man, quite hunchbacked, with yellowing teeth and unkempt hair. Christomanos was totally devoted to Sisi (she had a way of bringing about utter devotion from others). While her hair was being dressed or on long walks around the palace, Christomanos would listen to her declension of Greek words and occasionally correct her minor mistakes. He wrote three rather comprehensive books on his life with Elisabeth.[11]

As a young girl, Sisi grew up running through the woods and the white of snow to the delight of her father. "[S]he is a wonder of beauty — tall, beautifully formed, with a profusion of bright brown hair, a low Greek forehead, gentle eyes, very red lips, a sweet smile, a low musical voice, and a manner partly timid, partly gracious," the American envoy to Vienna first described Sisi.[12] From a very early age, she was not like most princesses encased inside their corsets and crinolines learning proper everything. Sisi, in today's vernacular would be called a tomboy — the darling of her father whose love for the outdoors, animals, horseback riding, and traveling was personified in his daughter.

Elisabeth adored her father. The two had a very good father-daughter relationship and spent hours talking about poetry and the arts and, of course, spent mornings and afternoons riding in the countryside. He reciprocated the feeling of affection that Sisi had for him. Out of an entire family whom he forever strove to escape, Sisi alone had a deep and lasting hold over him. And her father's influence is undeniable. Max seems to have set a pattern of rebellion with Sisi by preferring to spend his time in taverns rather than at court occasions or by traveling rather than being with his family. He flouted royalty as he and Sisi scoured the hillsides around Possi playing the zither in the huts of the peasants while they danced. From her father, Sisi took her love of poetry, while his tales of his travels incited wanderlust in her. Sisi shared her father's dread of confinement and became a partner in his numerous flights from reality. Very likely Sisi inherited her refractoriness, her restless spirit, and her hatred of discipline and pomp from him. Max's wish that Sisi's wings would not be clipped while the iron web of dynastic law closed in to make her its prisoner was never granted.

Many princesses kept diaries of their daily escapades; Elisabeth instead wrote poems to express herself. Her love for poetry took flight as a cathartic need to express just about anything from her loneliness to elegiac poems about her beloved Possenhofen to mourning the loss of her first loves to every one of her anxieties and annoyances. It was a therapeutic way to write down her feelings; only in her case, thoughts were styled in a rhyming set of poetic stanzas. She kept up her poetry writing all through her adult life, but each year it seemed to take on a more compulsive-writing frenzy. She had really no one to turn to — no friends or family — so verse became her sounding board. In later life just a few members of her intimate household, along with her daughter Marie Valerie, knew of her poetry writing. Elisabeth, as well as Marie Valerie, was quite convinced of the grand quality of her poems. She appeared to be unaware that her writing "was little more than dilettante rhyming."[13] An example follows:

Abandoned (Gödöllő Castle in Hungary, 1886):
In my great loneliness / I make tiny songs; / My heart, filled with grief and sadness, / Weighs down my spirit. / / Once I was so young and rich / In love with life and hope; / I thought nothing could match my strength, / the whole world was open to me. / / I loved, I lived, / I wandered through the world; / But never reached what I strove for.— / I deceived and was deceived.[14]

Her passion for poetry reached a new intensity when she began to read the works of Heinrich Heine. She read everything that she could obtain that was written by or about this poet, who is considered to be one of the most significant German poets of the nineteenth century. What attracted Sisi to him and his work were his honesty and sincerity, his realistic social criticism and irony, along with his insight into the human condition. "It was Heine's cry of pain and his scoffs at the heartrending illusions of life that had first struck a responsive chord in the heart of Elisabeth."[15]

Heine was constantly searching for real hope and change. Sisi wrote, "Heine is different from most other authors, because he despises hypocrisy; he always shows himself as he is, with the inherent good and frailty of humanity."[16] Also, the fact that he, too, was regarded as an outsider made him an identifiable hero to her. In 1933 there was a Nazi raid on the *Institut fur Sexualwissenschaft*, in which works by Heine, along with others, were burned. On the site has been engraved in the ground a famous line from Heine's 1821 play *Almansor*: "*Das war ein Vorspiel nur, dort wo man Bücher verbrennt, verbrennt man auch am Ende Menschen*" (That was but a prelude; where they burn books, they will ultimately burn people also).

Sisi's daughter Marie Valerie often complained of her mother's poetry writing obsession: "[S]trange life my mother's — her thoughts are occupied by the past, her activities deal with the distant future. The present is, to her, an insubstantial shadow, her greatest pride that no one suspects she is a poet."[17] Her verses from the 1880s would see publication, even though it was self-publication. She chose 1950 as the date of printing, a time when none of her contemporaries would be alive. Elisabeth wanted at least some understanding even if it were posthumously. She wanted justification, understanding, and fame — denied to her in her lifetime but perhaps granted to her in her death. In 1890 she sealed her poems in a casket, gave it to her brother Duke Karl Theodor, and through subsequent keepers her request was honored in 1951.

In her poems she often identified with the queen of the fairies, Titania, from Shakespeare's *A Midsummer Night's Dream*, a play, in part, about women defying men. Titania personifies a fairy in possession of many freedoms, one of Elisabeth's strongest desires. Sisi's fantasy expanded from poetry to reality. In 1881 Franz Joseph agreed to have a small villa built in a secluded part of the Lainzer Tiergarten. The villa was free from court ceremony and tucked away from the glaring public gaze. Franz Joseph paid for the villa from his personal funds and presented it to Sisi as a gift. Sisi duly called her husband's gift "Titania's enchanted castle."

As Sisi grew older, she continued to escape into a private world of fantasy, as her father still did as well as her second cousin Ludwig II of Bavaria. Both the Habsburgs and the Wittelsbach family lines suffered from a long history of madness and hereditary disease. The Wittelsbach eccentricity had a firm hold on Sisi's paternal grandfather, Duke Pius, who ended his years as a crippled, feebleminded hermit. His son Duke Maximilian Joseph, Sisi's father, shared Duke Pius's strange ways. Sisi herself doubted and feared for her sanity, fears that were justified, since insanity had afflicted Sisi's family (as well as Franz Joseph's). Sisi's sister Helene suffered from religious hallucinations.

Sisi was more and more haunted about passing on a taint of madness both to her children and to her grandchildren. To be an inbred Wittelsbach was bad enough; but then to marry into the Habsburgs and their incessant consanguinity was a double liability. In the course of a single century, between twenty to thirty members of the family became victims of madness.[18] King Ludwig II's brother, Otto, had already been confined in a padded cell for fourteen years in Furstenried Castle. And then there was Ludwig II.

Sisi had admired her second cousin Ludwig since he was a boy. During one summer, he had spent the whole month with the ducal Wittelsbach family at the resort of Kissingen. Sisi and he became inseparable, riding side by side through the forests, looking on each other's related beauty as once Narcissus looked on himself in the pool of legend. She called him the Eagle, while he named her the Dove. "Like her, he was irresponsible like her, a fugitive of reality; like her extravagant; like her, mistrustful where he might and trusted and wholly trusting where he could better have used caution. And like her, he was a being of exceptional magnetism."[19]

According to Marie Larisch (also known as Countess Marie Louise Larisch-Wallersee),

> In many things the Empress was very like Ludwig II, but unlike him, had the mental and physical strength not to fall prey to eccentric ideas. She was wont to say, half seriously, half joking: "I know that sometimes I am considered mad." As she spoke, she wore a mocking smile, and her golden-brown eyes flashed like heat lightening in restrained mischievousness. Everyone who knew Elisabeth well wrote about her pleasure in teasing innocents. Thus, with the straightest face, she could sometimes say the most outrageous things, or, with an enchanting smile, throw an elegant indiscretion at someone, in order, as she put it, to enjoy her listener's gape. Unless you know Elisabeth through and through, like Ludwig, it was sometimes hard to decide if she was saying something seriously or was only joking.[20]

Ludwig worshiped poetry, grand opera, Hamlet, swans, water lilies, Homer and a blond Lohengrin wig. He dwelled in fantasies. In this he and Sisi were one. Later in life, he was also plagued with phobias, which prevented him from leaving Neuschwanstein and his realm of fantasy. At the many turreted Neuschwanstein Castle, insomniac Ludwig spent many of his nights horseback riding by himself through the surrounding forests or wandering through the cavernous passageways of the castle dressed as a medieval knight from German folklore.

King Ludwig was betrothed to Sisi's sister Sophie Charlotte. Perhaps he was attracted to her because she was an enthusiast of Richard Wagner. On her acceptance of his proposal, they were frequently seen together and compared to Venus and Adonis. At six feet three inches Ludwig was a towering figure. Ludwig wrote ominously to Wagner: "I will be true to Sophie until death. But even in death, I will remain true to you, the lord of my life."[21] The wedding was continually postponed. Sophie knew that she could never be happy with such a man. She was aware of his romantic and homosexual nature, sublimated to a degree in his worship of Wagner and his building of fantasy castles. At one point in time Duke Maximilian Joseph realized the folly of it all and took it upon himself to break his daughter's engagement. Sophie would find another husband, the Wittelsbach princesses always did. Soon she was to marry Ferdinand, the Prince of Orleans and Duke of Alencon.

Ludwig was an extraordinarily handsome Adonis, a veritable Prince Charming. He was an artist, a poet and a fool. Ludwig himself had grown up in the storybook landscape of Bavaria, which gave wings to his fairy-prince complex. At the death of his father, Maximilian II, which put money and power in his reach, Ludwig succumbed to this fantasy complex, transforming it into castles dotting the Bavarian landscape — Hohenschwangau, Herrenchiemsee, Neuschwanstein.

In three castles of fantasy, he would enshrine the sets of operas in murals and stones. The influence of Wagner's operas was always the inspiration for the building of Ludwig's fantasies in architecture. The first of these was furnished in Gothic style with a ceiling reproducing the heavens containing an artificial moon that changed through its waxing and waning cycles. The second emulated the Bourbon Rococo of Versailles, while the third (inspired by Wagner's operas) captured a swan-like motif. Most of his residences were equipped with indoor lakes and other nautical paraphernalia, which caused an occasional shower upon an unsuspecting guest who sat in drawing rooms below. The castles were so enormous that meals had to be whisked from kitchen domains to an upstairs study traveling along two kilometers of secret passages. It is no surprise that the food was usually cold.

Ludwig lavishly attired himself as well, which so spectacularly personified the madness of the Wittelsbachs. He would flounce around the grounds of his castles in his troubadour bonnets, blue velvet breeches, pink hose and satin cape. Ludwig worried far more about the curls in his hair than about the state of Bavaria. His love of clothes and cross-dressing, of poetry and music, had not made him yet aware of his repressed homosexuality. Later, Ludwig had sexual encounters with stable boys and young soldiers. Each encounter was followed by solemn oaths that this would not happen again: "I swear today ... that what took place yesterday night was the last time forever; atoned for by the Royal Blood — The Holy Grail. Absolutely the last time under penalty of ceasing to be King."[22]

He had chosen Richard Wagner almost as a surrogate father because of his dreamland operas of *Lohengrin, Tannhauser* and *Tristan*. The composer feared that the "life of the young King must vanish like a fleeting godlike dream in this crude world of ours. He loves me with the fire and tenderness of first love."[23] The prophecy was correct. Ludwig's life was short and tragic, but he would assure Wagner's fame forever. The death of Richard Wagner in Venice in 1883 led the king nearer to the brink of sanity. "Frightful! Terrible!," he cried out at the news. He insisted that the coffin of his composer be brought through Munich to Bayreuth. Ludwig remained in one of his extravagant castles, Hohenschwangau, where he ordered all the pianos to be covered with black crepe.

The court physician, Dr. Bernhard von Gudden, said that King Ludwig was in an advanced state of mental disturbance known as paranoia: "Suffering as he does from this form of diseases, which has been gradually and continuously developing over a great number of years. His Majesty must be pronounced incurable and further decay of his mental faculties is certain.... His Majesty must be considered as incapable of exercising government; and this incapacity will last, not merely for a full year, but for the whole of the rest of his life."[24] His report allowed for a coup d'état to place the nearest sane Wittelsbach relative, the sixty-five-year-old Prince Leopold, on the throne. Sisi could not believe that the king was a madman and constantly maintained that he was only an eccentric who lived in a "world of ideas."

After dinner together one evening, Ludwig and the doctor went out for a stroll. The pair had not returned by eight o'clock; a search was made of the grounds. Two hours later, their hats and cloaks were found on the water's edge; their bodies were floating with their faces downwards in four or five feet of water. The struggle must have been desperate and fierce. The body of Dr. Gudden showed marks of great violence, his throat and forehead giving proof of the struggle.

Elisabeth's hysterical reaction to her cousin's death was such that for the first time her children began to question her sanity. On the evening after she had received the news, Valerie came into her mother's room to find her lying stretched out on the floor, sobbing and praying to "the great Jehovah, the god of vengeance, the god of hope, the god of wisdom. Her daughter's terrified screams brought her back to her senses."[25] For days after his death, Sisi would suddenly burst into tears and shout and accuse the Bavarian authorities of complicity in the murder of her favorite cousin, who had brought so much beauty into a pedestrian world. Crown Prince Rudolf was quite alarmed because of his mother's protracted grief. Sisi kept the memory of Ludwig II alive through years by wearing black crepe and requiring requiems in his honor. Life at court continued in a funereal mood.

The Wittelsbach trait of mental instability appeared to trouble Elisabeth as well. One can see her angst in her poems she wrote in the ensuing months after Ludwig's death, all show an obsession with death. Her thoughts on death were coupled with her thoughts on insanity. Two weeks before Christmas, she made a visit to Brundlfeld, the main insane asylum in Vienna, a most unlikely place for an empress to visit. When Franz Joseph asked her what she wanted for Christmas, she answered, "Since you ask what I would like, I will tell you: either a tiger cub — the Berlin Zoological Garden possesses three such — or a medallion. But what I would really like best would be a completely equipped insane asylum."[26] Madness held a certain amount of fascination for Sisi along with a paranoiac dread.

In one sense, the misfortune of the Wittelsbach cousins was to have enough resources to make their dreams come true. Both Ludwig and Sisi could have their fantasies turned into bricks and stucco. Sisi's classical follies were beginning with the planning of the Villa Hermes at Lainz, which she wanted to be Titania's enchanted castle. It is pompous and heavy, its décor overdone by the fashionable Makart, who obligingly pictured the empress as Shakespeare's Fairy Queen in the frescos.

She had always intended to construct her ideal of a palace. So, she bought the ruined Villa Braila near Gasturi to the south of the old Venetian fortress and port of Corfu. She would build her palace on a hill, which was Corfu's highest point. In the bay she built a jetty of white marble to ensure an easy debarking from the imperial yacht. Achilleion, a palace patterned after Phaeacian grandeur, was named for Sisi's favorite Homeric hero.

The palace consisted of 128 rooms, marble stairways, and a statue of Achilles standing in the marble entrance hall. On the ceiling Franz Matsch painted a huge fresco, *Achilles Triumphant*. Sisi had a completely free hand; whatever she desired took form. Bedposts modeled the bent forms of nymphs. Against the walls stood magnificent blue glass vases like those that are found in ancient graves. She used electric lights that burned bulbs in the shape of fruits, and surrounded her palace with terraces affording an unobstructed view of the ocean. She guarded her privacy with acres of gardens. As far as possible every piece of furniture was modeled on an original and made of the finest material. Chairs, like the one Adrastus set before Helen, were inlaid with silver and ebony and covered with a huge sheepskin.

A small temple was consecrated to Heine, consisting of a statue of the poet sitting in an armchair under the marble canopy looking out to sea. On a scroll, which he held, was a verse chiseled upon it:

> What use the solitary tear?
> It merely dims my sight
> A remnant of the olden times
> Left behind in my eyes.
> You ancient, solitary tear,
> Dissolve
> Now, too...

Sisi seemed, as did Ulysses, to prefer to be a vagabond accompanied by her tablet for writing poems. Her earlier works show her love for nature and her adolescent heart, which she lost twice. Hardly fifteen, she fell in love with a young man "with dark brown eyes" who gave her his picture. Ludovika found out about it; the young man was sent away but died soon after, not of a broken heart. Her second adolescent love was with a "Count F.R." (in her poem she included no name, just initials). He had blue eyes; more poems were the result. The count frequently visited the family's castle in Munich, but when her mother found Sisi's poems and lovesick expressions written down about him, the count was banished from the castle and Elisabeth never saw him again. Sisi was inconsolable; her broken heart grew heavier and she became quite depressed. She wondered if she would ever meet her "true love," as it appeared her older sister Helene had. Then they were off to Bad Ischl to meet her sister's presumed soon-to-be paramour, Franz Joseph.

Chapter Five

The Newlyweds

Much political wrangling surrounding the choice of the royal spouse would precede Habsburg weddings. For the most part, the choice of either the bride or groom was not based on a love match. One exception was the marriage of Maria Theresa and Francis Stephen of Lorraine. It appeared that he was an appropriate choice as he was descended from the Habsburgs and had been raised in the Viennese court. Maria Theresa had fallen in love with Francis Stephen when they were quite young; from then on, she insisted on marrying him. There were some misgivings about this marriage on the part of France. In order for the marriage to take place, Francis Stephen must give up Lorraine in order for France to acknowledge the Pragmatic Sanction and accept the marriage. Francis Stephen agreed.

In 1745 Maria Theresa became empress. Although a dedicated mother, she was not above using the marriages of her children for political alliances and advancement of the Habsburg Empire, particularly her daughter Marie Antoinette, who married King Louis XVI of France. Francis Stephen was cultured and quite handsome but was not particularly clever; thus, he did not play an integral role in ruling the Habsburg dominions. Francis, instead, dedicated his time to other pursuits, such as travel and building up the Habsburg-Lorraine fortune. When Holy Roman Emperor Francis I died in 1765, Maria mourned his death excessively, wearing black for the rest of her life and keeping his rooms untouched as a monument to him. There are several parallels between this royal couple and Franz Joseph and Elisabeth.

While marriages were predominantly arranged to strengthen the Habsburg dynasty and were mainly political alliances, both of these marriages were also love matches. Maria sought Francis Stephen and Franz Joseph felt an instant attraction to Elisabeth. Marie, like Franz Joseph, dedicated an inordinate amount of time to the affairs of state; both Francis

Stephen and Elisabeth resented the long hours spent in official duties by the monarchs. As a result, both Francis and Elisabeth sought outside interests, Francis through his affairs and Elisabeth through travel. Both of the women suffered losses from which they could not recover. Maria lost Francis and heavily mourned his death for the next fifteen years of her life. Elisabeth appeared to also be wearing black as she perpetually mourned death: her sister, daughter, son, and her cousin Ludwig II. The difference in these royal marriages was that Maria Theresa's marriage was a happy one; the marriage of Franz Joseph and Elisabeth, within months after their wedding, was doomed to failure.

In search of a suitable bride, Franz Joseph was on his way to Berlin where he was to meet Anna, Princess of Prussia and a niece of Frederick William IV. He thought she was quite a good choice as his future empress; his feelings, however, were not reciprocated. It so happened Princess Anna was already engaged to a prince of Hesse-Cassel. That could have been easily broken, if Franz Joseph would have requested it, but he decided to continue his search, or more precisely his mother would continue her search, for an empress. The dynasty had to be preserved, children had to be produced.

Sophie hated Hungary because it demanded parliamentary rule and a constitution of its own. For this reason the archduchess would have no Magyar brides for her son. The choice had to fall on a princess from a royal house, and since no candidates could be found in Russia or France, only one choice seemed possible — a princess of Bavaria. The Habsburgs must look to Germany. Sophie's quest was to find a royal princess, but there were other requirements: her future daughter-in-law must be easy to dominate, just like her son. An acquiescent bride was the only way for Sophie to satisfy her craving for power — power over Franz Joseph and the rest of her family, but also to attain political power. Therefore, Franz Joseph's future wife must be submissive and docile. Sophie's thoughts turned to her sister Ludovika's older daughter. In visualizing Helene, Sophie reflected how very different Helene's face was from that of her namesake, whose face was said to have launched a thousand ships. One thing was certain: Néné's beauty would never cause a Trojan war. But, she seemed to fit Sophie's other requirements.

In July of 1853, Ludovika received a very flattering letter from her sister Sophie, disclosing that she was looking for a wife for her son, the 22-year-old emperor of Austria, Franz Joseph. Remembering Helene's wonderful example of a refined young woman, Sophie had requested that

Helene come to the royal family's palace at Bad Ischl. For a long time Ludovika's thoughts had been occupied with marrying her eldest daughter to the most eligible royal bachelor of the day. And, no doubt, the most desirable bachelor would be Emperor Franz Joseph. Upon receiving Sophie's letter, Ludovika became an unquestioning and compliant handmaiden of her forceful sister. Bad Ischl, with its relaxed atmosphere, would be a lovely place for Franz Joseph and Helene to get to know each other.

Bad Ischl was a fashionable summer destination. Most of its holiday guests, who came from all parts of the monarchy, wished to spend the summer months in the same place as the emperor, where they just might get a glimpse of their monarch as a private individual. Franz Joseph loved Bad Ischl; he appreciated the landscape of the Salzkammergut with its vast expanses of forests and the tranquility of the surrounding mountains. It was a wonderful place for chamois hunting, which he pursued so passionately. In years to come, his annual summer retreat to Ischl would be "heaven on earth," a place to which he "could flee a paper-dominated desk-bound existence with all its anxieties and troubles."[1]

At the very last minute Sisi was invited to join the Bavarian entourage to Bad Ischl. For the past several days, Sisi had locked herself in her room at Possi so she could weep and write poetry about her second "lost love." So in order to help her shake off the depression, her father suggested (and her mother agreed) taking her along. The consummate matchmaker Sophie also thought that Sisi should become better acquainted with Franz Joseph's younger brother, Archduke Karl Ludwig. Since their meeting a few years ago, Karl Ludwig was obviously in love with his cousin Sisi.

Karl Ludwig was on the threshold of reaching his majority but had worshiped Sisi since they met in Innsbruck, where the royal family sojourned during the revolutionary spring of 1848. Sisi was just eleven years old; eighteen-year-old Franz Joseph, on the approaching eve of his accession, took no notice of her. From that time on, however, Karl Ludwig sent numerous and most ardent letters to Sisi along with an extraordinary variety of presents to the "goddess of his boyish heart." "There had been, in rapid succession, a handsome ring (bought with his own spending money), a dried rose, several dead butterflies beautifully mounted on cardboard, Marzipan, gummy licorice whips and a watch with a long chain. Sisi accepted these attributes with a causal gratitude; she wrote polite little notes on flowered stationary, thanking her young admirer, and telling of life at Possi."[2] So, perhaps Ludovika could marry off two girls into the prestigious and important Habsburg royal family.

Five. The Newlyweds

A rather romantic version of Franz Joseph's first encounter with Elisabeth was that he was walking in the woods around Bad Ischl before he thought the Bavarian contingent had arrived. He noticed a young girl clad in white, her long hair streaming down her shoulders, emerging from the woods with bunches of edelweiss in her arms; she saw him, and smiled with pleasure. At that moment, Franz Joseph was in love.[3] His brother Karl reported that when Franz Joseph entered the room where Helene and Sisi were having tea with Sophie, upon catching sight of Sisi, "an expression of such great pleasure appeared on his face so that there was no longer any doubt whom he would choose for his bride."[4] Sophie also noticed that her son "beamed, and you know how his face can beam when he is happy. The dear little one did not suspect the deep impression she had made on Franzl. Until the moment her mother spoke to her about it, she was filled by nothing but the shyness and timidity inspired in her by the many people around her."[5]

Ludovika had hoped Helene would make a splendid first impression on the emperor, but they had preceded the arrival of their luggage and on first presentation were still in their mourning clothes (they were mourning the death of their Aunt Sophie, who had died in the Parisian fire). Franz Joseph, of course, was impeccably dressed and a picture of aristocratic wonder from the top of his shining blond hair and imperial blue eyes to the sparkling spurs on his boots. He made a superlative impression. Néné should have been a vision of loveliness. But a critical survey disclosed that she was not even presentable: "Her straight dark hair, confined in the intricate web of a pompadour, hung here and there in dreary strands. Due to nervousness the girl's hands were clammy with cold and the tip of her nose was red. There was a frightened quiver about the thin lips, where large teeth gnawed at the flesh in an effort to draw more of the same color."[6]

At dinner on their first night, Franz Joseph sat next to Néné but "noticed and continually stared at Elisabeth,"[7] sitting far away from him, as the seats were set up according to titles and positions. Of course everybody noticed; Sisi blushed and could not eat. Rather quickly the news spread throughout the court that Franz Joseph preferred Sisi, not Helene. "Oh, but how sweet Sisi is, she's as fresh as a budding almond, and what a magnificent crown of hair frames her face! What lovely, soft eyes she has, and lips like strawberries." Sophie tried to bring his thoughts back to Helene: "Don't you think that Helene is clever, that she has a beautiful, slender figure?" Franz Joseph responded, "Well, yes, a little grave and quiet, certainly pleasant and nice, yes, but Sisi — Sisi — such loveliness, such exuberance, like a little girl's and yet so sweet!"[8]

Dinner on the second night, before the cotillion, was to celebrate Franz Joseph's birthday. "Néné swam in elegance in her white satin gown, kid gloves, silver slippers, and a fan of ostrich plumes."[9] Sisi, however, was in a rather undistinguishing pink dress without the stylish accessories worn by the other fashionable ladies at the table. Ludovika planned nothing for Sisi's wardrobe and nothing but the ostrich fan could have been borrowed from her sister, who was much larger boned than Sisi. Sisi was by no means in a happy state, not because of her plain dress but because she was terrified. The emperor's impetuosity frightened her. And if Sisi's unstylish dress would not cause gossip among the royal ladies the seating arrangement would. Sisi was sitting next to the emperor, while "Néné was down at the far end of the table with the vegetables where Sisi should have been sitting. She looked strange, Néné did, with her lovely satin gown and tiara on her head, yet all the while wondering why this had been happening to her."[10]

When the emperor entered the ballroom, the cotillion would commence with the first dance. The men were dressed in gala uniforms and the women were in their "globe" skirts, the latest fashion from Paris. Empress Eugenie, wife of Napoleon III, had recently introduced this fashion from France. (She had copied the design of the gown from a lampshade in order to conceal her pregnancy.) Wilhelm von Weckbecker, adjutant to the emperor, described the scene at the ball in his *Memoirs*: "His majesty did not dance the first dance. Neither did the two princesses. Helene who was intelligent but not pretty and Elisabeth who was pretty as a picture with her fifteen years, but still almost a child. During the second dance, a polka, I got a message from Duchess Sophie that I ought to dance with Elisabeth. Up to now she had danced only with a dancing master, and for her debut she would need somebody who could lead her firmly. Sophie introduced me to the Princess, who was adorable but ill at ease. She whispered to me shyly that she didn't know whether she could manage it without her dancing master. I reassured her, but I myself was a little uncertain…. After the dance I whispered to Donald, 'I think I just danced with our future Empress.'"[11]

The last dance of the cotillion was a telltale sign of Franz Joseph's intentions; the climaxing dance was tantamount to an engagement, and he chose Sisi. After the dance a signal was given and a large flower basket was brought in. It was an old Austrian custom; the royal was to select a nosegay for the lady of his choice before the remaining tokens were distributed among the other guests. Franz Joseph plunged both arms into the flowering mass and deposited his burden at Sisi's feet. Such a breach of etiquette was almost an official proposal, and Elisabeth was deeply embarrassed. Early the next morning Franz Joseph announced to his mother that he was going to marry not Néné but Sisi.

From that moment on Sophie raised all kinds of objections, first to the father of the bride. "True, he was the most popular Wittelsbach of his time; but popularity was hardly a quality with which to win the respect of Sophie, who thought in strictly dynastic terms." There were other problems with Maximilian Joseph. "Duke Max was not a man to turn up his nose at a pretty face, and he did not hold home life in very high regard.... [T]hen, too, Max openly expressed democratic views, if only to annoy those around him.... Max also paraded his liberal views in numerous articles on history."[12]

Then there was Elisabeth. "*Sie ist doch nur ein Fratz!*"[13] (She's still only a brat!) "She is too young—a child really, too giddy ... unable to fulfill the role as Empress," Sophie admonished him and said that he should think it over. Quite obviously, Sophie did not approve of his marriage to Elisabeth, but neither did Ludovika, who was somewhat embarrassed by this match, for she knew how immature and unprepared Elisabeth was for the role of Empress of Austria. Certainly Ludovika had some shred of happiness, as Sisi's engagement would definitely raise the standing of her ducal family: a Wittelsbach woman would stand beside a Habsburg emperor. As for Franz Joseph, for once he did not obey his mother. He had fallen in love with Sisi, and it was she or nobody.

Was Sisi in love with Franz Joseph? How can a fifteen-year-old, after knowing someone for such a brief period of time, know that she loved this person who for the past few days just simply and constantly stared at her? "She was overwhelmed by the honor, bewitched by the position, dazzled by the gold, allured by the crown, and she must have been attracted to the elegant cavalier that Franz Joseph then was."[14] To her father she announced, "I do love him if only he weren't an emperor." When her mother told Sisi of Franz Joseph's intentions, she burst into tears and assured her mother than she would do "all she could to make the Emperor happy." To the pages of her secret diary, she wrote the following poem, addressed to the swallow:

> O swallow, lend me your wings,
> Take me along to far-off fields'
> How gladly would I loose my chains,
> How joyfully the binding band [etc., etc.].

It is a girlish poem; it is not the poem of a girl in love.[15] Whatever her doubts, she accepted her role. Her time was to be occupied now, some eight months before the wedding, with much poem-writing, introspection, and learning the ways of the most strict and pompous court in all of Europe.

Before retiring that evening Ludovika sent off a telegram to Max: "Emperor requests Sisi's hand and your consent, he remains in Bad Ischl through August, we are all delighted."[16] Max had to be there to bestow his paternal blessing even if it meant canceling of the *Gesangveein* (choral song) jubilee to do it, and most certainly it would bring down his bowling average. But a man must make this sacrifice in the interest of his family.

On 18 August 1853 the engagement was made official: a jubilant time for the couple; a difficult time for the Austrian empire. In 1853, war broke out in the immediate vicinity of the Austrian empire. Determined to destroy Ottoman power in Europe, Russian czar Nicholas I sent his troops in July to sweep out Turks and occupy the Romanian principalities. Franz Joseph faced a difficult foreign policy decision. Moreover, the empire was riddled with unemployment, poverty, and lack of political freedom. The harvests of the summer of 1853 were bad and famine was prevalent. Then, too, a few months earlier, a serious attempt had been made on the life of the young emperor. Despite all this, perhaps, the royal wedding would lift the spirits of the Austrians — at least for a brief period of time. Pamphlets circulating in the country spoke of the misery and the hopes of the Austrian people. Several were hoping that the new empress would hear their pleas for help and justice: "We believe that you will become the mediator between him and us, that you will say what we, timid, do or dare to admit, that by your gentle hand any a matter will be steered to the good."[17]

It didn't take long for the citizens of Bad Ischl to gather in the small square outside the parish church simply to get a look at the girl who was to be their empress. The sounds of the Austrian national anthem were heard as they entered the church. "Franz Joseph was the happiest of bridegrooms, devoting every moment of his time that he could to his radiant fiancée."[18] He planned long drives and horseback rides and walks across the mountainside. Franz Joseph's essentially dry and matter-of-fact nature took flight and for a short time he was released from the iron cloak laid upon him by his imperial ambition and his overpowering sense of sovereignty.

On 31 August 1853, Elisabeth, her disappointed mother, and her depressed sister left Bad Ischl. As soon as she had arrived home, Elisabeth was consumed with lessons on how to be an empress. One of her tutors was a Hungarian, Count Majlath, who began the fire in her for Hungarian independence. Painters, designers, and jewelers flocked to the once calm and serene Possenhofen.

Franz Josef paid a visit to his fiancée at Possenhofen around Christmas of 1853, after three months of love letter writing. The courtship of Elisabeth by Franz Joseph, if one can call it that, took her to the age of sixteen. Franz Joseph found it sad that he should leap from the earthly paradise with Sisi to go back to Schönbrunn and his writing table and masses of papers. He commissioned a portrait of his betrothed and sent her a miniature of himself on a bracelet studded with diamonds, along with an imperial brooch of gems in a spray of rosebuds. He visited her at Possenhofen as often as he could. But, generally he could manage to stay only for a few days, as his duties in Vienna called him away from Elisabeth. Sisi was under regimentation of sorts as well; she no longer could flit about the fields of Possi, tending her various pets and cultivating ardent friendships with her neighbors. She was taken out of the woods and brought indoors "where ceremony hung in the stale air and where every gesture and every step dripped viscous precedent."[19]

Despite that, she appeared to be content and when she had completed her studies, she began the packing of her trousseau, which included 358 dresses, other clothing, shoes, combs, and many other fashion items. Splendid gifts arrived from Franz Joseph: his miniature in a diamond frame, an ermine coat, and a parrot from the Schönbrunn menagerie. He himself brought her the famous diadem, necklace, and earrings of opal and diamonds his mother had worn at her wedding. For weeks a steady stream of bundles and boxes arrived from Franz Joseph:

17 ceremonial robes
14 montant (high-necked) dresses
6 dressing gowns
19 summer frocks
4 ballroom crinolines
16 hats
6 coats
8 mántillas
5 mantelets (shoulder capes) of velvet
20 pairs of gloves (in every color and style).[20]

Sophie sent a rosary and objected when Sisi thanked her with the familiar "*Du*," and not the more formal "*Sie*" prescribed by etiquette. Sophie complained to her son about Sisi's irreverence. It appears that from the very start there would be trouble between Sisi and Sophie, and Franz Joseph did try to show his mother Sisi's improvements. Similarly, Sisi did try to comply with Sophie's wishes, even before the wedding, but thought it absurd that she should not say "*Du*" to her own aunt, her mother's sister and her fiancé's mother. Apparently, she simply forgot that Sophie thought of herself as Dowager Empress.[21] But Franz Joseph explained to her that even he addressed his mother with the formal "*Sie*," which appeared to pacify Sisi. Sisi's future epistles were models of stilted phraseology. This was not to be Sophie's last criticism, for new ones were forever cropping up. Sophie also criticized Sisi for having yellow teeth, and subsequently, she did her best to whiten them. Another one of Sophie's complaints was Sisi's "strenuous riding habits," which according to Sophie would endanger her health.

Sisi had just three more days at Possi to say good-bye to all that had spelled happiness — her beautiful gardens, the Lake of Starnberg, the distant Bavarian Alps, her four-legged creatures, her friends in the village, her old childhood nursery — childhood itself. On 20 April 1854, Elisabeth left with her mother and sister for Vienna, saying good-bye to her brother, sisters, her father, her pets, and Possenhofen. It seemed the entire town turned out for her carriage ride to Franz Joseph. "The provincial flags of blue and white fluttered from every housetop, signifying the pride her countrymen took in their princess."[22]

It was decided that Elisabeth would travel to the Austrian capital aboard a Danube steamer so that she could see some of the scenery of her new country and also, just as important, to be seen by her new subjects. Huge crowds gathered in Munich to watch her departure. On this same date, a crucial event in the Crimean War took place, unbeknownst to the future Empress Elisabeth. On this date Austria made a pact with Prussia to force Russia to retreat from the Danube duchies. Franz Joseph then placed Austrian troops on the Russian border. Further, he did not join the Western powers of Great Britain and France. By these actions, he antagonized both sides.

The journey down the Danube began on a rose-covered, steam-powered yacht named *Franz Joseph*. It took three days and nights, with official receptions everywhere. At Straubing on the Danube, Sisi and her parents would continue the trip by boat on a small steamer called the *Stadt Regensburg*. As they reached Linz, church bells rang out from the Postlingberg Basicilica Church. The town dignitaries paraded though the streets of the town; the military band played the Austrian anthem. Linz looked like one immense flower garden; there were bonfires blazing and torchlight processions. Work was suspended to mark the happy event, which allowed thousands upon thousands to turn their thoughts solely to the arrival of the expected princess. Franz Joseph was there to welcome her. Thousands watched as Franz, with heartfelt affection embraced his bride-to-be.[23] It was reminiscent of a marriage long ago between Maria Theresa and her "Franzl." Chroniclers did not fail to mention "they felt as if this time the gentle spirit of Maria Theresa floated above her illustrious grandson."[24]

After a performance of *The Roses of Elisabeth* at the Linz theatre and a torchlight parade through the town, Franz Joseph departed at 4:30 A.M. so that he could welcome his bride again, this time at the official reception in Vienna. Sisi was a floating Ophelia in a boat surrounded with flowers (the emperor had ordered every rose in Schönbrunn cut for this occasion). This part of the journey would take them to Nussdorf. Ducal cabins were hung with purple velvet and the deck was a perfect garden of flowers.

When Elisabeth arrived in Vienna, Archduchess Sophie introduced her to the court at Schönbrunn and her new entourage, including her handmaidens, ladies-in-waiting, and personal servants. At Schönbrunn, Sisi found that her entire staff had been selected for her, obviously by Sophie. First and foremost among her household was the chief Mistress of the Robes, Countess Eszterhazy-Liechtenstein, a matron of "fifty odd summers and a complexion the color of mottled parchment."[25] She was a severe and uncompromising woman and a close confidant of the archduchess. She served Sisi for nine years, until the emperor finally agreed to Sisi's request for her removal. This was quite a big step for Sisi after years of submitting to Sophie without remonstrating, just as the emperor had done since childhood. From that time forward, Sisi would have only women around her that she had personally chosen. Since Eszterhazy was Sophie's closest friend, the rift between Sisi and the archduchess widened.

Countess Eszterhazy presented Sisi with her evening reading material: *Ceremonial Procedure for the Official Progress of the Royal Highness, the Most Gracious Princess Elisabeth*. Two more documents would have to be read: "Most Humble Reminders" for the wedding procedure and the other a nineteen-page Book of Royals, detailing the various ranks of the guests and how and with what precise greeting they were to be received.

Elisabeth married Franz Joseph on 24 April 1854. She started her wedding day rising just before seven o'clock A.M. to once again look over the two tomes on the etiquette and the roles of her ladies-in-waiting, brought by Countess Eszterhazy the night before. Then, Elisabeth, accompanied by her mother and sister, set out to the Church of the Augustines where she would be married. The church was not even a mile away and yet it took hours for her carriage to get through the crowds. Just five years earlier, where the wedding onlookers stood, barricades had been raised along this street during the Revolutions of 1848. While the people were now shouting good fortune to Elisabeth, then the shouts had been for "freedom," and "constitution." But those voices had been quelled and the absolutist government prevailed.

On Sisi's wedding day, soldiers formed a continuous isle along the streets of Vienna; pavements were covered with flowers; flags waved from every house. Nearly a thousand people squeezed into the church. More than a thousand candles lit the scene. The ceremony was fixed for seven o'clock in the evening and by six o'clock all the invited guests had taken their seats. The archbishop of Vienna, Cardinal Othmar, Ritter von Rauscher, intoned the nuptial mass (the verbose wedding address earned Rauscher the nickname "Cardinal Plauscher," or blabbermouth). More than seventy bishops and prelates in their gold-embroidered vestments assembled in the sacristy assisted him. Then the master of the ceremonies had announced to his majesty that all was ready.

The procession passed through the rooms and corridors in the following order: Heralds, pages, chamberlains, privy councilors, the highest court functionaries, the archdukes, and finally the emperor himself. Sisi's white bridal dress, embroidered with gold and silver and decorated with myrrh flowers and white roses, was beautiful. At the moment when the rings were exchanged, a battalion of grenadiers mounted on the roof of the church released the first salvo, which was followed by a thunder of cannons, proclaiming that the couple were now man and wife, emperor and empress.

When the religious rites had finally been performed and the ceremonial procession had returned the bridal pair to the Hofburg, the machinery of court protocol was set in motion. First, Franz Joseph and Sisi must appear on the main balcony above the grand staircase, to be seen and acclaimed by all. This is known as *Repräsentazions-pflicht*, "the duty of keeping up a fine front." Sisi spent "the best part of an hour nodding to a mass of upturned faces."[26] Next, the victorious generals of 1848 were the first to be admitted to an audience with the imperial couple. In the audience chamber, the ambassadors and envoys were waiting. Foreign Minister Buol had the great honor of introducing each one to the new empress. After completion of this long audience, their majesties moved to the Hall of Mirrors. There the ladies of the diplomatic corps were waiting in full regalia to be introduced to the empress, advancing in the order of that nineteen-page book Sisi was given to read before her wedding night.

"Thereupon Their Majesties with the Imperial Family and the Royal Household on Duty proceeded to the Hall of Ceremony in order to receive the congratulatory delegation." The empress and emperor "were gracious enough to chat with those present."[27] The chatelaine made the introductions: the ladies responsible for the palace and the living quarters, the royal and imperial first steward and the gentlemen of the royal household. Thereupon the ladies were led up for the kiss of the hand. At the sight of so many strangers, Sisi panicked and fled, leading to just another episode for court royalty to talk about. The wedding ended with the illumination of the capital, and great crowds came from the outskirts to the inner city to witness the popular display. One chronicler reported, "The area around the gates was constantly enveloped in dense clouds of dust, caused by the movement of so many thousands." Another reported "there was much jubilation and expectant joy but behind the scenes there were increasingly somber, very somber signs."[28]

According to Sophie, "Louise [Ludovika] and I led the young bride to her rooms. I left her with her mother and stayed in the small room next to the bedroom until she was in bed. Then I fetched my son and led him to his young wife, whom I saw once more, to wish her a good night. She hid her pretty face, surrounded by the masses of her beautiful hair, in her pillow, as a frightened bird hides in its nest."[29] The wedding night for most women then was an anxiety-producing event and that is an understatement. Mothers in the 1800s were not considered a success unless their daughters received enough misinformation to turn any wedding night into the prelude for a nervous breakdown. Ruth Smythers wrote her instructions and advice to young brides in 1894, rather typical of the type of advice Sisi would have received:

> To the sensitive young woman who has had the benefits of proper upbringing, the wedding day is, ironically, both the happiest and most terrifying day of her life. On the positive side, there is the wedding itself. [On] the negative side, there is the wedding night, during which the bride must pay the piper, so to speak, by facing for the first time the terrible experience of sex. At this point, dear reader, let me concede one shocking truth. Some young women actually anticipate the wedding night ordeal with curiosity and pleasure! Beware such an attitude! A selfish and sensual husband can easily take advantage of such a bride. One cardinal rule of marriage should never be forgotten: GIVE LITTLE, GIVE SELDOM, AND ABOVE ALL, GIVE GRUDGINGLY.... While sex is at best revolting and at worse rather painful, it has to be endured, and has been by women since the beginning of time, and is compensated for by the monogamous home and by the children produced through it. Clever wives are ever on the alert for new and better

methods of denying and discouraging the amorous overtures of the husband. A good wife should expect to have reduced sexual contacts to once a week by the end of the first year of marriage and to once a month by the end of the fifth year of marriage.[30]

Misinformation regarding the subject of sex wasn't limited to the feminine world: "The young husband whose brides did not display the most garbled and fantastic notions on the technique of l'amour felt cheated. They had been taught to measure chastity by the degree of hysterics encountered in the marriage bed."[31]

Archduchess Sophie had made an earnest attempt to not interfere with her son's rule: "At my son's accession to the throne, I firmly resolved not to interfere in any matters of state; I felt I had no right, and I also know them to be in such good hands after a thirteen-year period without a ruler — that I am happy with all my heart, after the hard-fought year '48, to be able to sit by and observe current policy calmly and with confidence!"[32]

But apparently her noninterference policy did not apply to Franz Joseph's personal affairs. The couple was at breakfast the next morning when Sophie and Ludovika entered the breakfast room. Sophie noticed that Franz Joseph was beaming and all over was the picture of sweet happiness. Sisi was embarrassingly quiet, though most probably Sophie did not notice her social discomfiture. Nor, indeed, did Franz Joseph himself. Such intrusiveness came naturally to the archduchess. At first the archduchess briefly thought about leaving, but protocol-minded Franz Joseph asked them to stay "with a touching eagerness." Sophie had interrupted the couple's first breakfast, had inquisitively scrutinized their expressions, and then suddenly and politely announced that they were leaving. Sophie's diary continued with this revealing sentence: "Thereafter a confidential talk followed between each child and its mother."[33] This clearly meant that Sophie subjected her son to a detailed inquisition even while he was still at his honeymoon breakfast.

In the course of this talk Sophie would learn that the performance of marital duties had not yet been accomplished, a fact known all over the court before the day was out.[34] Some twenty years later Sisi would confide to her own handpicked ladies-in-waiting of the embarrassment she felt on that particular morning. Perhaps Sisi exaggerated how Franz Joseph was under his mother's thumb but there can be no doubt that they had very little intimate time with each other. Ruth Smythers noted, "It is useless, in most cases, for the bride to prevail upon the groom to forego the sexual initiation. While the ideal husband would be one who would approach his bride only at her request and only for the purpose of begetting offspring, such nobility and unselfishness cannot be expected from the average man."[35] But Franz Joseph was an exception to Smythers' advice, for Sisi became a woman on the third night of their marriage. For her "gallant efforts," she then received her "morning gift" (*Morgengabe*—a gift to compensate for the loss of her virginity) of 12,000 gold ducats ($240,000).[36]

Six days after the wedding, the couple finally left Vienna. They would spend their honeymoon at Laxenburg Castle, fifteen miles from the city. But even there Sisi would not have her husband all to herself. Each morning the emperor would rise long before she was awake and travel back to Hofburg to immerse himself in affairs of state, only returning to her in time for six o'clock dinner. Still, at Laxenburg the young empress could resume one of her favorite activities, riding, which provided exercise and fresh air and seemed to restore her vitality. Far too soon she had to return to Schönbrunn and its gloomy confines and once again be subject to the constraints of court life.

Just six months after the glorious wedding, there were more somber signs. For Franz Joseph, his desk at the Hofburg became more compelling than the marital bed. After his brief spurts of "reckless abandon," his imperial ambition and dominant sense of sovereignty regained control. Amid all the wedding excitement and the few celebratory weeks that followed, Sisi would never have guessed the tragic turns her role as Empress of Austria would take in years to come.

Chapter Six

The Royal Children

Once Sisi's condition of expecting the first royal child had been verified by three court physicians there was no holding back the Dowager Archduchess. She continued to be inordinately solicitous about small annoyances, this time for the protection of the unborn child. Her concern involved the pair of parrots living in a big cage on the veranda, an engagement gift from Franz Joseph. These birds worried Sophie so much that she wrote to her son warning him that if Sisi gazed too long at them, particularly in the first few months of her pregnancy, "she can bring about a resemblance to them in her children" (Sophie was being quite serious). "It was far better," the proud mother added, "for Sisi to spend her time of pregnancy admiring a photograph of Franz Joseph or the reflection of her own mirror."[1]

The things that Sisi loved, riding horses or taking vigorous walks, were considered verboten by Sophie. These active adventures were replaced by "calming carriage rides" with Sophie or leisurely strolls by the front gates so that those passing by might catch a fleeting glance of Empress Elisabeth and her advancing pregnancy and share in the joy and promise of a future heir. Thus, her once active lifestyle was reduced to the inert and sedentary life of an aging matron. Because Elisabeth was always an active person, she suffered tremendously under these restraints. Her complaints to Franz Joseph resulted in no changes. Sisi then became quite reticent and kept her complaints to herself. Sophie was thus given free rein to continue her micromanagement of Sisi's pregnancy. Once again, uninformed Franz Joseph spent his days, as usual, at Hofburg Palace — where the business of state came first — yielding to the concerns of the empire and seemingly oblivious to those of his wife.

Sophie not only was in charge of Sisi's daily health regimentation, she was also the commander supervising everyone from the doctors and their assistants down to the scullery maids and the seamstresses stitching the baby's layette. She had thought of everything and had a plan for the entire gestation period. Something came over Sisi and she simply gave in to every one of Sophie's demands.

During the beginning of the summer, Franz Joseph had to spend several weeks in Bohemia (now the Czech Republic). Bohemia had become a constituent state of the Habsburg dynasty when Archduke Ferdinand became king of Bohemia in 1618. During the Revolution of 1848, Czech nationalists called for their freedom from Habsburg Austria but their revolutionaries were defeated. After Austria's defeat in the Austro-Prussian War, Bohemia once again attempted to become a part of the "equality": Austria-Hungary-Bohemia. Their attempts at a tripartite monarchy failed but Franz Joseph periodically visited the country to assuage their frequent concerns.

Upon his return, Sophie was the first to greet her son, while Sisi followed shortly behind. After welcoming him home, Sophie presented her son with a piece of paper: "It was the title to the Marstallier Estate at Ischl, which would be remodeled into an imperial summer villa. She had bought the place out of her own pocket and was now placing it at the disposal of her son. The emperor was delighted with this new bauble."[2] The renovations were done by late July when the court moved to summer in their new villa at Ischl. Upon inspection of the villa, Sisi noticed that the nursery was off in another wing, quite far and almost inaccessible to her and Franz Joseph's rooms. "The design, of course, was deliberately done and speaks volumes about Sophie's feelings about Sisi's future parenting skills: 'Give her the child? When she cannot even discipline herself? Never!'"[3]

Sophie's tortoise-shell exterior slightly mellowed at the birth of her first grandchild: "Sisi held my son's hand between her own two and once kissed it with a lively and respectful tenderness; this was so touching and made him weep; he kissed her ceaselessly, comforted her and lamented with her, and looked at me at every pain to see if it satisfied me.... The child was born (after three o'clock) and cried like a six-week-old baby. The young mother, with an expression of such touching bliss, said to me, 'Oh now everything is all right, now I don't mind how much I suffered!'"[4]

Even in this touching situation, the birth of their first child, Sophie's paramount position was evident: "The midwife followed her every order; young Franz Joseph constantly looked at his mother's expressions for guidance and indications of the birthing progress, and seventeen-year-old Elisabeth whose mother could not attend, was wholly at her mother-in-law's mercy. Without consulting Sisi, the child was named after the Archduchess, who was also to become the child's Godmother."[5]

Sophie always had a very special place in her Grandmother's Sophie's heart: "Pages of her diary are covered with the details of infant care. Everything aroused the grandmotherly pride of the Archduchess, who was normally so cool. The slightest development, every new tooth became worthy of being recorded in the Archduchess' diary."[6]

A second daughter, Gisela, named after the Bavarian wife of the first Christian King of Hungary, Stephen I, was born on 12 July 1856. The disappointment at the fact that once again the hoped-for heir to the throne had not been born was great. The Viennese were probably among the unhappiest nonroyals. When an heir to the throne is born, the jubilant Viennese subjects receive generous benefactions from the Crown. Since times were particularly bad, the people were in desperate need for any court gratuities. More important, should Sisi continue to give birth to girls, the succession would pass to Franz Joseph's brothers and any male descendants they might have; for, despite the reverence shown to the memory of Maria Theresa, "legalistic pedantry" made the accession of a sovereign's daughter virtually impossible.

Archduchess Sophie was equally possessive of Gisela, who like her sister was primarily cared for by Sophie, not Elisabeth. When Gisela was just sixteen in 1872 she met Leopold, Prince of Bavaria. The wedding took place the following year. Archduchess Gisela was not a beauty but was rather philanthropic and became known as the Good Angel from Wien because of her charity work during World War I. Gisela turned her palace in Munich into a hospital and administered to the sick and wounded. Her husband was a field marshal who commanded German and Austro-Hungarian forces on the Eastern Front. Prince Leopold received the Grand Cross of the Iron Cross on 4 March 1918. In 1918, when revolution broke out, Gisela's family fled, but she remained to give assistance to the wounded and dying.

Shortly after the wedding, foreign guests began arriving for the 1873 Vienna Exposition, its motto *Koltur und Erziehung* (Culture and Education). Dignitaries began to arrive from London (the Prince of Wales and his brother) while Germany sent Crown Prince Frederick. Tsar Alexander II was present along with the Tsaritsa Marie of Hessen-Darmstadt. Perhaps one of the more interesting visitors was the leader of Persia, Nasiru'd-Din Shah, who, because of his love for curdled milk and goat cheese, brought his own goats and housed them in his hotel room. Colorful Persian customs caused much dismay among the staff: "On one occasion the atmosphere grew even more baneful when the Shah, weak from the exertion of a day's sightseeing, awoke at midnight with a pang of hunger. Then and there a sheep was slaughtered at his bedside and roasted in the open grate. Bones, viscera and hide were left in a bright silver wash bowl to be fetched away by a terrified chambermaid who fainted on the steps."[7] The shah came to Vienna with equal desires to see the exhibition and to see Sisi. When she appeared in a long white robe "embroidered in silver" and set off by a belt of purple velvet, a band of diamonds and amethysts bound her luxurious hair, the shah remained rooted to the spot and marveled at her beauty.

From the beginning, Sisi was never close to her second daughter—partly because of Sophie's intrusions and partly because of the death of her firstborn daughter, Sophie. In 1857, the children accompanied their parents on a state visit to Hungary. During this trip, both children fell ill. Gisela recovered, but Sophie became steadily weaker. For eleven hours, Sisi watched in despair as her child grew steadily worse and then finally died. One might think that as a result of her child's death Sisi would cling to her only surviving daughter, ten-month-old Gisela. But "Sisi withdrew from everyone, sought solitude, wept for days, even weeks, refused all nourishment, abandoned herself completely to her grief."[8] Franz Joseph sent a telegram to his mother, saying that the little one was an angel in heaven: "We are devastated."

Barely a year later, in December 1857, there were signs of a new pregnancy. It was a son! The young monarch performed an extraordinary deed; he had placed on the baby's cradle his own chain and collar of the Golden Fleece, Austria's highest decoration. In Bruges in 1429, Philip the Good, Duke of Burgundy, founded this order, which ranked as the most exalted and exclusive in the world. The Golden Fleece consisted of a small gold ram suspended from a starry flint stone emitting flames and topped by a jewel-studded chain, which was worn over a fur cape.

Rudolf was an attractive child but could not be called handsome. As an adult, however, Rudolf's future sister-in-law Princess Louise of Coburg wrote of him in her memoirs: "Though he was not conventionally handsome, he was irresistible to women. His moist eyes, the black mustache Hungarian-style, the straight back, the trace of melancholy in his expression, now and then wiped away by great laughter, his dashing style of dressing with his cap at a provocative angle, his vitality, as well as the fact that he was the Crown Prince." She further implied that their relationship was more than that of relatives, and continued her description as his being "more than handsome, he was seductive ... he was disturbing."⁹ But it is a paradox that none of Sisi's children inherited a trace of her great beauty. All were singularly somewhat homely, with plain features and lackluster eyes that had no expression.

Rudolf may not have inherited his mother's good looks, but he resembled her in mind and in his high-strung temperament. He always had a delicate constitution and was frequently ill. Extremely thin, he was quite fearful and anxious as well. "His father had wished for a bold, physically strong son, who would grow into a good soldier. Little Rudolf absolutely did not fulfill these hopes."¹⁰ When a father's wished-for temperaments don't match the child's, it is the child who suffers. "By the time Rudolf was ten years old, he was already the darling of the Court and the Viennese."¹¹ Under his grandmother's spoiling influence, however, he had developed a haughty and vain demeanor, character faults that were a great source of grief to his mother, who strenuously set herself to eradicate these consequences.

Rudolf grew into a slender youth with distinguished and sympathetic features expressive of unusual intellectual gifts. He proved to be highly intelligent and intellectually precocious. Even as a five-year-old he could make himself understood, as Archduchess Sophie proudly noted, in four languages: German, Hungarian, Czech, and French. Sisi took pains to instill in him her own ardent feelings for Hungary and continually remarked to all of their teachers, "Make my children as little German as possible!"¹² The Hungarian language was used as the medium of instruction, especially for religious knowledge: "I pray with my children each day in Hungarian, and you need not teach them to be orthodox, but rather to be religious; we all need the comfort of faith in our daily lives."¹³

Since the age of six Rudolf had been in the charge of Major-General Gondrecourt, a favorite of Sophie. Gondrecourt believed in a Spartan system of training the young boy and had Franz Joseph's blessing in administering such training. In the case of a sensitive child like Rudolf this led to grave consequences. In an attempt to tone up his circulation, Rudolf was subject to ice-cold showers; it was sheer torture and his teeth would begin to chatter uncontrollably. These were such horrendous experiences for Rudolf that simply hearing the sound of running water would drain his face of all color. Similarly the stern tutor would take his charge on frequent visits to the zoological park at Lainz, whereupon reaching the gates Gondrecourt "would rush inside and presently emerge on all fours, howling: 'Here comes a wild boar!'"[14] Before he was seven-years-old, Rudolf suffered spasms of hysteria. Sisi fought against these evils but, again, to no avail.

Since living under the strict, even sadistic control of his new tutor, Count Leopold Gondrecourt, Rudolf was almost a permanent invalid, suffering from fevers, angina, stomach colds, and similar ailments. The count drilled the anxious, sickly child to the point of exhaustion with military exercises and rigorous physical and psychological "toughening."

Both the imperial physician Dr. Seeburger and Sophie agreed that Sisi's sentimentalism toward the education of her son must be curbed, especially since the young empress would often give vent to excessive emotion while visiting the nursery, thus coddling and pampering the children, the prince in particular. Weary of discord, Sisi vacated the nursery and spent hours in despair over her writing desk, creating more poems. Finally, in a written ultimatum to her husband, she declared, "It seems ridiculous to terrorize a child, teaching him heroism by means of water cures. I can't stand it any longer. Either Gondrecourt goes or I go."[15] Gondrecourt went.

There is another statement made by the empress that casts a revealing light on the Emperor's family life during this period. Elisabeth handed the emperor the following ultimatum in writing: "I wish to have reserved to me absolute authority in all matters concerning the children, the choice of the people around them, the place of their residence, the complete supervision of their education, in a word, everything is to be left entirely to me to decide, until the moment of their majority. I further wish that, whatever concerns my personal affairs, such as, among others, the choice of the people around me, the place of my residence, all arrangements in the house etc. be reserved to me alone to decide. Elisabeth, Ischl, 27 August 1865."[16] The emperor agreed.

It took Sisi eleven years to achieve her emancipation from the intrusiveness of her mother-in-law, eleven years to find her strength rather than escaping through activities such as traveling. Her first task was deciding on a tutor. Colonel Latour, who had been such an effective supplicant in the cause of little Rudolf and who had, as the future was to show, genuinely taken the boy to heart, was her first choice. Sisi had full confidence in Latour. She knew that compared to the rest of the court, he held extremely liberal views. For this reason, he was mistrusted. However, he was interested not in military drill, but in education. Rudolf's drills were reduced to the most basic exercises and to riding and shooting. Intellectual training was given precedence over the physical, exactly the reverse of what the emperor had ordered a year earlier. With his new teachers, Rudolf took on a calmer persona.

Like his mother, he was a gifted linguist and learned the principal tongues of the old monarchy: Hungarian, Polish, and Czech, in addition to French and English. He traveled extensively and often corresponded with his mother in Hungarian. One of his travel companions was Carl Menger, founder of the Austrian School of economics. *Principles*, first published in 1871, is the book that provided a new basis for the understanding of value, utility, money, and the market process. Further, as heir to the throne, Rudolf received a thorough education in history and later, under Rudolf's direction, a huge work on the ethnography and history of the Habsburg empire was prepared: It ran to twenty-four volumes and, though subjectively patriotic, is still regarded as a valuable reference work.[17] Oskar Mitis, Rudolf's biographer, wrote that Rudolf read Descartes and Voltaire, studied botany and ornithology, geography, physics, sociology, history. Amassing of knowledge may have served Rudolf as compensation for an early life in which his Habsburg existence hindered normal access to his father, while absence estranged him from his mother.

After Condrecourt left, Rudolf's anger appeared to dissipate. He was no longer afraid. Little by little, however, his internalized anger externalized and he began to lash out and inflict violence on others. This streak of cruelty manifested itself in other ways; he drew scenes of mountaineer life, always with himself in hunter's clothing and in the center of the picture. Landscapes were strewn with bleeding pheasants, ducks or partridge. At age fourteen, crayons and toy sabers afforded no more thrills. He now had a shotgun that brought down live creatures, mainly birds. The weapon had been a Christmas present from Sophie. "It was this Rudolf, the childish killer, who horrified Elisabeth. Her own extravagant love of animals arose in protest. She resolved at once to alter his mode of life and to place him, like Marie Valerie, in the hands of Hungarian tutors. Bishop Hyazinth von Ronay, a friend of Andrássy's, henceforth took over the young Prince's education."[18]

As the tutors of Crown Prince Rudolf were changed from bullying generals to liberal doctors, Rudolf's thinking followed in kind. Rudolf, like his mother, was liberal, anti-aristocratic, republican, and a supporter of Hungary. Rudolf became a virulent critic of many of his father's policies, including the empire's ties with what the crown prince saw as an increasingly reactionary Germany. Over time Rudolf recognized the gap between his outlook, and the world of ideas in which he lived, and his father's. The inevitable result was that he became critical of his father; each lived in different worlds, the old and the new. In his father's world,

> The Habsburg Court came to be known for its strict ritual, its pomp, its exclusivity, and increasingly for its anachronistic nature. This was the result of the emperor's intentional effort to restore to his court the "majesty" lacking under Ferdinand, and thus, it was hoped, the authority which went with majesty. By all accounts majesty was indeed restored, and had the desired effect. The imperial family and the court aristocracy preserved their immense social prestige, and the strict ceremonial associated with such events as the *Hofball*, the Washing of Feet on Maundy Thursday, and most famous of all the Corpus Christ Procession, were eminently successful exercises in symbolic politics.[19]

One critic wrote, "Our emperor has no friends; his character, his nature does not allow it. He stands alone on his promontory; he discusses the official business of everyone with his servants, but a real conversation is carefully avoided. Therefore he knows little of the thinking and feelings of the populace, the views and opinions of the people.... He believes that we are enjoying one of the happiest epochs in Austrian history. He is told so officially, and in the newspapers he reads only the sections marked in red and so he is kept from any purely human contact, from any non-partisan, truly thoughtful advice."[20]

That critic was his son, Rudolf. Subsequently Rudolf was carefully kept out of all affairs of state and was distrusted at court, a situation he deeply resented. "The most minor court adviser has more to do with government than I do," he complained, "I am condemned to inactivity."[21] Rudolf began to mix freely with well-known liberals as Franz Joseph sent him off with a wave of his white-gloved hand.

As an adult, Rudolf would write to his wife, Stephanie: "Every year I become older, that is, less vital and less able ... this eternal period of preparing yourself, this continuous waiting for the time when construction can begin, sap my creative energy!"[22] Franz Joseph continued to deny his heir any responsibilities in the empire, even as Rudolf approached thirty, and his forced idleness made the crown prince increasingly frustrated. He rented his frustrations by hunting, traveling, and seducing willing maidens. He began drinking heavily and according to some historians became addicted to opium.

As he passed from childhood to adolescence, even his introduction to the topic of sex, like his lessons in history or geography, was planned. There exists a document, signed by several of his tutors, which described in dry official jargon, Rudolf's being told the facts of life when he was about thirteen.²³ His first love was the Princess Maria Anna of Tuscany when he was nineteen, but she died of tuberculosis. The sadness of it may have driven Rudolf to a need for intimate contact and conquest as compelling as Don Juan's.²⁴ Even in his first year of marriage, he had numerous affairs. Conversely, he was a jealous husband. Stephanie wrote, "The Crown Prince was extraordinarily suspicious. When he was at home, I could not leave him for a moment.... I was not allowed to write letters; even those addressed to my parents were read before their dispatch. The Crown Prince gave orders that during his absence no one except my ladies were to be admitted."²⁵

As a young boy, Rudolf was capable of some rather scandalous pranks, some of which were led by Archduke Otto, the enfant terrible son of Franz Joseph's brother, Karl Ludwig. On one occasion they came across a funeral procession. They bade it halt and amused themselves by jumping their horses over the coffin. The incident was aired in Parliament and Rudolf wrote to Stephanie: "The police gave me a few uncomfortable hours.... Now we are quite safe."²⁶ Rudolf also had a bad fall from his horse but begged his doctor not to tell his father. The fall seems to have worsened the headaches from which he was suffering, for the relief of which morphine was prescribed. It was a dangerous prescription.

As a baby he was spoiled by his grandmother's adoration; as a young child, he fell into an emotional abyss. As a youth he may have loved his father. However, Franz Joseph was not a father but an apparition and seldom seen. His mother concentrated her love on Marie Valerie. Despite the startling similarity in their views on politics, literature, religion, etc, Elisabeth and Rudolf were far from close. Indeed, after the ultimatum insisting on her being in charge of his upbringing, the empress showed no interest whatsoever in her only son. About a trip with his mother, Rudolf discussed his neglect in a letter to cousin Ludwig II: "I never manage to talk to Mama alone. During the journey she did not feel well, confined herself to her compartment, and appeared only at meals, which however, were partaken of in company of her suite. In London I never saw Mama alone."²⁷ He hated his father and didn't really know his mother. How sad it is to read the entry in the imperial daily diary kept for him in his early childhood: "10 to 11 A.M.—See Their Majesties."²⁸

It appeared that Sisi loved the crown prince, according to his old tutor Colonel Latour von Thurnberg. But the colonel added a strong caveat that she was never around in his nurturing years, when "a mother's hand was quite essential." Because of Sophie's sole proprietorship over raising the royal children, Sisi seemed to free herself of childrearing very early, at least in her feelings. Rudolf tried to gain her love; and in order to prove that he revered his mother, he paid an outrageous price for eleven Heine autographs (Sisi's favorite poet) and placed them under the Christmas tree for the empress. "Elisabeth, however, was so preoccupied with her daughter's engagement that she did not pay Rudolf's gift the attention that it had deserved and that he expected."[29]

Rudolf's marriage was purely a political alliance. Stephanie was the daughter of King Leopold II of the Coburg dynasty, who, like Franz Joseph, was "forever seeking to augment the power and wealth of the family through important marriages. Elisabeth detested the Coburgs, and Bismarck called them 'the stud farm of Europe.'"[30] Sisi warned Rudolf that he was being pushed into the marriage by his father, who considered the political aspects of the affair in his capacity as the ruler of an empire and not as a father. Franz Joseph wanted the heir to the throne to marry early despite Rudolph's youth and immaturity.

Stephanie was "plump, had red arms, small eyes, a sullen and haughty expression." At her marriage she walked down the aisle with "all the daintiness of a dragoon."[31] She's been described as a dumpy, uninspiring girl who, like Rudolf, had been brought up in a loveless atmosphere. Needless to say, the marriage did little to content the heir apparent. He continued to engage in short-lived affairs with society women; in the process he contracted — among other things — bad debts and, apparently, venereal disease, which he may have given to his wife.

Rudolf and Stephanie had in common a loveless childhood and phantom parents. She, like Rudolf, was quick in her feelings of being insulted and injured. Stephanie expected to find their rooms in the Laxenburg where they spent their wedding night to be newly renovated and furnished. Instead, she said, "As we entered, a musty clammy, icy air took our breaths away. Nothing seemed in readiness.... There were no rugs, no dressing table, no bathroom, just a washstand on a three-legged stool. What a night! What a disgust!"[32]

Rudolph did, however, spend enough time with Stephanie to produce a child — unfortunately not an heir to the throne but a daughter, also to be named Elisabeth. Stephanie would have no male heirs in line for the Habsburg throne. Because Sisi was so often vacant from court, the Viennese longed for a princess in their imperial house to whom they could give their affections.[33] Despite her appearance, Stephanie represented youth with all its hopes and desires, and the Viennese welcomed the royal bride with rapturous delight. When a daughter was born 3 September 1883, the enthusiasm of the people was an index to the popularity of both Rudolf and the crown princess.

The couple was so far apart, however, that Rudolf was said to have approached Pope Leo the Thirteenth for an annulment of his marriage, possibly in order to legitimize an heir by his mistress, Marie Vetsera. The crown prince was summoned by his father to the Hofburg and was told that his relationship with Marie Vetsera must end. Elisabeth was aware that her son's marriage was not a happy one but said, "Sometimes I have wondered what I could do. But I am reluctant to interfere, for I myself suffered so unspeakably under my mother-in-law that I do not wish to incur the reproach of a similar fault."[34]

Sisi's fourth child, Marie Valerie, was Sisi's sole caretaking responsibility. The archduchess made no claim upon the new baby, partly because Sisi watched over it like a tigress at bay but also because Marie Valerie had been born in Hungary. Marie Valerie was also very delicate as a child, and Sisi was a vigilant mother who was the first by her bedside every morning. When Marie Valerie was ill her mother refused to leave her, and could with only great difficulty be persuaded to take needful rest.

Mutzerl, as Marie Valerie was called, had inherited her mother's love of flowers, and as soon as she could walk, she had her own little garden in the grounds of the different castles visited by the Imperial Court. Ties of heart and mind closely united mother and daughter, and they were rarely apart. To Sisi, Marie Valerie was more than a daughter; it appeared that she was her only intimate friend.

Marie Valerie's education was her mother's main, and happy, preoccupation. She learned Hungarian and she and her mother most frequently conversed in that language. She was so "Hungarian" that Sisi was accused of bringing up not a Habsburg daughter but a Hungarian one. The paradox was that the son to whom Elisabeth paid so little attention was so like her, whereas the effusively beloved daughter Marie Valerie took a very different direction. She had inherited more of her father's temperament, was calm in judgment, devout, and rational; and like her sister Gisela, she was helpless in the face of her mother's flights of imagination. Of most significance, however, this "Hungarian" child, born in the royal castle in Budapest, raised by Hungarian tutors, developed a strong aversion to Hungary when she was still a very young girl. Of course, she did not dare to reveal her dislike of Hungary and all things Hungarian in the presence of her mother.[35]

Six. The Royal Children

"Marry a bricklayer or a chimney sweep," said the empress with a sprightliness that was a trifle grim. "I shall be the last to stop you!"[36] And, apparently, Marie Valerie listened, as she was the only child of the emperor and empress who married without court considerations and for love. She married Archduke Franz Salvator of Tuscany. The archduke was a doctor of medicine, a cavalry general in the Austro-Hungary army, and held the prestigious title of Knight of the Order of the Golden Fleece. The wedding took place in Ischl on 31 July 1890. The *London Morning Chronicle* reported:

> In anticipation of this event the country around Ischl presented a brilliant scene last evening, when the thirty-eight peaks of the mountains that are within sights from this enchanting city were illuminated with colored lights and fires. Bonfires were burning on every prominent height, and from the roofs of the houses and villas of the surrounding country there waved the colors of Austria in flags and in bright lanterns. The narrow streets were crowded with sight seers.
>
> It was the special desire of the Emperor and Empress that the marriage be celebrated at this place, although it was known that the imperial villa is far too small to accommodate even those in immediate attendance on their Majesties, while the town itself cannot find room comfortable for one-half the people who are here. For the past week the rooms in every hotels of any prominence have been secured by emissaries of the Lord Chamberlain for the royal guests, who included all the members of the Hapsburg family....
>
> The bride is twenty-two years old, has a graceful figure, and a face full of intelligence, although one that would hardly be considered beautiful. She has been highly and carefully educated, and her teachers all speak in the warmest praise of her goodness, her amiability, and her literary abilities. Of the last quality she has given evidence by the production of several charming poems and some admirable essays, which found a publisher, and enjoyed a sale. Wherever she goes she plays the part of a fairy godmother to poor children, strewing gifts and bestowing bounty where she feels they will give the most enjoyment and be the most welcome.
>
> The groom is twenty-four years of age and a son of the Archduke Carl Salvator and the Archduchess Maria Immaculata, a daughter of King Ferdinand II. The groom is therefore a descendant of the Tuscan branch of the Hapsburgs. He is tall, well built, has a dark complexion, is a bold rider, a good soldier, and enjoys a large share of popularity.[37]

This happy day was followed by one of the unhappiest days. It was January, and the day began in its typical fashion: "Sisi was being tutored in modern Greek; Marie Valerie was having her piano lesson, the Emperor was working in his study. Count Josef Hoyos's carriage pulled up to the inner courtyard. He brought the sad news."[38] On 30 January 1889 Rudolf and his seventeen-year-old mistress, Marie Vetsera, had committed suicide in his hunting lodge at Mayerling. The events of his life provided an overflowing cup of bitterness, frustration and despair, which prompted him to finally make the decision after contemplating it for years. He had asked his wife Stephanie to prove her love by joining him in a suicide pact. She told Franz Joseph about this request but she simply received a polite rebuff. Both Franz and Elisabeth failed to notice the tragic decline in Rudolf's appearance and demeanor. Nor did they do anything to help him overcome his addiction to alcohol and morphine. Elisabeth was the first member of the imperial family to be told of the crown prince's death, and at first she bore up well, breaking the news herself to the emperor, Mary's mother, and others.

Three versions circled Vienna: the poisoning of the crown prince by his mistress, his suicide with hers, and death by natural causes. Marie had been killed at short range by a single bullet in her forehead, although her hair had been arranged loosely over her shoulders. A rose had been placed between her folded hands. Marie's body was spirited away from Mayerling and secretly interred at a nearby cemetery. Not even her mother was allowed to attend the burial. It wasn't until the following day that Franz and Elisabeth learned from Dr. Hermann Widerhofer, their personal physician, how the couple had really died. Widerhofer "saw the girl's folded hands — and Rudolf in a half-sitting position, the revolver on the ground, fallen from his stiffened hand, nothing but cognac in the glass. He laid down the corpse, long ago turned cold, the skull cracked, the bullet in one temple, out the other. Same wound in the girl. Both bullets found in the room."[39]

Rudolf had left letters to his mother and his wife and others, but not to his father. To Stephanie, he stated that she was rid of his presence and burden; she should live happily in her own way. He was going calmly to his death, which alone could save his good name. Yet to Marie Valerie he wrote, "I do not die willingly."[40] While Marie Valerie knew already Rudolf was mentally disturbed, the empress would not hear of that. No one took the thirty-year-old Rudolf's frequent mentions of his imminent death seriously. Elisabeth had to turn away from that thought for if she acknowledged it, she would accuse herself of passing on to her son the Wittelsbach strain of insanity. Historian Heinrich noted after his interview with Marie Festetics in 1909, "I could not refrain from telling the Countess that, no matter how deeply her statements moved me and filled me with sympathy for the Empress, I could not comprehend how a mother as deeply sensitive as the Empress could remain ignorant of what was disturbing the Crown

Prince and how she could not know how far he had strayed. The Countess then repeated emphatically a remark she made several times: You must never forget that persons of high rank live quite differently from other people, that they find out less and that actually they may be called very unhappy because the truth reaches them only rarely and never completely."[41] For Franz Joseph, Elisabeth was his strength and he solemnly remarked that without the help of his wife, who displayed superhuman strength, he felt he would literally not have made it.

Rudolf lay in state in the Hofburg Chapel for two days before being taken to the burial shrine of the Habsburgs, the Capuchin Church. Gisela accompanied her father, the emperor, to the funeral; neither Elisabeth, Marie Valerie nor Stephanie could bear to go. The *New York Times* reported: "During the service the Emperor stood perfectly calm, looking about him with quick movements of the head, as his custom is. After the chanting of the *Libera*, however, His Majesty stepped out from his place and walked to the coffin, knelt down beside it, and with clasped hands remained for a moment or two in prayer. This was a moment of poignant emotion for all present. Not a sound was heard. Nobody coughed, not a dress rustled, not a scabbard clanked on the flagstones. An entire stillness pre-vailed till the Emperor rose from his knees and walked back calmly to his place."[42]

Unhappy and dissatisfied with every part of his life, the heir to the Habsburg throne had decided there was only one honorable thing left for him to do. The crown prince had long been a disappointment to his father. The tradition-bound emperor was at a loss to understand Rudolf's liberalism, let alone his opposition to the church, his contempt for aristocracy, his questioning of the legitimacy of the Habsburg state. His son's profligate lifestyle angered and dismayed him. Rudolf's physical health was also a concern. Ever since his boyhood fall from a tree, he had suffered from blinding headaches. He also suffered from persistent bronchitis and "rheumatic pains that left him so weak that the Emperor insisted he should spend a month on the island of Lacroma, off Dubrovnik, to build up his strength...." From there Rudolph wrote to Stephanie; "I am keeping the cough under control with morphine, although it is a dangerous drug.'"[43] But nothing the crown prince had ever done in all his thirty years had prepared the emperor for Rudolf's final act, which would shock Franz Joseph like nothing else and rock the empire to its very foundations.

Of all the motives given for the tragedy, the revenge of Rudolf on his father is the most likely. His killing of himself was a lethal protest of impotence and defiance. Specifically, the wish to wreak vengeance on a parent by destroying oneself is one of the strongest drives leading to suicide. "Finally, and perhaps best known, are the fantasies in which suicide represents the ultimate act of revenge aimed at a disappointing object, or real or imagined persecutor. Here, in effect, suicide is homicide which has been turned against the self."[44] Freud postulated that in pathologic depression the subject "identifies with a hated and loved object. When, as a result of loss, disappointment or rejection, the love turns to hate, the tendency to suicide may be overwhelming."[45]

On 31 January an official bulletin announced the crown prince's "suicide by revolver." His death, the bulletin claimed, had occurred while Rudolf was "in a state of temporary derangement,"[46] thereby clearing the way for a church funeral. The catalyst may well have been a botched abortion on Marie Vetsera. The deluge of blood on their funeral bed was too great to have come from their official head wounds. The act appears to have been premeditated; an onyx ashtray was in the Hofburg rooms of the crown prince, on which Marie scrawled, "Better a revolver than poison."

After the tragic death of her only son, Elisabeth became more and more embittered, and receded into her own world. Contrition for never understanding him grew in her. She became unsociable and inapproachable. From then on she would wear black exclusively. At the first court reception that Sisi attended two years after Rudolf's death, the wife of the British ambassador was astonished to observe that the empress was dressed like a nun. She was heavily veiled, with a necklace of black beads that seemed to resemble a rosary, although a medallion containing a lock of Rudolf's hair replaced the cross. Her last official appearance was in the year 1896 on the occasion of the millennium celebrations in Budapest.

Kalman Mikszath, present at the reception at Budapest Castle, described his impressions: "There she sits, in the throne room of the royal castle in her black, lacy Hungarian robes. Anything and everything on her is somber. From the dark hair a black veil flows down. Hairpins black, pearls black, everything black, only her face as white as marble and unutterably woeful ... a *mater dolorosa* (sorrowful mother) ... it is still her, but the grief has embedded its mark upon this visage.... Not one stir, not one glance reveals concern. White as marble, resembling a statue."[47]

After the first few days, however, Sisi's grief exploded in rage at her daughter-in-law, whom she accused of being responsible for Rudolf's death because she hadn't loved him, along with a great deal of self-accusation. She blamed herself not because she had shown her son no more (and perhaps even less) affection than his wife had, but because Rudolf, as a suicide, had to be declared insane in order to be given a church funeral. The empress believed that it was the Wittelsbach inclination towards mental illnesses that Rudolf had inherited from her and which was ultimately at fault, and she began to fear even more than before the manifestation of such a family history within herself. She wore mourning for the rest of her life. She seemed to abandon herself to and felt born to misfortune. Elisabeth's increasing longing for death saddened all those close to her. Marie Valerie said, "Mama will probably never again be as she was at one time; she envies Rudolf his death, and day and night she longs for her own."[48]

In October 1889 a circular was sent to all the Austrian representatives abroad informing them of the empress' wish that any felicitations on her name days be omitted, not only in the immediate future but for all time. At the end of 1889 the official year of mourning was coming to an end. Only a few weeks after the anniversary of Mayerling, Gyula Andrássy, whom Elisabeth regarded "as her last and only friend, died at the end of a long and painful illness. His death brought back a flood of memories, all the passionate emotions of the time of the Austro-Hungarian Compromise, when in loving Andrássy she had learnt to love his country and he in turn had sacrificed their love to his patriotism."[49] Shortly afterward, the empress gave away all her light-colored personal items, ranging from clothes, shoes, and scarves, to umbrellas and purses. She kept only the plain mourning outfits and for the rest of her days she did not wear colored dresses again. Her only concession was a simple pearl-gray dress at Marie Valerie's wedding and at the christening of Marie Valerie's first child, little Elisabeth (Ella).

Toward the empress, Franz Joseph's chivalrous devotion was redoubled; he submitted his will wholly to her wishes. He allowed her even greater freedom than before in the ordering of her own life. Sisi suffered in silence; she was never really able to escape from the pain caused by the death of her only son. Franz Joseph became more reserved and detached, like a man who expects no good from life and the world, and began to age rapidly. He was becoming *der alte Herr*— the old gentleman.

Franz Joseph ordered the destruction of Mayerling and the building of a convent of Carmelite nuns in its place. He commissioned the Viennese artist Joseph Kastner to paint an ornate fresco above the high altar, which stood directly above the room in which Rudolf and Marie Vetsera went to their deaths. Kastner was to show the patron saints of those dearest to

Franz Joseph grouped in adoration of the Holy Trinity. The boy-martyr Saint Rudolf is prominent in the fresco.

Sisi desperately mourned the death of her son:

> There is a moment in the life of each one when the spirit dies,
> and it by no means follows that this need be at the time of physical death.[50]

Chapter Seven

The Royal Mistress

After Mayerling, the succession order to the throne changed. The next heir to the throne should, in fact, have been the emperor's fifty-five-year-old brother Archduke Karl Ludwig. But Karl had not taken an active part in Austrian politics and he was quite as devoid of ambition as his own father had been. It was widely assumed that he, like his father before him, would relinquish the throne to his son Franz Ferdinand. But, shortly after the death of the crown prince, his father died from typhoid contracted on his pilgrimage to the Holy Land. Franz Ferdinand now held the coveted position of heir to the Habsburg empire. Most Austrians knew very little about Franz Ferdinand and, thus, his elevated position did not excite any expectant hopes for a better constitutional future under his reign.

Princess Maria Annunciata of Boubon-Two Sicilies gave birth to her first born, a son named Franz Ferdinand, in Graz in 1863. As a young boy, Franz Ferdinand suffered from tuberculosis, which, in most cases, was a death sentence. He inherited the disease from his mother, who subsequently died when Franz Ferdinand was just nine years old. Because of this illness, it was generally believed that there was little or no chance that Franz Ferdinand would become heir to the throne. Even though he was known to be oppressed by his illness, with grim determination he soon let it be known that he was not prepared to renounce the throne. Partly to cure his lung ailment and partly to enlarge his knowledge, Franz Ferdinand went on several cruises, one of which took him around the world. When he returned from this long journey, in spring of 1889, his doctors declared him cured of the last of his several tubercular relapses. As an embodiment of vigor and health, he then hastened to assert his rights to the succession. He often saw his cure as a sign that he would become emperor. And now after Mayerling, this came to pass.

It was almost a rite of passage for Habsburg males to join the army. Thus, Franz Ferdinand joined the Austro-Hungarian Army in 1883, serving in Hungary, Upper Austria, and Bohemia. His military career included service with an infantry regiment in Prague and with the hussars in Hungary. While in the army Ferdinand received several rather quick promotions: captain (1885), major (1888), colonel (1890) and general (1896). His genealogy was impeccable; unfortunately, his character did not match his royal family pedigree. He was not an especially cultured man; at times, he was prideful and mistrusting. He simply lacked the charisma to make him socially and politically popular.[1] He had a strong tendency towards political intrigue, and an innate dislike for everything anti–Catholic. His religious beliefs were fervent and he observed all the externals of religion very scrupulously from his childhood. Franz Ferdinand had a long-standing contempt for Viennese high society. He was opposed to all the liberal ideas, and he was fiercely opposed to republican and anti–Catholic France as well. The differences between him and Franz Joseph were quite apparent.

The emperor had grave doubts about Franz Ferdinand, in particular his temperament. His short temper and suspicious nature ensured that truly talented advisors did not last long in his cabinet-in-waiting. To illustrate, he was not a great linguist and the Hungarian language was almost impossible for him to master. When he was in command of the Hungarian Hussar regiment, he became furious when they persisted in speaking Magyar and not German. Alan Palmer had this to say about it: "A responsive, astute colonel might have charmed the less truculent officers into cooperation. But not Franz Ferdinand. He reacted like a frustrated child; his rage knew no bounds.... His incandescent temper soon made the prejudice public, with ominous consequences for the dynasty as a whole. For over a period of some twenty years, the personal authority of the Emperor-King among his Hungarian subjects was diminished by their fear that his heir would remain a rabid anti–Magyar once he came to the throne."[2]

Archduke Frederick and his wife, Isabella, had five marriageable daughters and Franz Ferdinand appeared to be interested in their eldest daughter, Marie Christine. Since all of the daughters were acceptable Habsburg brides, discreet wedding plans were being made. Franz Ferdinand at last made his choice known; it was Isabella's lady-in-waiting, Sophie Chotek. Although Sophie came from the higher nobility, she was not of equal birth by the terms of the Habsburg Family Statute. To be an eligible partner for a member of the Austro-Hungarian royal family, one had to be descended from the House of Habsburg or from one of the ruling dynasties of Europe. For this reason, Franz Joseph initially refused to agree to the marriage; he would not tolerate a dynastic wedding to a minor noble. Yet when his minister Count Goluchowsky told him that if he did not give way he would face another Mayerling and when his sister-in-law Marie Theresa whom Franz Joseph respected, asked him to consent, he relented. There was an important caveat attached to his approval; the couple had to agree to a morganatic marriage in which their future offspring would have to renounce their claim as heirs to the throne. Perhaps as a small compensation, a few years later Franz granted Sophie the title of Duchess of Hohenberg. Franz Josef did not attend the wedding. Nor did his brothers or their families. Franz Ferdinand became more reclusive following his marriage to Sophie Chotek von Chotkova in 1900. Contrary to his public persona, he was a very happy husband and devoted father. It was this morganatic marriage that Franz Joseph insisted upon and his attitude taken during Ferdinand's illness that turned the archduke against his uncle: "Henceforth Franz Ferdinand would run counter to the emperor in all things."[3]

Within a few months after the death of the crown prince, Franz Ferdinand was fulfilling official engagements which would normally have been entrusted to the emperor. He soon began preparing himself for a goodwill mission to St. Petersburg; a trip that Rudolf had begun to prepare for himself shortly before his death. Franz Joseph was reluctant to give any authority to the heir apparent. But Franz Joseph had other more important things to attend to and as before when disaster struck Franz Joseph battled on, doing his duty. He continued on with his pressing chores of state and on somewhat more pleasant endeavors as well.

No one was up at this ungodly hour — four o'clock in the morning. There was a light in the window in one of the houses on Maxingstrasse, and a young woman was waiting for the familiar knock. Their loving making was quick; the sexual affair, however, lasted thirteen years. Franz Joseph was not in love with Anna Nahowski; she was a convenient release when Sisi was traveling, Sisi was always traveling. Anna was by no means an Austria beauty; she was rather plump and had brassy blond hair but she had a kind face and was accommodating and gracious to the emperor.

Anna had once been a young wife of a railway official who periodically beat her after a night at the local tavern. They separated. She met Franz Joseph in the park at Schönbrunn when both were taking their morning walks. Franz Joseph had other affairs, dalliances really. Countess Isabella Potocka was a Viennese beauty and was suspected of captivating the emperor's fancy for a short while, but none of these mistresses amounted to much of anything.

Franz Joseph's affairs were with ladies from the highest aristocratic circles down to the women on his own staff. Remuneration was generous for those women who rendered "services" to the emperor and ranged from advancing the careers of their husbands to receiving more handsome salaries. Or, when the affair was over, many were given some extortion money enabling them to buy commodious accommodations in remote villages tucked away in the countryside outside Vienna. One affair received a more official status and that liaison was with Katharina Schratt. Katharina appeared to play a light-hearted social role, a role that Elisabeth was incapable of or declined to play.

At the beginning of her marriage Sisi had been jealous and possessive. If Franz Joseph paid attention to any other woman, she initially made her hurt and angry feelings known.[4] Her pregnancies also became another wedge separating the couple. She retired into seclusion hating the temporary loss of her figure. Her husband looked elsewhere for his satisfaction. Somehow Sisi always thought that it all had been pure gossip about her husband's infidelities — until she had become infected after his sojourn in Italy.

Contracting syphilis was a common nightmare for women in the 19th century. Sisi, quite passionate about her physical condition, summoned Dr. Seeburger to check out the swellings around her wrists and knees along with other internal ailments. She was told that she had contracted a venereal infection. She justifiably blamed Franz Joseph. Dr. Seeburger and other medical advisers could not cure her. The remedy for that disease at the time was a poisonous metal, a compound known as quicksilver. As the saying went, "One night under Venus, a lifetime under Mercury." Sisi's horror at the harm that had been done to her led to hysterical demands for escape at all costs from the Viennese winter and the stifling court. In his remorse, Franz Joseph could refuse her nothing.

The mercury cure badly affected Sisi's teeth. She made every effort to conceal the tiniest flaws in her appearance but her bad teeth seriously marred her beauty. Her teeth had never been beautiful; Archduchess Sophie had noted and criticized this defect even before the engagement in Bad Ischl. But even the most expensive dentists that Sisi contacted, then and throughout her life, could not fix her teeth. (In later life, she wore dentures.)

Elisabeth's self-consciousness because of this blemish was so great that she parted her lips as little as possible whenever she spoke. Her enunciation was therefore extremely indistinct, almost unintelligible, and she spoke so softly that, as many contemporaries complained, she was given more to whispering than to speaking. This habit made conversation in the salon extremely difficult; hardly anyone could understand the empress's words.[5] Sisi kept her lips tight over her smile for most of her life; when amused, she looked as enigmatic as the *Mona Lisa*.

In every country through the years royal mistresses were a national institution. The queens of England had to recognize the kings' mistresses and often have them as maids of honor or women of the bedchamber. When Queen Caroline was dying, she begged King George the Second to marry again. The king burst into tears and said, "No — I will have — mistresses." "My God," the dying queen said, "marriage doesn't stop that."[6] Over the years, Sisi mellowed and Franz Joseph's affairs did not cause the angst that they once did. As a matter of fact, Sisi helped to pick out a mistress for him, someone to keep him company while she was traveling. While Sisi was away, Franz Joseph was mesmerized by an actress, Katharina Schratt. Sisi was not around enough to observe that the romantic glow of their friendship had begun to burn into a steady flame.

Franz Joseph would often attend plays at the Burgtheater, his visits there had always been one of the few pleasures accorded to him. Attending plays was quite convenient; he didn't have to bother with security or transportation as the old Burgtheater was connected to the Hofburg Palace. This particular evening a young actress was making her debut in Vienna. She would be playing the ingénue Lorle in the play *Dorf und Stadt* (Village and Town). She was a success with the audience and, in particular, Franz Joseph. Because the Burgtheater was subsidized by imperial funds, it was customary for the cast members to meet with the emperor after the play on opening night.

Katharina was to be the cast's spokesperson, and she had devoted almost as much time to rehearsing her speech to the emperor as she did to her leading role. She role-played her speech to the theater manager, Paul Schulz: "Your Majesty it is so gracious...." Schulz interceded: "Do not cross your legs; do not sit down; say your piece and exit quickly." Upon Katharina's being introduced to Franz Joseph this is what transpired: "Your Majesty it is so gracious...." "My Dear Lady, wouldn't you like to sit down?" "I thank you your Majesty; it is so gracious...." "But why won't you be seated?" "Paul Schulz won't let me." The emperor laughed loud and long, so loud that the people waiting in the anteroom for their visit with the emperor were utterly astonished by hearing this unaccustomed laughter coming from him.[7]

Twelve years were to go by between their first visit and their next. In the interim, Katharina married Nicholas Kiss von Itebbe, a handsome Hungarian spendthrift. Nicholas enjoyed the good life and lived well beyond his means in a fourteen-room apartment in Vienna's plush Gumpendorferstrase. They had a son, Toni, but soon the unhappy marriage ended. Kiss, however, was heavily in debt. His gallant way of dealing with his creditors was to flee, leaving Katharina to face the bailiffs and a debt of thirty thousand gulden.[8] One of Katharina's influential friends and admirers was Edward Palmer, president of one of Austria's biggest mining companies. Palmer started a subscription fund among his friends to collect money for Schratt's debts. Although he gave the largest contribution, twenty-three thousand gulden was collected on Katharina's behalf. Resolving these financial issues, she moved to America, leaving her son with her parents in Baden. For a year she could capture only small acting roles in New York City. Perhaps the language barrier had prevented her from becoming a Broadway star. Dejected, she returned to Vienna and the Burgtheater the following spring.

She and Franz Joseph met again in February 1885 at the *Industriellenball*. It was a rather grand occasion with the czar and czarina of Russia attending. Franz Joseph monopolized the actress in a long conversation. It was on this occasion that Katharina reunited with Franz Joseph and was presented to Empress Elisabeth for the first time; Sisi put her seal of approval on the projected liaison. There is very little doubt that Elisabeth encouraged the Franz and Katharina relationship. Her beloved poet Heine, however, may have influenced her. Heine's last year of life was noticeably bleak due to failing health and financial reverses. His ending days, however, became more bearable because of his platonic friendship with Elise Krinitz. Empress Elisabeth was hardly ever resident in Vienna, spending her time traveling. She felt bad about leaving Franz alone and may have thought that his loneliness would be partially assuaged by the relationship with Katharina Schratt.

Franz Joseph made more frequent visits to the Burgtheater, where Katharina was promoted to leading roles. She was not considered to be a great actress by her audiences nor her critics but "she had spunk." Her great warmth and charm made up for her lack of depth and she was thus able to carve out a rather successful career playing the role of a comedienne. Knowing of her husband's interest in the actress Sisi took her daughter

Valerie to see Katharina perform as well. Sisi and Franz Joseph visited Katharina at the theater and her home to such an extent that she advanced to the position of "friend of the Empress."

It was Empress Elisabeth's kindness that brought the actress Schratt into the emperor's life. But there was a reason for her kindness. As Elisabeth often escaped from her worldly frustrations by traveling, and knowing how lonely Franz Joseph was while she was away, she wanted to find a woman who could be a friend and companion for him. Sisi felt almost grateful to her rival for consoling her husband when she left Vienna on these extensive travels. Her kindness may have been a way of placating her conscience and of giving her the freedom she most desperately needed. Katharina was perfect; royal or aristocratic ladies would not do, for their ambitious relatives might use them to exact favors from the emperor. Sisi's choice fell upon the actress, whose loveliness, gaiety, and unaffected charm already seemed to have enchanted Franz Joseph.

Others were aware of Katharina's visits at least two or three times a week to the Hofburg, where she had afternoon coffee with the emperor, chatted or merely sat while he continued working. He gave Katharina the house at 9 Gloriettegasse, backing the gardens at Schönbrunn and built in the baroque style with a conservatory, which led Katharina to call the place "her glass palace." In the summer, Katharina rented a holiday villa not far from Ischl, and while the emperor was at the imperial resort he took advantage of every opportunity to visit her. He did not try to conceal his early morning visits to her at Ischl but he did have a special door built in his villa from which he could walk directly to the garden gate of her villa, the key to which he always carried in his pocket.

He came at seven or eight o'clock in the morning, and she was always ready and dressed, with a light breakfast prepared. There would be flowers on the breakfast table and she always presented herself in a state of carefully arranged disarray. On these occasions, despite the time of day, Katharina would slip into a light comedy role, vivacious, sharp-witted and enlivened by mimicry. The best performances of Schratt's career may well have been at her breakfast table at these very early morning tête-à-têtes. The emperor wrote, "Breakfast, so modestly offered and eagerly accepted, was superb. Even the mediocre cigars seemed excellent when smoked in the company of a delightful young woman who for a brief hour had made me forget the dispatch boxes waiting for me on my writing desk at Ischl."[9] The Sunday morning of 9 July 1886 was the first of a series of visits that Franz Joseph referred to as "those unforgettable hours at Frauenstein."

Perhaps it was Katharina's humorous demeanor that enabled Franz Joseph to become a different person in her presence: "He seemed to lose his stiffness; he almost appeared quite easygoing, amenable, even humble, showing a modesty, which went beyond the *'politesse des rois.'*"[10] He truly profited from her infectious gaiety, discovering how to chatter over trivialities in an easy, intimate manner he had not experienced since boyhood — and then only rarely. Then, too, being removed from the protocol and etiquette of the court no doubt contributed to Franz Joseph's being able to relax and enjoy simple pleasures — a comfortable armchair, rich pastries, hot coffee. Back in Vienna, the relationship continued and intensified.

Actors were not always highly revered; subsequently one may conjure up a picture of a loose and free-giving person living a Bohemian life. Katharina was nothing like this stereotypical image; she was methodical, a good housekeeper, an excellent cook, and a devout Catholic. Her favorite way to pass time was doing jigsaw puzzles and on a large table in her apartment a ten thousand-piece puzzle was always a work in progress.

Katharina was not as beautiful as Sisi; indeed, she was, in many ways, the antithesis of Sisi. Frau Schratt was a "real Viennese girl, round and soft, fed by an inner spring of gaiety, light-hearted, vivacious, the kind of girl who when she walked arm in arm with a man molded herself along his frame and looked up into his eyes. She was neither exceptionally handsome nor exceptionally clever; yet without being out and out coquettish, she made the most of her femininity through her conviction that a man must be catered to."[11] Katharina by most standards would be considered rather plump. In her desire to be more "svelte," she experimented with a certain diet quite popular throughout Europe at the time. The diet, based on a book by Herr Kuhne on how to be slim, prescribed eating sand. Elisabeth was quite impressed by the diet and lost several pounds. Franz Joseph put a stop to Katharina's attempt to lose excess poundage; he liked her "chubby and gay."[12]

Schratt cooked for the emperor and supplied him with expensive Cuban cigars, which he liked to smoke but was too frugal to buy for himself. She was always thinking of gifts to give him — a plaid rug, a woolen jacket and, one Christmas, a mechanical nightingale, no doubt a reference to "The Emperor and the Nightingale"[13] — all gifts that any bourgeois wife might give her husband rather than a successful actress one of the richest monarchs in Europe. She made his workroom more pleasant with the first violets of spring and arranged with Max Schling, court florist, to deliver a pot of four-leaf clovers. She gave the emperor a small mirror, which he kept on his desk and on which she had engraved in her handwriting *Portrait de la personne que j'aime.* He told her of being plagued by thirst one night but that he didn't want to wake his valet. She then arranged for him to have a bottle of iced champagne and a box of biscuits by his bedside each night.

Elisabeth arranged for a portrait of Katharina to be done by Heinrich von Angeli as a present for the emperor. It was immensely flattering to Katharina to have her portrait painted by an artist of the royals. When it was presented to Franz, on 14 February 1888 he wrote to Katharina, the first of hundreds of letters:

> You no doubt already know that I adore you This affection has done nothing but grow since the day on which I was fortunate enough to meet you. Were I not so old and had no cough, I could shout with joy at the idea of meeting you again tomorrow. If one has so much work, so many cares, so much heartache as I do, a casual, frank, and cheerful talk is a true joy, and that is why the moments I am allowed to spend with you are so infinitely precious to me.[14]
>
> To my greatest joy I received this morning your long, sweet, dear letter of the 12th, for which I thank you with all my heart.... If I didn't know that you are always truthful with me, I could doubt its contents, especially when I look into my mirror and see my old, wrinkled face.... You must know that I adore you, you must know. At least you must feel it. My feeling grows all the time, ever since I experienced the great happiness of knowing you.[15]

They quarreled very infrequently. One quarrel — the direct cause is not certain — caused Katharina to leave town. Franz wrote the following letter:

> My dear good friend. I really do not know whether I may still use this form of address or whether I ought to write "Honored Lady." All the same I cannot relinquish the hope that the black thundercloud of yesterday will pass and that our old and happy friendship will be restored. You refused stubbornly and passionately all my suggestions and pleas, though they were well meant and offered in both our interests. Finally I lost control of myself with vehemence which I regret and for which I beg your pardon with all my heart.... Give me a sign which lets me hope that everything will turn out well, that we will be able to see each other again — I hope before long — either here or in your house. God bless you.... Your profoundly loving Franz Joseph.[16]

The quarrel was forgotten.

Katharina was treated quite well financially by Franz Joseph. She was given a yearly allowance of 30,000 gulden — about $60,000, an enormously high sum in comparison to her annual salary of a mere 8,000 gulden she received at the Burgtheater. One of her pastimes was gambling and Franz would pay her gambling debts; but he encouraged her to give up this habit. Many of his officers were ruined by gambling debts. He would also "buy" her expensive pieces of jewelry. She would go to the jeweler, pick out the piece she desired, and the jeweler would bring selections of jewelry to Franz. The one she had chosen would always be in the bottom right-hand corner. (The sale of a diamond dragonfly Katharina bequeathed to her niece paid for the restoration of an apartment house destroyed by the Russians in World War II.)

Even when Franz Joseph's son died, Schratt provided the distraught father with soothing words and tenderness Elisabeth could not. When Katharina arrived at the palace, Elisabeth told her, "You must go to him. You must try and help him. I can do no more."[17] With Rudolf's death, Franz Joseph lost his legendary self-control; he seemed to become a fragile version of his former self, and he was forever grateful to Katharina for her compassion: "Your true friendship and your tranquil sympathy have been a great consolation to us both in these awful days."[18] Franz Joseph's relations with Schratt, documented by many letters to her published after her death in 1940, showed him at his most human. With her he could relax, be comfortable, and express feelings that had been once buried so long ago.

In 1896 the dynasty was to play an important symbolic function. It was the one-thousandth year jubilee of the kingdom of Hungary. "Everywhere throughout the Magyar realm festivities were planned in honor of the glorious anniversary; no nation in Europe could look upon so long and honorable a past, England, Italy, Germany, Russia, France were all mere infants compared to the gerontic tribe of Attila."[19] Elisabeth and Franz attended the opening of the great Millennium Exposition in Budapest. Elisabeth had aged considerably; she styled her hair with bangs to cover up the telltale wrinkles and wore a more modern-style taffeta dress, yet still in black. But the Hungarians saw her as their regal, lovely and ageless queen. The Magyar Millennium was to be Elisabeth's last triumph. Before the ceremonies commenced she signed, "I feel a thousand years old myself." The queen whom Hungary had glorified as none before would not be seen in Hungary again.

Franz Joseph did not keep a detailed journal of the affairs of state. Instead, daily records of his personal life are found in long letters to Elisabeth and Katharina. To the empress he normally wrote every other day when she was away on one her travels: "Between September 1890 and September 1898 not less than 474 of these letters have survived, clear testimony both to his diligence as a correspondent and to the frequency of her absence from Court."[20] (Katharina received more than two hundred letters during the same eight-year period. They are lighter in character and ring with mocking self-pity but they reveal more about his inner feelings.) Few of the letters to Sisi make for captivating reading: many of them discuss mundane events like the weather or the seating arrangements for an upcoming formal dinner, along with news of their daughters and granddaughter Erzsi, who lived with the crown princess at Laxenburg. Almost every letter from him during these periods of separation also refer to walks or talks with the *Kriegsminister* (War Minister), their code name for Katharina.

The empress may not have been as philanthropic about Katharina as one might suspect. Sisi, from time to time, would amuse her ladies by making snide remarks about Schratt's "robust body." While Sisi may have strongly supported her husband's love affair, that did not mean she found Schratt as likable and lovable as Franz Joseph did. If her husband's infatuation did not rouse her to jealousy, it nevertheless seemed to give rise to her mockery. Her feelings towards Katharina showing less generous appraisals are found in her poems as well. There are also verses that reflect pangs of guilt but, on the other hand, the marriage was shattered. The emperor and empress no longer had anything to say to each other. Some poems simply question what her husband finds so gratifying about this second-rate actress who most likely was feigning her simplicity with the emperor. But like Franz Joseph, she, too, needed Frau Schratt, for in a short while, she would be off again—perhaps sailing down to the Island of Corfu. It was good to know her husband would not fret in her absence. The closer the emperor's relationship with the actress became, the less the empress felt obliged to spend time in Vienna.

Katharina was given the privilege of eating with the immediate family and dined rather often at the Hofburg. The frequent foursomes included Franz and Elisabeth and Katharina and her husband. The other royals found these dinners most distasteful, as Elisabeth often ignored official court dinners and yet she would dine with an actress. Such a thing had never been done in the Habsburg court before. Elisabeth was unfazed by these criticisms but Valerie was most dismayed when Katharina joined Franz, Elisabeth and Valerie for dinner: "Frau Schratt dined with us, took a walk with us, and remained until evening. I cannot say how embarrassing such afternoons are for me, how incomprehensible that Mama finds them rather cozy."[21]

Was the emperor's relationship with Schratt a platonic one? Some historians simply bypass this issue; others flatly deny that any sexual encounters occurred between the two; and some vehemently maintain that the couple was sexually intimate:

> She was his best friend and often his only friend. There is little doubt in my mind that Schratt took the place of a wife, that they shared sexual as well as companionable experiences, that he not only loved her but also was in love with her, at least for some years. I cannot prove this statement, since proof does not exist. I derive my belief from his behavior toward her and from the tone of his letters.... His letters are not love letters yet they are letters of love. He was too introverted a man to pour out his feelings in passionate streams, and he was too circumspect and sometimes too embarrassed to pen eloquent endearments. He must have known the probability that these letters would be perused by posterity. Letters of love outweigh their moralistic assertions that they were "not doing anything wrong" and that they were "just good friends." Whom was he fooling — himself?[22]

Another historian has noted, "there was no amatory intimacy; he enjoyed sitting together and chatting in the comfortable room at Ischl.... There was too much to risk ... cheapening the honour of his newly found friend."

There runs though Franz Joseph's letters in this second winter of close friendship an apologetic strain of self-deprecation, mingled with the happiness at his good fortune: "To see you again would make me happy, but of course only if it pleases you, if you feel well and if you can spare the time." "With what delight I saw you look up several times to my window," he wrote after he had watched her cross an inner courtyard of Hofburg on her way to early Mass. A fortnight later he proclaimed, "Were I not so old, I could shout with joy at the idea of meeting you again tomorrow — I hope."[23] To some, then, their relationship was platonic. Katharina and Franz both called her *die freundin*— the friend. Other samples of the imperial correspondence also shed light on a platonic relationship:

To Frau Katharina Schratt:
   29 August 1899: Six A.M. Did you arrive in Ischl and how are you? Franz Joseph
   17 October 1899: Most cordial thanks for yesterday's letter. How are you today? I beg you to keep strictly to yourself the information which I wrote yesterday. My heartiest greetings.

On St. Valentine's Day in 1888, Katharina offered to become his mistress: "It was probably a gesture dictated by tenderness and generosity rather than by passion. But she can hardly have expected a reply which was at once a declaration and a renunciation of love."[24] (Elisabeth still exercised a powerful influence over Franz, who kept on worshipping at an empty altar.) He mentioned in his letter that he was flattered, "especially when I look into the mirror and my old wrinkled face stares back at me," and he told her openly that "you must at least guess ... that I adore you." But he insisted that their relationship "must remain for the future as it has been until now, for I love my wife and do not wish to abuse her confidence and her friendship with you." He then added, "I am too old to be a brotherly friend, but treat me as a fatherly friend."[25]

In his correspondence to Katharina, Franz Joseph never used the word "*Du*," nor did he ever employ one of those love-struck diminutives reserved by all-important men for dealing with their intimates. The world's best have at one point in time, when emotionally stirred, achieved sophomoric-type, over-the-top endearments. But that's a moot point as this is beyond what one can expect from such a cautious man. The only thing we know for sure is that Franz Joseph was in love with Katharina Schratt.

Katharina was not the only refuge for Franz Joseph. Since Rudolf's death, he had been grooming one of his nephews to become his heir to the throne. It was not Karl Ludwig, his brother, but Otto, Karl's son, who was Franz Joseph's choice: "Otto had long been known as the most dashing officer in the Austrian Army; he was charming, gay, beloved by young and old. Also he was what Franz Joseph called a *hallodri*, an incorrigible knave."[26] His fall from grace occurred because of his performing a few dancing steps sans clothing at Sacher's, quite a famous café on the Ring patronized by many royals who, of course, were there and witnessed his entertainment in nature's garb.

Katharina did play a small part in the politics of the day. The *New York Times* noted, "Katharina Schratt, the actress, then became a participant in affairs of State, playing behind the scenes but wielding an influence over the aged Emperor that made Austro-Hungarian statesmen eager to gain her counsel. In politics, she was at first an opponent, and then a partisan, of the Hungarians, who desired greater legislative privileges than the dual monarchy permitted."[27] Hungarians' ire was rising once again — and they "were damned if they would allow themselves to continue to be saddled with a portion of the expenses of running a monarchy, of contributing to building a railroad that would run from Vienna to some place not in Hungary, of paying for that army in which German was spoken."[28]

It was Katharina who persuaded Emperor Franz Joseph in 1905 to receive in audience Franz Kossuth, son of the great Hungarian patriot and radical leader. Franz Kossuth was one of the leading spirits of the Hungarian Independence Party: "They were against the customs union, wanted a separate army, recommended that teachers require their pupils to hand in their homework only on Hungarian paper, that houses be heated only by Hungarian coal, and similar nonsense. A boycott of Austrian goods began. Yet in spite of the orating ... in Hungary, in Bohemia, Dalmatia, and Galicia—the house did not collapse. The quakes were sufficient to keep things tottering but not powerful enough to destroy."[29] The majority once again accepted the status quo and remained loyal to Franz Joseph.

Schratt was given a mansion on Vienna's gloriettegasse and a three-story palace on Karntner Ring to which she completely withdrew after the emperor's death. She died at the age of 86 and was buried in the Hietzing Cemetery in Vienna. The *New York Times* wrote, "Katharina Schratt was described as an extremely handsome woman of the brunette type—tall and classically formed. Her eyes were large and blue, and she had a wealth of dark hair. She was possessed of much personal magnetism, and her manners were said to be charming.... The perfectly innocent character of the relations between the monarch and the actress are known to every one here who has the slightest acquaintance with Austro-Hungarian court life."[30] The *Catholic Herald* wrote, "In an age when intrigue was rife in Vienna, she never abused her position and used her influence discreetly behind the scenes for the exclusive purpose of helping the imperial couple. No breath of scandal was ever attached to her name and she always retained her unique position."[31] According to Haslip, "Where another women may have wished to advertise her illustrious conquest with the emperor, she on the contrary affected to be more anxious that the emperor to prevent any form of *Tratsch* (gossip)."[32] In the eyes of Katharina's admirers her discretion was perhaps the most appreciated of all her attributes.

But, for now, Katharina's death was in the distant future and Elisabeth could depend on Frau Schratt to appease Franz Joseph. Thus Elisabeth occupied more and more of her time with an obsessive concentration on her beauty. Her loneliness was, in part, of her own making and it expressed itself in an intensive pursuit of her own person and her own beauty. Her most crowning and significant feature was her hair and when undone it would reach almost to her ankles. In the 1800s, the hair, as Lyndall Gordon writes in his book *Vindication*, would be teased and frizzed so that it stood straight up from the head. This would then be sprayed and powdered, creating a haven for lice, as washing one's locks was rarely done. White was the "in" color, not in fabric but in the white lethal lead paint that formed a chalky foundation sculpted over the woman's face. To this ghostly look would be added spots of red rouge on the cheeks and a black patch at the corner of the mouth, which was thought to be scandalously alluring to men.[33] Fortunately, some of these cosmetic enhancements faded into history.

Bathing was considered to be unhealthy; so, women would generously douse their bodies with pomatum, an ointment whose fragrance was little better than the "fragrance" it was supposed to camouflage. Bathing took on a more hygienic role in Sisi's time and was done at least once a week. Unfortunately, however, women's bodies were still encased in layers and layers of fabric with an infrastructure of corsets and whalebone stays. To this were added large, wire hoops at the hips. Women had to learn to glide like a geisha girl in order to prevent that dreaded seesaw swaying at the hips. The waist was the focal point of attraction — the tinier the better. Sisi would have her corset pulled so tight that she often suffered from shortness of breath. She endured; apparently, it was more important to have a 19½-inch waist than it was to breathe.

"How beautiful she is!," shouted the Shah of Persia against all etiquette, when Elisabeth received him in 1873. Men and women of her time enthused over Elisabeth's fabulous beauty. She was blessed with Helen of Troy looks and cursed with the Cassandra complex. Beauty, however, is often in the eye of the cultural decade in which it is being judged. Thin was not considered beautiful even in Sisi's time, so technically the Austrian empress did not fit the beauty pattern of the day. It was also a time when plump waddling females flouted their large breasts; Sisi didn't measure up on that count either. Thinness was not the beauty norm in earlier periods of history. During the Renaissance and even up to the 1900s, beautiful women were shapely, soft, and round; we might consider them — well, chubby. If you were "well-endowed," you were considered to be well provided for. If you were pale, it meant you didn't have to work and you could remain inside, as being outside was not considered good for your health.

It was a fashion statement to have voluminous hair. Wealthy women who could not grow as much hair as Sisi often wore wigs — large wigs. Sometimes these wigs were three feet high and held together by a wire cage in the center. Blessed (or cursed) with an abundance of hair, Sisi did not have to wear these cumbersome wigs. The maintenance of her hair, however, was exceedingly time consuming. For three hours every day, it was combed and braided and was so heavy that Sisi suffered from "mysterious" headaches. Her hairdresser was Franziska (Fanny) Feifalik. Sisi had noticed the beautiful hairstyles of the actresses at the Burgtheater and discovered that Fanny was the hairdresser responsible for the ornate waves and curls neatly assembled on the top of the actresses' heads.

Sisi paid Fanny a yearly salary of two thousand gulden, a veritable fortune. University professors made only roughly half that. Fanny was the most sought after hairdresser, and women of society virtually sued for Fanny's favor so that they too, on special occasions, could obtain her services. When Fanny was conducting her magic, she had to wear white gloves over ringless fingers. The empress sat at a table that was moved to the middle of the room, and underneath it was a white cloth. After combing and braiding Sisi's hair, Fanny would carefully gather up all the "lost hairs" from the white sheet, the clothes, the brush and the comb, and place them in a silver bowl. A look of profound dismay would occur on Sisi's face if she felt that too many wayward strands had fallen from her head. Her niece once remarked that the hairs on her aunt's head were numbered.

Every fortnight, Sisi's hair was washed, a procedure that took the entire day. The cleansing formula was composed of egg yokes and cognac. Ketterl, the valet de chambre, considered the treatment of her long tresses as quite an affair, for in addition to a large number of yokes of eggs, twenty bottles of the best French brandy were used every time. While all of this was going on Dr. Christomanos would read to Sisi or continue with her lessons in Greek or Hungarian.

At night, Sisi almost always would wear a mask or some pasty cream. When strawberries were in season, she would cover her face with crushed strawberries. Or, in an attempt to preserve her skin, she would wear a mask with raw veal in it. When she bathed, her baths were in ice-cold water; on occasion she bathed in warm olive oil in the afternoon. She sometimes slept in a mummy-wrap of wet rags soaked in cider vinegar, thinking that this would preserve her thinness. Her bed was stiff and hard and she slept without pillows.

In order to maintain her admired beauty, Sisi would test countless beauty formulas. There was not one magic recipe she would swear by and for most of her life she kept trying something new. She would often use creams that were either produced in the court pharmacy or prepared by a lady-in-waiting in her own apartment. One of her favorites was Crème Celeste, which was made from spermaceti, sweet almond oil, and rosewater. Another cream was called cold cream and it was made from almond oil, coca butter, beeswax and rose water. It owes its name to the cooling and refreshing way it affects the skin: given that the water-oil emulsion is unstable and slightly breaks on the skin, the water evaporates faster, making the cream feel pleasantly cooling. Sisi never used perfume, nor would she allow her ladies-in-waiting to use perfumes. She wore no rings on her fingers, even her wedding band, but strung them on a chain she wore around her neck.[34] Unlike her contemporaries, Sisi rarely used facial cosmetics; she wished to showcase her naturalness.

As she aged, her beauty became an obsession. Sisi wanted to be the most beautiful woman in the world. In fact, she started collecting photographs of beautiful women around the world, including those from Turkish harems (collecting, perhaps, photographs of her rivals). Later in life, the preservation of her beauty became more paramount and her struggle became more strenuous and demanding. When she ventured out, she often hid her face from others with a fan or her umbrella. She would often close herself off from others in her private chamber, the walls of which were covered in floor length mirrors. "The admiration of her beauty, which came close to autoeroticism, consoled her for an unsatisfactory marriage and served as a defense against Sophie."[35] Many have said she was the most beautiful woman in the world and the public image of her beauty was never to be challenged: after the age of thirty-two, she allowed no pictures to be taken or portraits of her to be painted.

Chapter Eight

Hungary

As an aftermath of the Revolution of 1848, Hungary was forcibly brought into line and for the next twenty years was an insurgent, unquiet province ruled by and administered from Vienna. Hungary was a conquered and occupied country after the defeat of the Hungarian Revolutionary Army and the liquidation of the Kossuth government with Russian help in 1849. The constitution of 1848, granted by Emperor Ferdinand, which made Hungary an independent kingdom within the monarchy rather than an Austrian province, was forfeited. Hungarian opposition continued with occasional rebellions for the next two decades.

Franz Joseph would simply not budge from his insistence that Hungary remain a province ruled like all the other Austrian provinces with representation in a central parliament in Vienna. The Hungarians showed their opposition to Franz Joseph's dicta by not sending delegates to parliament, and with equal tenacity and resolve they wanted their freedom. In Hungary, political opinion ranged from the desire for compromise to the radical demand for separation from Austria and the founding of an independent Hungary. As Caesar had thought about Cleopatra's Egypt, Franz Joseph also thought about Hungary: it was a shame to lose, a risk to deny their demands, and a headache to govern.

But Franz Joseph's thoughts were beginning to change in favor of giving Hungary its freedom. What appeared to bring about a reversal in his thinking was, in part, his obsessional thoughts of revenge against Prussia. After the decisive battle of Koniggratz in 1866 when the Austrian army was royally defeated by Prussia, Franz Joseph wanted to regain his German hegemony. His obsession made him do things that he ordinarily would have found "dishonorable." He curried favor with Napoleon — the archenemy of Austria — perhaps hoping that Napoleon might join him

Eight. Hungary

in his war against Prussia. The idea of preserving a centralized Habsburg empire was slowly dissolving. If Hungary were given its independence according to the 1848 constitution, a consideration which until now Franz Joseph had rejected as utterly impossible, he could preserve the monarchy and with Hungary's support succeed in his plans of Prussian revenge. Eventually, however, Emperor Franz Joseph abandoned his policy of revenge against Prussia and his changing thoughts about Hungary paved the way for the 1867 Compromise.

While Franz Joseph was not a popular sovereign among the Hungarians, his wife was. The hatred toward the reigning monarch was softened by the genuine love and affection that the Magyars had for Sisi. It was a mutual attraction. Perhaps her love of this country had its roots in her opposition to the Viennese Court and to Archduchess Sophie, whose dislike for the Hungarians was widely known. Perhaps it began when her oldest daughter, Sophie, died in Budapest — her tears and those of the Hungarians showed openly shared sorrow. While the Viennese did not like Elisabeth, she was clearly honored in Hungary. "Their "éljens!" for her were loud and came from the heart; those for Franz Joseph were forced and came from hesitant lips.

Several events led to this love affair between Hungary and Elisabeth. It may have begun on Madeira with Imre Hunyady, who taught the empress her first words in Hungarian.[1] Years of friendship with Imre linked her to the woman's sister Lily. It is certain that Lily, one of the empress' favorite ladies-in-waiting, talked to the empress about her homeland during the many lonely hours on Madeira and Corfu. Sisi's love of Hungary was certainly enhanced due to one of her Hungarian servants, Ida Ferenczy. Ida became much more than a servant; she became Sisi's closest friend and confidante. Ida knew all her secrets, was the go-between for her most private correspondence, and was altogether indispensable, not only as a servant, but also as a close friend. Ida was a liberal with strong, positive thoughts about an Austria-Hungary compromise.

The Viennese Court had carefully scrutinized several Hungarian noblewomen to become a part of Sisi's staff. Six had passed the test. When the calligraphied list was presented to Elisabeth, mysteriously a seventh name had been entered in another hand at the bottom of the list. Elisabeth without a great deal of thought picked that name — Ida Ferenczy — simply because she liked the sound of the name. But there was a small problem: Ida was a country girl and didn't have the right pedigree to become a member of Sisi's retinue. A subterfuge was thought of and the girl was given the title of canoness, which at least entitled her to become "reader to the Empress." She never carried out that role.² Ida stayed far away from all gossip, remained aloof, even distant, from everyone at court, and was devoted with her whole heart and soul to her mistress and friend (and remained so even after Elisabeth's death). No wonder that Ida Ferenczy soon became one of the most bitterly hated people in the Hofburg. Given Sisi's unshakable affection, however, the dislike did not particularly trouble Ida.³

Another person who would ignite the empress' love of Hungary was Max Falk. In addition to his role in the Hungarian Diet, Max was an editor for the newspaper *Pesti Napló*. The empress had asked Max to become her tutor and teach her Hungarian. Max replied, "Thank god, I was long since past the time when I was forced to 'give lessons.' But her Majesty's wish, I added, was not only my command, but also a high honor."⁴ What Max was able to do was to give Sisi a wonderful literary education introducing her to the very best Hungarian authors in addition to a first-rate education on the history of Hungary, particularly the Magyars.

The nomadic tribes of the Magyars were descended from the Finn-Egric people, who first settled in the eastern part of the Frankish Empire. They remained there for centuries with the various Ural-Altaic peoples such as the Huns, Turkic Bulgars, Alans and Onogurs. In time, the Magyars adopted many cultural traits and customs of these people. In 890, under the leadership of Arpad, the Magyars finally ended up at the outer slopes of the Carpathians. For the next fifty years, they were the scourge of Europe, ferociously attacking other areas of the continent and inflicting a great deal of damage on Europe. As the centuries passed, they became herders and farmers but continued their raids on neighboring villages. They conquered Moravia and penetrated deep into Germany. In 955 they were defeated by the Holy Roman Emperor Otto I.

In 970 C.E. Arpad's grandson (Taksony or Toxun) died and was succeeded by his son Geza, who would eventually be responsible for uniting all the many tribes of the Magyars into a single unit. Geza's son Vajk continued his father's work. He fought against Bavaria and gained a substantial victory, then was crowned in Esztergom by the pope, who granted him the title of apostle. Vajk applied to Rome for recognition as king on Christmas Day in 1000 C.E. (Vajk was canonized in 1083, becoming St. Stephen.)

Hungary was now a Christian nation and each Christmas this is celebrated in the "renewing of the empire." It is considered to be the most important day in Hungary's history and St. Stephen is one of the most important figures in Hungarian history.[5] In the Hungarian language Magyar and Hungarian are identical; however, in non–Hungarian languages, the term Magyar is frequently used to distinguish the Hungarian-speaking population of Hungary from the German, Romanian, and Slavic minorities.

Falk was simply amazed at Sisi's diligence and enthusiasm. Beginning with one lesson when Elisabeth handed him her assigned Hungarian translation and remarked, "I was engaged the whole of yesterday with receptions, and in the evening there was a state concert, after which I was so tired I went to bed. Then I suddenly remembered that I had not written my Hungarian composition, so I tore a leaf out of an almanac on a table by my bedside and translated a tale. Pardon me that it is written in pencil."[6]

Empress Elisabeth had visited Hungary for the first time with her husband and two daughters in 1857, and this visit left a deep impression. In Hungary, she had received a political object lesson. As one of her German biographers, Karl Tschuppik, wrote: "It was the first time that Elisabeth had met with men of character in Franz Joseph's realm, and she became acquainted with an aristocratic independence that scorned to hide its sentiments behind courtly forms of speech.... She felt her innermost soul reach out in sympathy to the proud, steadfast people of this land."[7] Her visit to Hungary so impressed the empress that from the very beginning, she wanted to learn Hungarian.

In 1866, the empress went with her children to Budapest to escape the unstable situation in Vienna and to carry out Franz Joseph's request to drum up some support for the dynasty. She reported to Franz that the revolutionary spirit prevailed in Budapest. The people were *against* Habsburg rule but *for* something as well: Hungarian probity, piety, and self-control. Sisi warned Franz that unless he came to terms with the Hungarian leaders Deák and Andrássy there would be another revolution. During her stay, Elisabeth bombarded her husband with pleas, ever more insistent in tone, that he do what he did not have "the faintest intention of doing," seeking a compromise. She could not bear to watch "incompetent men," prompted by "senseless hatred," run the imperial wagon deeper into the mud: "Would he not at least see Deák and Andrássy and listen to their ideas?"[8]

Both Max and Ida were good friends with Ferenc Deák and Gyula Andrássy. Ida's admiration for these "sages" was passed on to the empress. "Ida was not only an enthusiastic partisan of Deák, she also knew him through her family. In June 1866, Ida sent to Hungary for a portrait of Deák with his signature in his own hand. His picture hung over Sisi's bed in the Hofburg until her death."⁹

The Hungarian statesman Ferenc Deák (1803–1876) was one of the creators of the Austro-Hungarian Compromise of 1848 and was often called the "Sage of the Nation." In 1833 Deák became one of his country's representatives at the national Diet at Pozson and from that time forward, he was irrevocably linked with Hungarian polities. The 1800s witnessed a rise in Magyar nationalism calling for more liberal social and political changes. In the 1830s Deák, who was once a lawyer, became the leader of this nationalistic movement calling for liberation of serfs, Polish liberties, freedom of speech, elimination of corporal punishment and the death sentence, and more religious freedoms. The liberal Hungarians, praising Deák for his integrity and his dedication to the aforementioned progressive goals, turned to him to set up a program of the "united opposition." This formed the basis of the "March-April Compromise" of 1848, transforming Hungary into a parliamentary state with its own new Batthyany government. In December, Deák was unable to negotiate a compromise with the commander in chief of the Austrian imperial forces, Prince Alfred Windischgratz, and retired from politics.

However, in 1859, Deák regained his leadership role and began serious negotiations with Franz Joseph. The Hungarian position was further strengthened when Austria lost the war with Prussia in 1866. Deák's revolutionist views of complete separation had changed; he now believed that complete separation would spell Hungary's death, "a death without resurrection."¹⁰ Thus, he broke with the hard-line nationalists and advocated a modified union under the Habsburgs. Deák took the line that while Hungary had the right to full internal independence; questions of defense and foreign affairs were "common" to both Austria and Hungary under the "Pragmatic Sanction."

Andrássy had also been one of the leaders of the Hungarian Revolution and had been sentenced to death. In exile, first in London, then in Paris, Andrássy flourished. Unlike so many of his compatriots, he had no need to earn a living by odd jobs. His mother sent ample funds from Hungary, and the fact that he was not only an aristocrat but also a most witty companion, with splendid good looks and fluency in Hungarian, German, French, and English, opened the doors to all the distinguished homes. In Vienna, however, he was hanged in effigy. In 1857 Franz Joseph proclaimed his amnesty, largely on the urging of Elisabeth. He was allowed to return to Hungary, where he promptly resumed his political activities. He, like Deák, abandoned the extreme line of the still exiled Kossuth, joined the more moderate Deák and became his confidant and close collaborator. Andrássy adored Sisi, whom he called "Hungary's beautiful Providence."[11]

Gyula would certainly have been called a ladies' man; he was quite used to the most beautiful women in Paris and London. He thought Sisi, however, was "the prize of all womanhood." She in turn fell under his spell, as well she might. He seemed to her the very symbol of "romantic insouciance," glowing with the light of his own past and his country's history. In court assemblies his tall figure towered above all others, and he bowed with the ease of the "man of wealth to the manor born." He was a delightful conversationalist but he could also bore into a difficult problem with utmost seriousness, "his dark eyes assuming a scholar's intensity."[12]

Elisabeth was fascinated by the brilliant mind and Hungarian character of Count Gyula Andrássy, who, in the meantime, had become Deák's partner in the negotiations with the court. These difficult negotiations were broken off repeatedly only to be resumed with the help of Elisabeth. She was in total agreement with Deák and Andrássy, and she urged the emperor to grant concessions to the Magyars. As she once said to Andrássy, "If the Emperor's cause goes badly in Italy, it pains me, but if it goes badly in Hungary, it is death to me."[13] During the protracted negotiations, the queen suggested to her husband that Andrássy be made the premier of Hungary as part of a compromise and wrote a most serious letter to the emperor to bring the two men together: "I have just had an interview with Andrássy. He set forth his views clearly and plainly. I quite understood them and arrived at the conclusion that if you would trust him — and trust him entirely — we might still be saved, not only Hungary, but the monarchy, too.... I can assure you that you are not dealing with a man desirous of playing a part at any price or striving for a position; on the contrary, he is risking his present position, which is a fine one. But approaching shipwreck, he, too, is prepared to do all in his power to save it; what he possesses — his understanding and influence in the country — he will lay at your feet. For the last time I beg you in Rudolf's name not to lose this, at the last moment."[14]

When Elisabeth gave birth to her son, her influence at court increased considerably. This change of position, coupled with her sympathy toward Hungary, made Elisabeth an ideal mediator between the Magyars and the emperor. Andrássy noted that if their cause met with any success at all,

Hungary would owe greater thanks to our "Beautiful Protectress who watches over us." And, indeed, this appeared to be true.

When Jókai, a Hungarian novelist, was presented to the empress, she said to him, "I have long wished to make your acquaintance; your works have been known to me for some time. I consider *Kárpárthy Zoltán* the finest of them" (a book in which Jókai embodies the spirit of national idealism). "I understand nothing about politics," continued the empress with a smile, whereupon Jókai responded with a ready wit: "The highest art of politics is to win the heart of a country, and Your Majesty understands perfectly how to do that."[15]

As a result of the compromise, there were now two capitals, Vienna and Budapest, two parliaments, two cabinets. Only the minister of war, the foreign minister, and the minister of finance served both sectors. Austria and Hungary were two equal and constitutionally independent political entities. Hungary was virtually autonomous in domestic affairs, while holding on to the concept of unity in international matters. The monarchy was divided into Transleithania (Hungary — Lands of the crown of Saint Stephen) and Cisleithania (Austria — Lands represented in the imperial council) with each sharing the army and the navy. The emperor offered Deák the post of minister-president in the first Hungarian government but Deák, because of his age declined, urging the appointment of Count Gyula Andrássy, who indeed became the first prime minister.

The Austro-Hungarian Compromise (*Ausgleich*) was ratified on 29 May 1867. It marked the end of wholly centralized government but it preserved the Austrian Empire and the Habsburg dynasty. Franz Joseph was to be the sole dual monarch known to history. The compromise also decreed that the economic compromise should be renegotiated every decade.

The other peoples of the empire did not share Hungary's joy. A separate parliament and government for Hungary would mean a privileged position for Hungary among the nations of the empire. Consequently, there was general resentment against the preference accorded to the Hungarians. Franz Joseph had given in to the people who had been his enemies from the day he ascended the throne and slighted those who had fought for him. About 6.5 million Czechs living in Bohemia, Moravia, and Austrian Silesia made up the largest and most restless minority. The Czechs were the most advanced in their national development and felt they had been "sold down the river," and the Poles likewise resented the Hungarian compromise.

It was only a matter of time until they too, like the Hungarians, asked for equality — technically, the Kingdom of Bohemia. Franz Joseph made an effort to reconcile the Czechs and proposed giving them equal status as he had done with Hungary. Immediately, Andrássy argued with the emperor that such an action would cause Hungarian revolts. He hastened to add that Hungary was the largest country under the Habsburg rule, even larger than Austria itself. As such, Hungary should rank above all the others. The Magyars were descendents of the thousand-year-old empire of St. Stephen and that entitled them to a superior status over the peoples of other Habsburg domains. The Habsburg dynasty continued to reject Czech national demands until the end of the empire in 1918.

It was not just Bohemia that demanded more equality. The other remaining constituents — Croats, Slovakians, Poles — could they be ignored while Hungary received all the compensations and freedoms? The Slavs in southern Austria, for one, revolted; Austrian troops had to be called to put down their insurrection. An immediate and continuing response to the Hungarian Settlement was that other nationalities in the empire also demanded similar "settlements." None were granted. But many of these resurrections were caused by a small number of revolutionaries. The majority of the peoples comprising the vast dominions, according to historian Alan Sked, were concerned with practical matters. "Despite the fact that there was indeed much dissatisfaction with Habsburg rule, the nationalities directed their attention primarily to the issues that directly affected their daily lives. No major leader or party called for the destruction of the Monarchy."[16]

As a reward for agreeing to the Hungarian Settlement, and in order to solemnize this historic compact with fitting ceremony, a magnificent coronation was arranged for 8 June 1867. (While Budapest festively engaged in preparing for this celebration, Prague was under martial law.) The ceremony began at four o'clock A.M. Cannons exploded over Budapest to proclaim a spectacle such as the city had never seen and "every house was decorated with the Hungarian flag, the display of which had up to now been forbidden."[17] "The frenzied 'éljens' to the beautiful young *Queen Erszebet* brought tears of pride and joy to the eyes of her [sic] who had no small part in bringing about all this joyousness."[18]

Weeks before the coronation, the preparations began with packing great quantities of boxes and chests; even carefully wrapped state coaches were loaded onto Danube steamers going from Vienna to Budapest. From precious pieces of china to flatware to table lines and furniture, everything necessary to housekeeping at the imperial court was being shipped; even carriages and horses for the equipages were being shipped by the same route. In Budapest, different types of arrangements were being conducted. Certainly one of the problems in this overcrowded city was lodging. Many places had to be found that were suitable for royalty, accompanied with high prices suitable for royalty. Police were kept fully occupied with clearing Budapest of suspicious characters and followers of Kossuth during the festivities. A week before the coronation, Sisi complied with an ancient tradition, which required her to repair the royal vestments:

> The mantle of Saint Stephen to be worn by Franz Joseph, as well as the coronation socks (once woven by historic Gisela the Good), must now be mended by the Queen's own fingers. If by chance these garments showed no recent damage a few threads were loosened in order that the symbolic tasks might be performed. After hours of mending and darning came the fitting of the crown; it had once been stolen and was bent out of shape. A pad had to be inserted to keep it from toppling off the anointed brow. Next Elisabeth donned her coronation gown, which was fortunately less archaic, for it had been fashioned by Worth in Paris for the modest sum of five thousand francs. The ceremonial gown consisted of white and silver brocade with a black velvet surplice hemmed in diamonds. Over this there was draped a long cloak of the same velvet lined in white satin. Since no separate crown for the Queen of Hungary existed, Elisabeth was to wear the coronet of Maria Theresa.[19]

The coronation took place at the Church of St. Matthew in Budapest. At seven o'clock, the coronation procession set out from the castle. Eleven standard-bearers, chosen from among the highest nobility, preceded Gyula Andrássy, wearing on his chest the large cross of the Order of St. Stephen and carrying the holy crown of Hungary. He was followed by gonfaloniers and finally by Franz Joseph. The undisputed highlight was the queen, whose appearance was described in the newspaper *Pester Lloyd*: "On her head the diamond crown, the glittering symbol of sovereignty, but her expression was one of humility in her bowed head — thus she walked — or rather floated — along, as if one of the paintings that adorn the sacred chambers had stepped out of its frame and come to life."[20] The appearance of the empress at this holy site produced a deep and lasting impression, particularly for the composer Franz Liszt. In writing to his favorite daughter, Cosima, he noted that he had never witnessed such pageantry. Empress Erzseget looked like a vision from some barbaric tale. Liszt was close enough to see her eyes brimming with tears.

The great moment arrived when Andrássy, serving as Paladin of Hungary, held the crown above Franz Joseph's head and with it brushed the shoulder of the queen. Thus in a classic ceremony of Asiatic splendor the Magyar nation signalized its king and queen.

Thunderous acclaim rang through the cathedral and echoed from the choir loft to the vast central dome, as the senior bishop of Viszprim intoned the benison. He heard a thousand throats cry out, *"Eljen Erzsebet!"* The reception was touchingly described by Kálmán Mikszáth, the famous Hungarian novelist, in the *Pesti Hírlap* and is worth quoting in full:

> And now the President of the Parliament, D. Szilágyi. began to speak. Slowly and cautiously, full of reverence for the throne.... Still nothing could be read in the face of Elisabeth. It remained pale and impassive. But now the orator pronounced the name of the Queen. She moved an eyelid: suddenly a cheer broke forth such as the royal palace at Buda had never heard before, as though a storm of emotions burst from every heart with a ring of wondrous sublimity which can neither be described nor told.... And now that majestic head, 'til then unmoved, was seen to stir. Gently, almost imperceptibly, it bowed in gratitude. A wondrous grace was in this gesture. Louder still rang the cheers, and for minutes they refused to be silent. As roar after roar went up, the vaulted roof quivered.
>
> The magnates of the realm waved their hats. Still the cheering would not abate. The orator was forced to pause, and the Queen inclined her head. Her snow-white cheek was flushed faintly. Its mild whiteness was tinged with pale rose, and then a crimson wave surged up, flooding it with a living red. As though by magic, a Queen appeared in all the hues of life seated at the side of the King. Her eyes dilated and flashed with their former splendor. Those eyes, whose captivating smile had once power to console a sorrowing land, now filled with tears. Once more the current of sympathy flowed back and forth. The land now happy had succeeded in consoling its Queen. But only for a moment. Majestically she raised her lace handkerchief to her eyes to dry tears. The orator resumed his speech. Slowly the flush of life faded from the Queen's countenance, and soon by the King's side there sat once more the woman shrouded in mourning, the *mater dolorosa*.[21]

Seven days of feasting brought the Budapest visit to a close. The newspaper *Budapest Lloyd* brought particularly glowing tributes, referring to Elisabeth as "the most captivating woman on earth."[22] When she was allowed to follow her instincts, "Elisabeth impressed everyone by her inimitable charm, her tact and sweetness, her royal grace and kindliness, not to speak of her extraordinary beauty."[23] A new seriousness came over Sisi and courage. At last she had made a place for herself, beyond wife and removed mother; at last she knew that she could be useful.

Her delight after her coronation as queen of Hungary had led to a reconciliation with Franz Joseph. Sisi's greatest gift to Hungary and to her husband was her readiness to abandon her stubborn refusal to have another child. All the same, the fact that she offered this great sacrifice exclusively for the Hungarian nation was left in no doubt, to understandable anger in Cisleithania. Nor did she conceal the fact that she was determined to see this child treated differently from her older children, who were raised by Sophie.

Although the emperor was religious, he was not a bigot and his just treatment of the Hungarians were exemplified in several ways: he allowed himself to be "crowned by Gyula Andrássy, a rebel who had been hanged in effigy; he donated the 60,000 gold pieces he had received as a coronation gift from the nation to the home of the invalid Honvéds of 1848, and arranged for the remains of Kossuth, Thököly, Rákóczi and Ilona Zrínyi to be brought back from Italy and Turkey."[24] The Compromise of 1867, however, was a trying time for Franz Joseph and his letters to Elisabeth show the toll of these times. He used to sign his letter "Your ever-loving Franz"; his letters now were piteously signed, "Your devoted little man," Your manikin" or "Your little one who loves you so much."

As a coronation gift from the Hungarian nation, an eighteenth-century baroque castle constructed by Count Grassalkovich, an intimate of the Empress Maria Theresa, was given to the king and queen. Gödöllő, a splendid country residence, was just twenty miles east of Budapest. It was a structure of about hundred rooms, surrounded by a forest of roughly thirty thousand acres eminently suitable for hunting. To Elisabeth's delight, the horses could gallop to exhaustion. There were excellent marshes for shooting snipe when the emperor came to stay.

Sisi was rapidly adopting the Hungarian mode of life, which suited her temperament most admirably: "Here all pomp and show was dispensed with; here her laws prevailed, and they had little to do with questions of rank and protocol; here she was entirely her own mistress, unrestrained by Court ceremony, surrounded by her favorite ladies-in-waiting."[25] Here were a people who loved horses as she did, a people who grew up in the saddle. She surrounded herself with horse-loving people, one of whom was Nikolaus Esterházy, whose huge estate adjoined Gödöllő. Esterházy was famous for his thoroughbreds and was the ranking horseman of Austria-Hungary for many years as well as the undisputed master of the hunt. He joined other of Sisi's friends who were young, rich aristocrats who spent their lives almost exclusively at racecourses and on hunting and had no obligations or work of any kind. Andrássy was also a frequent visitor.

She would return from her restless wanderings to visit Hungary time and time again, to spend the days of early autumn in the quiet solitude of Gödöllő, knowing that in no other country in the world was she loved so deeply as in the land of the Magyars. In her favorite residence she passed peaceful days, without a care, enjoying her large hunting parties and being mistress in her own house. A great part of the seventies was spent in this home, and when there it was her custom to rise at four o'clock, to be in the saddle by five, and to ride till eleven, when she would return to breakfast.

The following year, Elisabeth spent 221 days in Hungary, alternating between the charming residence at Gödöllő and Buda, much to the chagrin of the Austrians, who felt neglected by their empress. Elisabeth was expecting a child at the time and the Austrians resented rumors that, if it were a son, she would call him Stephen after the patron saint of Hungary. As it happened, Elisabeth gave birth to a little daughter, Valeria. During her stay in Hungary, the queen took lessons to improve her Hungarian and read Hungarian authors with avid interest: the poems of Vörösmarthy, Arany and Petfi, and the novels of Baron József Eötvös and Mór Jókai. She conversed primarily in Hungarian with her lady-in-waiting, Ida Ferenczy.

Since the queen surrounded herself more and more with Hungarians, the Austrian and Slavic papers began complaining that Elisabeth now lived in a world which was wholly Hungarian, that she always spoke Magyar, admitted only Hungarian ladies to her intimacy, and had chosen as nurses for her little Valeria those who could sing Hungarian folk songs to the princess. When Elisabeth was obliged to return to Vienna in 1869, she wrote to her mother: "I am desperate at having to be here, and long for Buda constantly, where it is so much more beautiful and pleasanter in every respect."[26] She told Ida Ferenczy that when she was abroad, she would suffer from a "terrible homesickness" for Hungary.

The last demonstration of that mutual love occurred in Budapest at a state reception on 8 June 1896, the year of the millennium and the anniversary of the coronation. This was the last time the Magyars saw their queen in Hungary, so it would be considered a tearful farewell.

When the agencies of the joint Austro-Hungarian government met on 21 December 1867, the official rhetoric emphasized the unity of the empire; but the fact was that this unity had been ended. After that the empire was unified in appearance only, if in that. Perhaps this was all Franz Joseph cared for, appearances always being of prime concern to him. It was his achievement that he held on for another half century to this appearance and to whatever reality was left of his empire.[27]

Was the compromise a good thing? Opinions as to whether it was positive or negative from the Austrian point of view are divided to this day. Of course, one must consider that the alternative in all probability would have been the secession of Hungary. The factual evidence is subject to differing interpretations but the general consensus appears to be that the dualistic system was not beneficial to Austria, Hungary, or its minorities. In 1895, Karl Lueger, who had been mayor of Vienna for thirteen years, expressed his views on the compromise. In his address delivered to the Lower House of the Austrian parliament, he vehemently noted that dualism was one of the greatest misfortune that his "fatherland" had suffered. But while the compromise did not bode well for the Austrians, according to Lueger, it was the only option that Franz Joseph and his government had. What other alternative did the Habsburgs have to keep their empire together?

Economically, according to John Komlos, an economic historian, Hungary was the beneficiary and the "Austrian economy could have done as well without its Hungarian partner."[28] The implication was that Austria was the exploited one, not the other way around. David F. Good concurs, emphasizing the development of Hungarian rail networks, the expansion of the banking and credit system and Hungary's increasing regional market integration.[29] Hungarian demands became bolder following each decade when the agreement was reviewed: "If it had not been for First World War, it is likely that Hungary would have become independent by the time of the renewal of the Settlement in 1917."[30]

Chapter Nine

Repräsentazions-pflicht: "The duty of keeping up a fine front"

Johann Strauss the Younger aptly reflected a precarious mood in his operetta *Die Fledermaus* (1874): "Illusion makes us happy." Indeed, there were a number of illusions surrounding Franz Joseph's Austria and the House of Habsburg. At the Congress of Vienna (1814–1815), Austria was proclaimed a dominant power among the European nations. By the time Franz Joseph stepped onto the throne, Austria's power position was already in serious decline. Several factors contributed to Austria's situation, beginning with the Crimean War. Many wars have been based on flimsy excuses or started under hollow pretexts and that was the case with Crimean War (1853–1856).

In brief, Russia wanted control of the Black Sea region and thought it had enough power to win that control. This would have been a coveted prize that would have given Russia superb military and commercial advantages. Russia, however, was unequal to the strength of the opposing nations: France, Great Britain and the Ottoman Empire (present-day Turkey). The war ended with the signing of the Treaty of Paris (1856), which required Russia to surrender lands it had taken from the Ottoman Empire. The determinate was the war's toll: "suffering, starvation, cholera, useless bravery, and death for almost half a million young men. Nobody won the Crimean War; the country which, politically lost most through it was the one least engaged in it: Austria."[1]

Austria remained neutral during the war and didn't come to the aid of its ally Russia, to which they owed a deep debt for its intervention, upon Franz Joseph's request, in Hungary in 1849. Austria's policy originated largely with Franz Joseph, who appeared to be torn between ingratitude to Russia for its help in quelling the Hungarian rebellion in 1949 and siding with Great Britain and France and the advantages of doing so. The abandoning of the close alliance with Russia, done with Franz Joseph's clear agreement, seriously damaged the Austro-Russian relations — to Prussia's advantage. Franz Joseph's revealing statement justified his action: "One must above all be an Austrian."[2] His actions were no doubt in keeping with his most confident advisor — Sophie. With Teutonic truculence Sophie sponsored the "lone world" policy of government, spurning alliances and mistrusting friendship. Her maxim of "we need no one" was a dangerous one for Franz Joseph to follow. Franz Joseph's action gained no friends among the Western powers for Austria and lost the good will that Czar Nicholas I had once held for Franz Joseph.

The price Franz Joseph paid for keeping his army uninvolved in the Crimean War was that he became known as the man who breaks his word. Austria would have to pay dearly for her political isolation during the subsequent wars waged by Franz Joseph in 1859 in the cause of Lombardy, and in the cause of Venice in 1866. The lingering Russian ill will was a factor in the July Crisis (1914), which led to the outbreak of World War I.

If there is a brighter note to war, it produced two literary masterpieces: Tennyson's poem "The Charge of the Light Brigade," and the *Sebastopol Sketches*, which established the young Tolstoy's early fame (Sebastopol was a Russian naval base that fell to ruins after a full year of fighting). The war also began the nursing career of Florence Nightingale, known as the "Lady of the Lamp" because she ended her long day inspecting the British wounded and dying late each evening. Her legendary work with hygiene cut the number of deaths nearly in half.

Certainly another factor providing a threat to the future of the House of Habsburg and Austria was the unification of Italy, or *Italian Risorgimento*. The unification of Italy was a chain of political and military events that produced a united Italian peninsula under the Kingdom of Italy. Subsequently Austria lost nearly all of its Italian possessions, such as Lombardy and Venetia. Further, two defeats — in 1859 in the Austro-French Piedmontese War and its 1866 loss to Prussia in the Austro-Prussian War — resulted in the rise of Prussian dominance and the weakening of Austria, making it the lesser of these two German powers. Austria was never to rise in status again.

But throughout these events and those beyond, the illusions continued. The mighty portrait of Franz Joseph, now with a receding hairline and graying sideburns, still graced the halls of all prominent buildings, still capturing the illusion of a strong and vigorous Viennese future. In 1908, Franz Joseph celebrated his diamond jubilee; he had reached the zenith of his power and popularity. Vienna appeared to look upon him as a father figure, loved and revered by all. The city was given over to festivities for their emperor, "but the most popular of all the festivities was the great historical pageant representing six centuries of Habsburg rule, when twelve thousand men drawn from the various races of the Empire, with the exception of the Czechs who had refused to participate, paraded down the Ringstrasse. Marching to the sound of clarions and drums, the procession, which ranged from the armoured knights of the first Rudolf of Habsburg to the veterans of war passed in front of the Emperor, who stood for three hours firm and erect on a dais."[3]

It was a city of illusions as well. The public spaces, even the whole city, became a stage. Its appearance was quite opposite of its reality. The Ringstrasse, lined with the Gothic Rathaus, the Renaissance museums, the classic Parliament house and the baroque theater — all with sumptuous facades — gave the illusion of a secure and prominent country and monarchy. Its mortar splendor, however, masked the huge problem of housing, housing for a population that had increased by leaps and bounds since the industrial revolution. Then, too, the buildings masked the political conflicts that were constantly occurring between the royalty and the bourgeoisie — the liberals and the working class, the Jews and the anti–Semites.

The court continued with its festivities to create an illusion of wealth and power. To the Viennese, and perhaps to the outside world, the Habsburg dynasty was a vision of pomp and extravagance. The aim was to impress the public at large but also to convince the great powers of Europe of the continued existence and prosperity of the empire.

Like Scarlet in *Gone with the Wind*, most Viennese simply chose not to worry: "Illusion makes us happy." And it did as they continued with their usual pleasures of attending the theater, eating warm apple strudel, sipping dark Viennese coffee. The leading heroes and heroines of the day were the actors that swept them into further worlds of illusion. In art, Makart, much admired for his presentation of female beauty in the setting of semi-historical compositions, became a symbol for the eclectic and often superficial make-believe tastes of the period.

If the truth were known, Austria was lagging behind in technical progress — far behind Germany. While there were an equal number of outstanding and creative talents in Austria as in Germany, those from Austria were brought to a standstill as a result of the "stability" system of Franz Joseph. This, of course, led to repression of anything new. In contrast, Germany nurtured these talents: "The educated workforce found employment in industries which had begun to exploit science and technology. The Prussian universities turned out scientific pioneers and the system of technical colleges trained generations of engineers who could apply science to industry. The German colleges with its doctorates, seminars, research agendas and the technical colleges pushed Germany further ahead in the struggle for dominance in Europe."[4]

Franz Joseph, however, could not relinquish his patriarchal government. This paternal method of government, which may have been adequate in the eighteenth century, was entirely out of place in the second half of the 19th century. The central government in the mind of Franz Joseph was to serve the populace as a protectorate. He could not visualize the role of common citizens beyond their vegetative one. The common citizens could, however, and their new social forces, ideas of law, education, and science were exercising a deeper and stronger influence than Franz Joseph could ever have imagined. But keen observers could see the approaching disintegration of the rigidly bureaucratic absolutism of Emperor Franz Joseph.

Some historians claim that Franz Joseph from the very beginning was ill prepared and ill equipped for government and write of his veneer rather than a gestalt understanding of the issues.[5] He often, for example, did just a casual perusal of newspapers or read written summaries from his staff in order to save time. He appeared to not be in touch with the everyday citizen, confining most of his time receiving kings, archdukes or princes. Thus, he rarely connected with knowledge of life beyond his aristocratic circle of intimates.

It is clear from a perspective of many years that the continuation of an irresolute style of government caused the Habsburg empire to slowly but surely crumble. The Austro-Hungarian Empire would soon live up to its label as "the sick man of Europe." If there had been more recognition of liberty, a stronger sense of the national autonomy and identity within Franz Joseph's empire, the empire might have flourished — perhaps in similar fashion as the British Commonwealth and its self-governing dominions such as Australia and New Zealand. "When Austria-Hungary in condoning the war with Serbia committed suicide ... the dual monarchy lost the only chance it had to survive: namely by the help of time itself. The decline could probably have been slowed down or ever stopped.... When the brittle political body of the empire joined the war, a time limit was set for its continued existence."[6] Some historians claim that Franz Joseph was beginning to "see the light," and had he lived longer the nationalism development would have naturally, through the course of time, come about.[7] In 1914, Franz Joseph seemed to be "much closer to a president than to an autocrat, and he knew it"; and if only he had been a little younger, perhaps, more fit and mentally sharper, he might have transformed his dynasty and beloved nation into a true constitutional monarchy.[8]

Some historians are rather harsh in their criticisms of Franz Joseph, who "was not clever enough or far-sighted enough, let alone tough enough, to be the absolute monarch he styled himself to be; nor was the Habsburg Monarchy strong or rich enough to perform the role that he and his advisers, and Habsburg tradition, demanded of it. In their minds, Austria was a first rate, and an indispensable great power, the anchor of legitimacy and the international settlement."[9] In short, Franz Joseph felt himself, his empire, and the Habsburg dynasty to be invincible.

Illusions contributed to the demise of the Habsburg empire and illusions were apparent in the personal lives of Franz Joseph and Elisabeth that led to the demise of their marriage. *Repräsentazions-pflicht*—"the duty of keeping up a fine front"—began with their wedding and the customary kiss on the main balcony above the grand staircase, to be seen and acclaimed by all. The royal couple's happiness was an illusion from the start.

Sisi's youth, background and home life provided none of the qualities needed to fulfill the role of an empress at the Habsburg court of Vienna. Her life around Possi was one of freedom to do as she pleased. From frolicking around the bucolic hillsides surrounding Posenhofen, she now needed to comply with the strict regulations of the Viennese Court. This transplant from her beloved Possi to court was difficult and she did not make the adjustment. Those who are accustomed to freedom are often least able to realign themselves in circumstances where regulation rules: "Elisabeth experienced the strict daily routines, hierarchies at the court, continual intrigues and her official duties, as disagreeable restrictions on her lifestyle."[10] At court she was always in the spotlight, which was again difficult for her. Her introverted character and shyness in public made her dislike social appearances and social conventions. She abhorred ceremony and disliked the strict etiquette surrounding everything one did at court— just as the unfortunate Queen Marie Antoinette had done.

And the court was not always kind and accommodating to Elisabeth. At her wedding there was the Kissing of the Hand ceremony; the court's finest ladies lined up to be introduced to the new empress. The distinguished ladies bowed and scraped in sycophantic delight, but what they were now saying behind her back was not quite so flattering. In fact, life at court was quite difficult, as Sisi suffered from out-and-out rejection and defamation. Though Elisabeth's family, the Arenbergs, was of high aristocracy, they were not royal. Having qualified for the first two requirements of an impeccable pedigree — money and property — they lacked the essential third condition: an impeccable genealogy. Thus, Sisi became the object of reserve; where she had looked for open hearts, she found herself "entrenched behind a barrier of coolness, ill will and intrigue."[11]

The Austrian court and aristocracy were the most exclusive in Europe and Sisi's self-appointed mentor was her mother-in-law, who attempted to groom Elisabeth as an empress according to her own notions. Sophie's interventions, however, made court life even more difficult for Sisi.[12] It appeared that Sisi was always rebelling and Sophie's customary response was always "it is not fitting for the Empress" or "it is the custom" — the usual reply by staff members. Admittedly, there were some rather questionable court customs. One was the custom of wearing slippers just once and then discarding them. Sisi won this titanic battle and wore her shoes and boots for weeks, sometimes months. This, of course, lead to the spirited dismay of her help, who were the usual recipients of the wear-once slipper policy. Another custom was eating while wearing one's finest white gloves. Sisi also refused to yield to this fashion of nobility. When she was told that she could not deviate from this rule, she dared reply, "Then let the deviation now be the rule."

She never showed herself without exciting uncharitable remarks: "Her erect dignified carriage was construed into pride, her delicate complexion was due to cosmetics, and her simple style of dress was unsuited to her position."[13] Even the light-hearted Viennese did not forgive her for disappointing them in the enjoyment of festivals because she was always away from court. They began to treat her with marked coolness on the few occasions when she appeared in public. They called her proud and cold and it cannot be denied that Sisi certainly tried the patience of the Viennese by the indifference with which she treated them. The common people were disturbed at the stories of the great sums of money she spent traveling. The diplomats joined in the general chorus of outrage. So along with rejection by the aristocracy, the middle classes no longer accepted her either.

The fact that she was not popular troubled her not at all and Franz Joseph very little.

It would be difficult to find two women less capable of understanding each other than Sophie and Sisi. Sophie had a craving for power and a desire to rule, neither of which ever attracted Sisi in the least. Sophie ruled the emperor, but the priests directed her. Sisi worshipped God in nature but generally ignored most of the festivals of the church. Sophie clung to church ceremonies. Their mutual antipathy was deep-seated and irreconcilable. Sisi called Sophie "Madame Mere" to the courts and "that bad woman" to one or two friends that she trusted. Sophie called Sisi "that Bavarian provincial." As the years went by, the chasm between the two deepened, and it was never to be bridged.

Countess Marie Festetics wrote about the Archduchess Sophie: " Her ambition always made her come between the two married people — always forcing a decision between mother and wife, and it is only by God's grace that an open break did not occur. She wanted to break the influence of the Empress over the Emperor. That was a dangerous gamble."[14] Sophie was accustomed to making all the decisions in the family and in political matters. And she was accustomed to commanding obedience. Her husband depended on her mind, and her children never resisted her.

Sophie could not help being offended, even outraged, at the way in which the young empress looked on her high standing as only a burden and something that robbed her of her personal liberty. She paid no attention whatever to Sisi's very obvious depression; she did not even take it seriously. Sophie saw her as an opponent. She was always trying to force the imperial couple to separate: "She was so successful that in the sixties, the Emperor and Empress were virtually living apart and hardly ever saw each other for nearly seven years…. She now had the Emperor's children also in her power. Her victory was complete. The Archduchess Sophie left no stone unturned to make people forget her [Sisi] altogether."[15] To some historians it seemed, however, that Sophie's malice may have been somewhat exaggerated. Upon an examination of Sophie's diary it appeared that she meant well even though she employed the wrong means.[16]

Sisi tried to meet the demands of Sophie, for a time anyway. But over time she, too, became antagonistic. While Sisi initially refused to develop any social activities at court outside of official functions, she now, in the spring of 1860, held balls in her apartments. She never invited more than twenty-five couples but did not invite their mothers, as was the court custom. This meant, of course, that Sophie was excluded as well. Moreover, at the close of the Vienna Exhibition Sisi had taken into her service a little black child named Mahmoud, who had been a messenger in the Cairo house. Mahmoud did his mistress's bidding and was happy to be near her. The empress treated him with the greatest kindness and nursed him during an attack of inflammation of the lungs induced by the cold of Vienna. Sophie and the rest of the aristocracy were incensed when they discovered that the Archduchess Marie Valerie was allowed to play with the black child.

Sophie never managed to train Elisabeth according to her precepts: "The long, embittered struggle, however, deprived the monarchy and the imperial family of a highly promising, talented personality by driving Sisi into isolation."[17] Her ladies in waiting made fun of her "eternal promenades in the evenings alone in the little garden." As often as she could, she refused all company, getting her way, for example, in "being allowed to go alone through the gallery into the Oratorium, which was contrary to court protocol."[18] An empress had to be an empress at all times, with appropriate entourage; she could not scurry alone through the long corridors of the Hofburg like a shy doe, as Sisi liked to do. But Elisabeth did take part in the most important functions — appearing at the court balls and at the Corpus Christi processionals — and promptly became the center of a crowd.

The proud family — Franz Joseph, Elisabeth and their three children — stood for a photograph, a picture of a beautiful and loving family, which was another illusion, Sisi and her children. She took little care of her family, often withdrawing into her creative dream world. Gisela she did not love, and Rudolf she loved only from afar.[19] Even after Sophie's death she was unable to establish a meaningful relation with them. Nevertheless, Marie Larisch, niece and confidante of Sisi, may have put it too harshly: "The Empress says that she became Rudolf's mother only through an accident. Everything, which has been written about her great love for him, is sheer fiction. Mother-love was an emotion unknown to my aunt. Marie Valerie, however, was the exception. Elisabeth believed that her children aged her."[20]

Similarly, the royal marriage was an illusion from the start. Franz Joseph and Sisi were different not only in temperament and upbringing but also in their tastes, which became increasingly clear as the years passed. *A Midsummer Night's Dream* was a favorite play of Sisi's, so much so that she committed great sections of it to memory. Franz Joseph wrote to his mother: "Yesterday I went with Sisi to Shakespeare's play in Burgtheater. It was quite boring and very stupid. Only Beckmann wearing a donkey's head was amusing."[21]

Sisi's outward appearance was one of great beauty and health, but this, too, was an illusion. She began ailing from her wedding day. Three pregnancies within four years had exhausted her body, especially the difficult birth of the crown prince in 1858.

Following the birth of her third child, her personal physician diagnosed lung disease and ultimately recommended recuperation at a spa resort. She was troubled with sciatica and in later life her sufferings were at times so excruciating that her physician declared she needed "almost superhuman patience to bear the attacks without shrieking."[22]

It would seem that some of her suffering was from a mental illness rather than from any disease, and that the physical symptoms she showed were attributable to emotional causes. For years, she suffered from severe coughing attacks, which increased ominously in the winter of 1860 and probably led to the diagnosis of pulmonary disease. Her cough, which she could not shake off, may have been as much a nervous gesture as a symptom of the throat or lungs.

Her stubborn refusal to eat not only caused her to suffer from "greensickness" (anemia) but also kept her physically exhausted. Affected by nervous breakdowns and unrelieved starvation diets, Sisi became so fragile by the end of October 1860 that Dr. Josef Skoda, a lung specialist, determined that she would have to seek out a warmer climate at once; he felt her condition to be acutely life threatening. She could no longer, he advised, endure the Viennese winter. During the preliminary consultations, the physician recommended Madeira as a suitable wintering place. Sisi agreed. "I must go far, far away, right out of the country," she told Franz Joseph. She wanted a remote island where no one could reach her. Madeira was her choice, a beautiful island in the Atlantic.[23] But on her return, the symptoms would come back: "Since her return, the Empress has the deepest aversion to any kind of nourishment. She no longer eats anything at all, and her energies are exhausted all the more as the cough persists and severe pain robs her of the sleep that might still be able to keep up her energies."[24]

Nothing could be found in Sophie's diary concerning the nature of Sisi's illness, only regret that the empress was abandoning her husband and children for so long. "She will be separated from her husband for five months, and from her children, on whom she has such beneficial influence and she really raises so well," wrote Sophie of all people.[25]

Sisi's discontent grew. There was no one to whom she could have poured out her heart. According to Sophie's expressed wishes, Sisi was not allowed to confide in anyone, for to do so would have compromised her sovereign position as empress.²⁶ Franz Joseph could not see the isolation from which his wife suffered as anything out of the ordinary. Her place at court had no attractions for her, but she did devote herself to indefatigable work in the hospitals, where she earned the name of "the Angel of the wounded."²⁷ She visited every military hospital and inspired the wounded soldiers with fresh hope and courage, speaking to them in their mother tongue, enquiring about their relations and personal circumstances. Wherever she went she made "a highly favorable impression by her gracious condescension and kindness."²⁸ Perhaps because of her excursions into the villages around Possenhofen with her father as a young girl, Sisi had a simple and natural manner in which she was able to speak with people from the lower classes.

She was doubly a Wittelsbach by birth, and possessed their distinctive traits in a remarkable manner. Neurasthenia was the hereditary malady of the Wittelsbachs in an acute degree and had manifested itself in one generation after another and it is a fact that where nerve trouble is inherited it is likely to increase in intensity. Similarly, Elisabeth's "craving for solitude, her repugnance to mix with others, her restlessness and continual change of residence, may certainly be looked upon as at least partially inherited."²⁹ Her strong personality revolted against allowing her will to be molded and fashioned by mere court routine. Moreover, life at the Hofburg, with each day precisely like the preceding one, was wearisome to her eager mind.

Sisi missed the whole carefree existence of Possi; she felt trapped in a gilded cage. The jewelry and beautiful dresses were merely a burden to her, for they meant fittings, making choices, constant dressing and changing. She did not like to have the waiting women dress her. She had been raised to be independent and she was very shy; the lady's maids were still strangers to her. Elisabeth's melancholy was more pronounced in the first stages of her marriage, when she was still trying to find a way to make the union work.³⁰ She was still attempting to be a wife, and still earnestly learning to be an empress. Later, she did find some solutions which removed her, body and soul, from the struggle. She withdrew through traveling and confiding her sadness in awkward poems:

> What are the delights of spring to me
> Here in this far and foreign land?
> I long for the sun of my home,
> I long for the banks of the Isar.³¹

Nine. Repräsentazions-pflicht: "...keeping up a fine front"

Sisi was sad and often suffered from melancholy, a prominent Wittelsbach trait. Marie Valerie noted in her diary, "Mama showed us the desk at which she wrote so much to Possi and cried so much, so much, because she was homesick."[32] Similarly, Marie Festetics wrote in her diary, "Elisabeth went from room to room — said of each what it was — but without more detailed commentary, until finally she stopped in a corner room where a desk stood between windows and a desk chair before it; she stood quiet as a mouse for a long time — suddenly she said: "Here I wept a lot, Valerie. The mere thought of that time constricts my heart. I was here after my wedding.... I felt so abandoned, so lonely. Of course the Emperor could not be here during the day, early every morning he went to Vienna. I was alone all day long and was afraid of the moment when the Archduchess Sophie came. I was completely *a la merci* of this completely malicious woman. Everything I did was bad. She passed disparaging judgments on anyone I loved. She found out everything because she never stopped prying."[33]

Franz Joseph equally lacked the necessary qualities or skills to support her against the constant pressure of her over-bearing mother-in-law, who sought to control and influence their lives. Franz Joseph had been prepared from childhood for his future role as emperor, and often showed no understanding for the needs and fears of his consort.

He was a poor lover but he was incapable of giving better. "He was being too much the Emperor and too little the man. He was a clumsy lover."[34] They were both immature, he completely dominated by Sophie and Sisi just a child, closer to the nursery than to womanhood. Sisi came increasingly into conflict with the conventions and rules of the Viennese Court, personified by her mother-in-law. The emperor did not respond because he could not see the emotional needs of his young bride; he was raised in an emotionless world. The rigid formality was a matter of everyday practice, perhaps indispensable to demonstrating the power of the crown.

The emperor permitted himself no rest; he was simply accustomed, as he had been from childhood, to fulfilling his duties. He expected the same readiness to meet obligations from his young wife, whose knowledge of those obligations was almost nonexistent. The fact that an infinitely complex political situation (the Crimean War for one) happened to coincide with the emperor's wedding and the early years of his marriage is surely not without it tragic aspects. The emotional and mental stress on the emperor left him far too little time for his young wife. His constant absences allowed the differences between Sophie and Sisi to grow into irreconcilable antagonisms, which had their full effect on the imperial marriage.

Franz Joseph had no intention of letting his young wife share in his worries.[35] He continued to discuss politics only with his mother, never with Elisabeth, who was developing opposing opinions. Annoyed, the empress had to accept a situation in which she was pushed aside and her suggestions were not even acknowledged. The tug of war between Sisi and Sophie grew fiercer than ever.

In all these decisions the young empress was not only bypassed but treated like a child: "She was to do her duty; appear in public until she dropped, and have a baby as soon as possible — although she was only sixteen. That she had desires and needs that she wanted to be acknowledged as a person in her own right, not even the enamored Emperor recognized."[36]

Sisi, an excessively sensitive, highly cultured woman given over to fantasy, was tied to a man who was practical and industrious but had no understanding of her complicated emotional life. As they grew older, abysses opened to separate them, chasms that could be bridged only precariously by outward cordiality and formal politeness. The more eccentric Sisi grew, the more pedantic and sober, taciturn and imperial grew Franz Joseph. More than ever Sisi complained of his obstinacy and lack of sensitivity. Franz Joseph idolized Sisi; yet, he neglected her.

One day a family member, Archduchess Maire Mainer, explained to Marie Valerie Sophie's system, which was to isolate Papa and his brothers, to keep them far from any intimacy with the rest of the family. Keeping them on an island, she thought she was providing them with greater authority over the others, preserving them from influences. Valerie's response is also recorded in her diary: "Now I see the reason why Papa stands so very alone, takes no pleasure in dealings with relatives, is therefore dependent on the advice of strangers, often unreliable. I always thought that I should blame Mama for it."[37]

Repräsentazions-pflicht — illusions — so apparent in the Imperial Court of Vienna and in the dynastic lives of its principal players. Sisi believed that lives ought to be so arranged that they can never dispel the illusions one brings into them. But while illusions, for a time, may make us happy, eventually the inevitable reality reigns.

Chapter Ten

The Fates

Elisabeth would become Empress of Austria and Queen of Hungary during a time riddled with problems, the fin de siecle of the Habsburg dynasty. Lacking balance or moderation in all things would pattern the Empress' life, a life that never achieved the elusive states of happiness, satisfaction or peace. She too, like the empire, would show a state of decline, retreating to a world of escapism through travel, poetry and self-solitude. These were her ways of dealing with an imperial husband who indefatigably was devoted to the Habsburg dynasty and to his beloved Austria; an archduchess and court whom she never was able to please; and children who emotionally were never her own. Did she suffer from madness? Or was she wise and an instrument of Divine Providence?

Empress Elisabeth seemed to be a fighter in some ways, with her ultimatum to Franz Joseph that she, not Sophie, would be in charge of the children or that Rudolf's grim tutor, Gondrecourt, had to leave or she would. She even stood up to some of the strict etiquette policies of the court and occasionally to Sophie's incessant demands. She tried to be a good wife — a good queen, but little by little, she seemed to be losing the battle.

If young Elisabeth had any adolescent notions about being an empress, those would soon vanish. It became very clear to her that she was a pawn — an Austrian commodity, at least in the eyes of Archduchess Sophie and members of the Viennese Court. Her life and her existence were similar to the pamphlet that she read shortly after she was married:

> The natural destiny of a Queen is to give an heir to the throne. If the Queen is so fortunate as to provide the State with a Crown Prince this should be the end of her ambition — she should by no means meddle with the government of an Empire, the care of which is not a task for women.... If the Queen

bears no sons, she is merely a foreigner in the State, and a very dangerous foreigner, too. For as she can never hope to be looked on kindly here, and must always expect to be sent back whence she came, so will she always seek to win the King by other than natural means; she will struggle for position and power by intrigue and the sowing of discord, to the mischief of the King, the nation, and the Empire.[1]

Elisabeth was to do her duty, put her finest foot forward at all state occasions, follow the strictest court protocol, give the royal wave, smile, and above all, give the empire an heir or possibly two.

Between July 1859 and the autumn of the following year, only a half dozen years since her wedding day, the marriage bond was irreparably torn. When Franz Joseph was separated from Sisi, his letters to her were protestations of love and idyllic worship. Paradoxically, when he returned and they were face to face, his tenderness, softness, and love seemed to vanish. His letters were totally contradictory to his behavior when they were in each other's presence. In keeping with the notion that absence makes the heart grow fonder, for Franz Joseph absence indeed increased his love. But once Elisabeth was back and encapsulated within the Habsburg walls, his love was blocked or driven to a latent existence hidden by his primordial law of service to his country and the House of Habsburg. Maybe Sisi could have learned to understand this kind of love but when she discovered that the rumors about Franz Joseph's affairs were true, the marriage, in every sense of the term, was over. Sisi had now lost her only potential confidant at court.

Losing her children to Sophie was another poignant occurrence that caused her to abandon any motherly feelings for them, except for Marie Valerie. Other experiences, the tragic deaths of her child Sophie, her cousin Ludwig II, and her sister Sophie mixed in with the inherited Wittelsbach traits were the final chips to fall that led her to the abandonment of her marriage and children and being empress of one of the mightiest nations on earth. Her life was a search for peace, happiness, and satisfaction, none of which she ever achieved.

Sisi was never to be satisfied. She built her beautiful villa, Achilleion, on the highest hill in Corfu. No expense was spared in its construction or in furnishing it. The cost was millions; it was pretentious but her joy in her palace was brief. She regretted turning the ruined Villa Braila into the palatial Achilleion, for it had lost its solitary charm under its great trees. Her dreams should have been left as dreams for when they turned to reality, they gave Sisi no pleasure. Her satisfaction was always fleeting. She asked for Achilleion to be blown up. In the search for dynamite, it was discovered that high explosives were obtainable only with a special permit from the Corfu Island government, which kept the Empress's mad behest from being carried out.

The beautiful island of Madeira was her sanctuary. She reveled in the delights of this tropical paradise like a young child on a seaside holiday. But all too soon, she became bored and needed to move on. Like Corfu, Madeira captured her fantasy: "I love it; I could renounce all travel and remain here forever."[2] Soon, however, she tired of it.

Empress Elizabeth was never to find happiness. The happiness in her marriage was short-lived. The king and queen had been married just four years when real and serious misunderstandings occurred; by 1862 a final break occurred. She never again found happiness in her marriage nor in any other intimate relations. Some biographers write of her love for Gyula Andrássy.[3] He was a Hungarian statesman who served as prime minister of Hungary (1867–1871) and subsequently as foreign minister of Austria-Hungary (1871–1879). Andrássy and Elisabeth's paths first crossed in 1866 when she was twenty-eight years old and he was forty-two.

He stood out as a man of the world and she a beautiful princess. It appeared that the two had deep feelings for one another, but several historians deny that they had a sexual affair or that he was the father of Sisi's fourth child, Marie Valerie.[4] It would have been too dangerous for Andrássy, who was totally devoted to his country and too ambitious to lose everything—even his life—with such an affair. Sisi based a great deal of her identity on her virtue and did not appear to have a strong sexual drive. Then, too, Andrássy was under constant observation, especially when he visited Vienna. And it was not possible for him to call on the empress in private. Sisi, however, was a willing tool of Andrássy and his policies and he did a splendid job of flattering Sisi, proclaiming that she was the savior of Hungary.[5]

The empress tried and for the most part succeeded in creating happiness through intellectual and artistic interests and threw herself passionately into these endeavors. She read, or more precisely was read to, nearly everyday. She loved Shakespeare and could not get enough of reading about her favorite poet Heine. She was a superb linguist. Her reader Dr. Christomanos must have been a good teacher or Sisi a good student because she was able to translate Heine into classic Greek and *Hamlet* and *King Lear* into modern Greek, an utterly astonishing feat. For the most part, however, Sisi seemed to live the lines of Heine's poem: "Where I am not, there lies happiness." She was constantly burying a dream but would then restlessly seek a fresh one.

She lacked balance and moderation in all things. Elisabeth was always in motion, as deftly put by one of her ladies-in-waiting: "If one lacks inner peace altogether, one thinks that keeping on the move will make life easier, and she is by now only too used to this."[6] When she engaged in any activity, she went in for it to extremes. She loved to walk and when she walked she walked fast and far, occasionally walking for more than eight hours, up to ten hours at a time. Her pace was so quick that often her companions, ladies-in-waiting Ida and Marie, were panting and exhausted. They often just surrendered and with the empress' permission traveled via sedan chairs or horses. Her private physician would come along traveling behind them on his donkey.

It was in 1885 and she was the first of the crowned heads of Europe to visit the East and become acquainted with the site at Troy. Her endurance as a traveler has hardly its equal among women. Once again, while most of her ladies accompanied her on horseback, "the Empress walked eight miles at a stretch in burning sunshine, over wretched roads with very little food, and yet without any apparent sign of fatigue."[7] Periodically, her feet became swollen from those long marches and pained her a great deal. Although she contacted her physicians, who generally forbade her not to walk for at least a period of a few weeks, she didn't obey; keeping in motion was essential to her being.

Riding was another pastime and, like walking, it became an obsessive pastime. She wanted to become the best equestrian and to be revered for her outstanding horseback riding skills, surpassing the only aristocratic rival on horseback, Empress Eugénie of France. She looked wonderful in her riding outfit, as sleek and thoroughbred as the horse she was riding. Most mornings would find her at the imperial riding school and for hours on end she would exercise horse after horse. Similarly, many afternoons strolling Viennese would see her in the park or riding on country roads around Schönbrunn. Adding to her exhaustion, she scarcely ate or slept, spending whole days on the bridle path in the woods about Vienna. She was so devoted to the sport of horseback riding that she took lessons from a circus rider and learned to ride without a saddle, kneeling on horseback, and even standing. As a result of her circus-riding endeavors, she was nicknamed by the Viennese bourgeoisie "The Circus Rider."[8] Perhaps these lessons and circus-trick riding brought back fond memories about her father and his riding school in Munich.

She rode passionately and would at times ride all day, especially when she went to England to ride with the hounds and used up three horses a day.[9] She was always in the lead or at least ahead of the field. She threw herself into the saddle with a blind and dangerous passion and frightened the gentlemen appointed to watch over her safety, leading them to a point of apoplexy as they witnessed her hair-raising, daring jumps. She was never thrown once, but in 1885 she suddenly developed fears. From that time on, she was afraid to mount a horse. She never rode again. But an equally compelling reason for her giving up this fond passion may have been due to the severe pain that she suffered from sciatica.

Very little about Elisabeth's lifestyle was done in moderation and that included her extremely rigorous, disciplined and compulsive exercise habits. Every castle she lived in was equipped with a gymnasium; the Knights' Hall of the Hofburg was converted into one. Even mats and balance beams were installed in her bedchamber so that she could practice on them each morning. Even the imperial villa at Ischl, which was their place to simply relax, was fitted with exercise equipment and gigantic mirrors so that Sisi could correct every movement and position. Women, let alone an empress, engaging in exercise or any sporting activity was extremely unusual and often considered bad because of the fragile nature of women.

Women in the mid–1800s had figures that resembled those portrayed in Michelangelo's Sistine Chapel, i.e., they would generously be called "full-figured." Sisi was an exception to that; even her waist measurement hardly changed at all in her lifetime. The reported hip measurement was 24 to 25 inches but that may be open to doubt; apparently at the time the measurement was taken higher up on the body. Sisi was about 5'7" and generally weighed around 110 pounds. By all average accounts, in today's world, this would be considered underweight; in Sisi's time, it would be considered grossly underweight. Elisabeth was a fanatic about her weight. She would look in the mirror and the reflection she would see was someone who was overweight and needed to diet. Her diets consisted of only drinking milk, six glasses a day and nothing else. Or she would consume a few oranges and that was all she would consume for days.

Even at state banquets she was satisfied with a couple of slices of wheat bread, a cup of bouillon and some fruit. On the exceptional occasions when the empress did appear at the table (e.g., in Schönbrunn or Bad Ischl) she ate nothing. She had her own cook and her own meal hours, and her caloric intake was similar to that of a jockey in training. In ordinary life as well as during her travels, she frequently went without a real dinner, when her refreshment consisted mainly of a glass of milk and a couple of biscuits. Paradoxically, she was particularly fond of sweet things and was never without her box of bon-bons. She abhorred and never touched wine of any sort, even at gala dinners, and could hardly be persuaded to take it.[10]

All of these characteristics would give her a modern-day diagnosis of anorexia nervosa, a disease not recognized in Sisi's time. Anorexia is a label given to those who consume as few as 300 to 500 calories a day and are constantly fighting an imaginary weight problem. Anorexics are tormented by hunger but if pressed to eat more, they become very tense and irritable, just as Sisi did. But, there were some aberrations in Elisabeth's diet such as binge eating that are characteristic of another eating disorder, bulimia. On one occasion in 1878 the empress astonished her traveling companions when she unexpectedly visited a restaurant incognito, where she drank champagne, ate a broiled chicken, an Italian salad, and finished with a "considerable quantity of cake." She may have satisfied her urge to binge in secret on other occasions; in 1881 she purchased an English country house and had a spiral staircase built from her living room into the kitchen so that she could reach it in private.

For the most part, though, she was as frail as a ghost; her weight at times wavered around 100 pounds, seldom an ounce above. Sisi starved herself so effectively that she developed symptoms of hunger edema. As she aged, she became even more restless and obsessive, often weighing herself several times a day. In addition to consuming meager amounts of calories, she regularly took steam baths to prevent weight gain. When she was in her late fifties, she had wasted away to near emaciation, reaching her lowest point of 95.7 pounds.

Sisi had a sweet but shy demeanor. Her temperament was to be one of her virtues but that didn't turn out to be the case, for there are degrees of shyness. Sisi was at the extreme end of the spectrum and being around others was a form of sheer torture for her. Perhaps this was so because when she appeared among crowds at various court functions, she was always on display — always being scrutinized, her clothing, her jewelry, her hair. Everything about her furnished endless matter for discussion among the lords and ladies of the court. Every flaw, even the slightest, in her looks or her dress was noted and commented on: "Every second, Elisabeth had to live up to her reputation as the greatest beauty of the Monarchy. But there is not the least indication that she enjoyed the splash she made, as others in her situation would have done. Quite the contrary: her innate timidity and unsociability were not relieved by these public appearances; instead, they were reinforced to such a degree that she developed a virtual terror of strangers."[11]

She would have great beauty: this prophecy was to be a prescient one as well, and her beauty was acclaimed throughout the empire and beyond. But Sisi's entire identity was predicated on her beauty and being the most beautiful woman in the world and, of course, this became yet another obsession. The bane of her existence was her teeth — the "sole flaw in her beauty." Perhaps as a result of her bulimia or her malnutrition there was a striking deterioration of her teeth and this is why she constantly carried a fan, in order to hide her teeth. Her attempts to camouflage this problem simply added to the gossip of the court. Her day was centered on her obsession with beauty:

> In summer, she would rise around five, in the winter around six, and she began her day with a cold bath and massage. This was followed by gymnastics and exercise and a meager breakfast, sometimes taken with her younger daughter, Valerie. Then while her hair was being dressed, she used the time for reading and for writing letters and for studying Hungarian. Then came dressing, either in her fencing costume, if she intended to fence, or her riding habit, if she were going to the riding school to practice. All these activities amply filled the morning. At dinner, however, the Empress made up for lost time; her meal, consisting of no more than a thin gravy, was consumed in a few minutes. After the meal, she went for a walk lasting several hours — more accurately, a forced march at great speed over huge distance on which she was accompanied by a lady-in-waiting. Around five in the afternoon, after another change of clothing and hair combing, Valerie came to play. This was followed by the family dinner around seven o'clock — the only time of day she saw her husband. The meeting did not last long; for Sisi retired at the earliest opportunity, to indulge in her daily chat with her friend Ida Ferenczy, who also prepared the Empress for bed and loosened her hair. The Empress lived entirely for her beauty and health.[12]

Preparing herself for each day took an inordinate amount of time. Sisi needed as much as three hours a day for dressing (occasionally several times in one day). The famous lacing of her corset alone frequently took an hour, until her waist achieved its proverbial thinness. She had herself sewn into dresses each time she changed clothes. While other queens and empresses may have had to endure the layering of wire corsets and clothes, they did not have the sobriquet of being known as the most beautiful woman in the kingdom and the said queen and her retinue tolerated slight imperfections. Not so for Sisi. she could not appear in public without being perfect — at least in her eyes. All her appearances were occasions for her to continually secure her reputation for her supreme beauty.

She would never find peace. Elisabeth would always fall back upon the same panacea for her ills — locomotion. She was always saying goodbye. She would remain empress in name only. Nothing Franz Joseph could do or say had the power to stop her, for all was over between them. They faced each other like strangers. Doctors gave her the first opportunity to escape court life due to her health. Two doctors, Fischer and Skoda, examined the empress, who showed listlessness, loss of appetite and an intermittent cough; the doctors recommended a warm tepid climate. Thus, she embarked on her travels to Madeira and Corfu, followed by a speedy improvement in her health. Franz Joseph proposed several of the resorts of southern Austria. She would have none of them; nothing Austrian, nothing familiar would satisfy. The official medical bulletin informed the public that Her Imperial Majesty was suffering from a grave infection of the lungs, which required her to winter in a warm climate. Maurice Barres, a French novelist, wrote as follows: "Her voyages did not resemble the peaceful and deliberate regularity of migrating birds; they were rather the planless darting to and fro of an unanchored spirit which beats its wings, allowing itself neither rest nor design."[13] G.R. Marek also wrote of the situation: "There was no fixed goal. She went to Portugal, to Gibraltar — where Elisabeth walked for eight hours in the heat, exploring town and fortress, while Marie dragged along — to Tangier, Oran, Algiers, where having barely touched the coast, she decided to swerve to Corsica to visit Napoleon's birthplace, to Marseilles, Florence, Pompeii, and Capri. They were all cooped up on the small boat, half-dead from the heat, bickering among themselves. Finally at Naples she declared she had had enough of the *Chzalie*"[14] (a chartered British cutter). After Rudolf's death, her life reached a mad crescendo of restlessness and haste. All that mattered was to keep going.

When she was not in Vienna, she wandered all over Europe. Where was she not in those years? "The mere itinerary is dizzying: the Riviera, Baden-Baden, Heidelberg, London, Athens, Smyrna, Corfu, Wiesbaden, Amsterdam, four times in England, in Ireland, Munich, the palace of Miramar (Triests), Budapest, Rome, Normandy, up and down the Adriatic and the Mediterranean."[15] Often she changed her destination on short notice, causing considerable confusion.

In search of sun and warmth, she went to Egypt. There she haunted the bazaars, walking at such a pace that the policemen who were secretly detailed by the Austrian ministry in Cairo to follow and protect her could not keep up with her and demanded carriages, protesting it was impossible to shadow her on foot. In Alexandria she met Frederic Barker, a handsome young man of a prominent Anglo-Greek family. She was attracted by his looks, his youth, and above all by his knowledge of languages. A year later, she asked him to join her on an eight-week voyage, to teach her Greek literature. The eight weeks stretched into 13 months, and later Barker became her official reader. That was the end of Christomanos.

Trains, ships and coaches henceforth became her home. Her trips, which were certainly also motivated by health concerns, became ever longer, and her stays at Hofburg became ever shorter. She scurried at random to many locations on one prolonged and pointless migration. In time, Franz Joseph visited Sisi at Corfu. He reminded her of the predicament in which she placed him and the entire Habsburg clan. She needed to understand, he implored, that some compromise was necessary to check the wave of ugly scandal: people were calling her "mad." When he asked if she could choose some place closer, she chose Venice. Franz Joseph was delighted. Perhaps the tranquil lagoons of Venice would bring peace, opening the way to her own stormy heart.

The expense of any one of her voyages, traveling as she did with her own retinue of horses, milk cows and goats, was documented at 106,516 gulden (more than 200 thousand dollars, a fortune indeed). A businessman wrote her saying that what she spent in one day of traveling would finance his entire business. All too often she would arrive unannounced at the height of the season, bringing her sizable entourage, demanding a great many rooms, and at times the entire hotel, with a private entrance and hundreds of complicated security precautions to protect herself from curiosity seekers. Her arrival became a matter of dread. "Her Majesty grows more demanding by the year, and with the best will in the world, it is not possible to satisfy her; the people are so astonished at us that I blush," Marie Festetics[16] wrote from Interlaken to Ida Ferenczy in Hungary in 1892.[17] But Sisi's vast travels did not release her from her depression.

Rudolf's suicide prompted Elisabeth to wear only mourning from that time on and to give away all her jewelry. Her ever-deepening depressions, in the last years of her life, were thought to have developed into a kind of death wish. She never recovered from the death of Rudolf. "Black was all she wore.... Only her face was marble-white and ineffably sad. It was the same face as of old, well known from her bewitching portraits, hair cut short in front and waving around her brow like a silken fringe and above this her luxuriant braids, the loveliest of all crowns. Lashes drooped over her sweet eyes, once so full of life. Still and impassive as though seeing and hearing nothing. She was racked by nerves and insomnia."[18] Sisi, however, would soon find peace. She would die because she refused protection. She spurned security whether she was at Schönbrunn or engaged in visiting the villages of Belgium. Against her wishes, however, some foreign governments assigned police protection. But she was not afraid of assassins or even strangers as most members of royal families were.

On 9 September 1898, Elisabeth paid a visit to Baroness Julie Rothschild. After her visit, Elisabeth, under the pseudonym "Countess of Hohenembs," and her companion lady-in-waiting, Countess Irma Sztáray, registered at the Hotel Beau Rivage in Geneva. Elisabeth was recognized by the hotel owner and in the first edition of the *Journal de Genève,* all of its readers knew that the empress of Austria was a guest in their city. Those readers included the Italian anarchist Luigi Lucheni. Luigi was the son of an unwed mother from Alvaraeto in the Apennine province of Liguria. As his mother was unable to care for her son, Luigi spent his early life in orphanages. At an extremely early age, he was on his own; at age nine he worked for the railroad. Luigi was young but he could hold his own in serious brawls. There was a large chip on his shoulders and a first-rate hate for those better off than he — which was just about everyone — and a deep disdain for all who had title, power, and money. He joined the army and fought the Italian campaign against Abyssinia and was decorated for bravery.

The purpose of his being in Geneva was to assassinate Henri d'Orléans, pretender to the throne of France. Henri, however, changed his plans and was not in town. The name of the only royal aristocrat in Geneva was staring back at him in bold, black newspaper print. In his wildest thoughts of becoming a martyr by killing off some rich aristocrat, he had never thought of killing a woman, certainly not a queen or an empress. But now, he was staring at Sisi's picture and his reservations about killing a woman vanished. After all, she was a good personification of the wealthy — those whom he hated, those who lived in palaces, traveled on deluxe trains, and wore silks and satins while the poor rabble had not enough to eat or drink or warm clothes to wear. For Lucheni the prominent aristocrat Elisabeth was an equally suitable victim. She would provide him with the notoriety he craved, a victim prominent enough to attract media attention. The Italian anarchist now prepared himself for his "great deed."

He had purchased his murder instrument, a file that he had ground to a triangular shape and given a sharp knife-edge.

When Elisabeth and Countess Sztaray came out of the Beau Rivage, they crossed the park and headed towards the Quai du Mont Blanc, where they would catch the boat. Lucheni followed them. The two women had no protection at all. Lucheni then saw his chance and by the balustrade on the lake, he stumbled in front of the empress, who was hiding behind her umbrella, and stabbed her in the heart with a sharpened file. Sisi fell on her back but the force of the fall was broken by the weight of her heavy, pinned-up hair. The assassin fled, but was captured by a passerby and taken to the police station.

When Countess Sztaray came to her side, she asked Sisi if she felt pain or if she was wounded. Sisi's reply was that she was fine but terribly frightened. Then they continued to walk the remaining hundred yards to the boat. Once onboard ship, Elisabeth collapsed. When her clothes were loosened, two small drops of blood and one a little larger of very light red color were noticed on her chemise; on the body itself was only a small wound, but no blood was visible. Countess Irma Sztáray de Sztára et Nagymihály, Sisi's sole companion at the assassination, exclaimed in consternation, "The Empress has been stabbed!"

Elisabeth was brought back to the Beau Rivage. Frau Fanny Mayer, the wife of the proprietor, was asked to assist. In her words, "It was two o'clock when the Empress was brought to the hotel and carried into her bedroom. I was called to give such assistance as was in my power. The Empress was lying with a pale face and closed eyes upon her bed. Soon after she arrived in her room she sighed twice deeply: These were the last signs of life. She lay on the stretcher as if asleep, and with no outward show of pain. When we removed her from the litter to the bed she was evidently dead: she must have died when still on the stretcher. Two physicians, Dr. Golay and Dr. Mayer, arrived at this moment, and also a priest; but all remedies proved vain."[19]

The autopsy by Dr. Golay showed why the empress had been able to walk to the steamer after her fatal stabbing. So sharp was the file that it caused slow bleeding. The pointed file broke the fourth rib in her chest, pierced the lungs and the pericardium, then passed through the heart to come out in the left ventricle.

The women and girls of Vienna tried to avenge Sisi's death; sixteen thousand women signed a petition of hate for her assassin. The fearful crime committed against their beloved empress brought legion of Viennese together. If Elisabeth at one point curried the disdain of the common people for her extravagant travels and spending and her withdrawal from their presence as their empress, she now became a cult icon after her murder. Statues of her were set up all over the city; these were covered with garlands. She became the symbol of the sorrowing mother, almost a Madonna, one who had also lost her son — and her own life — most tragically.

The tragic occurrence, in broad daylight in an open thoroughfare of a large town, aroused the horror and dismay of the whole world. It was a senseless and purposeless murder. Sisi, with the exception of her incessant pleadings for a Hungarian compromise, had never exercised the faintest influence, either direct or indirect, upon politics and was perfectly ignorant of most of the laws and measures affecting her country. Her assassin was condemned to life imprisonment but committed suicide in 1910. His head was for a long time preserved in "the *Narrenturm*, the home of the Federal Pathologic-Anatomical Museum (*Pathologisch-anatomisches Bundesmuseum*)" in Vienna, before finally being laid to rest in the Anatomical Graves at the Central Cemetery (*Zentralfriedhof*).

Frau Schratt was immediately there at Franz Joseph's side and was a great comfort to him. But, their long-lasting liaison was not the same as it had been before. While Sisi was alive and Katharina was known as a friend to the Empress, the "affair" was more or less condoned by the court and Sisi's family. Indeed, Elisabeth had told her daughters that if anything ever happened to her that they should continue to nurture their father's relationship with Katharina. With her mother gone, however, Valerie now openly disapproved of the liaison. Katharina soon realized how much she owed the empress, for now that she was gone and Schratt was bereft of her protection she found herself exposed to petty humiliations of a jealous court and an unhappy empress' daughter.

While the whole empire was plunged in grief, no country mourned her in deeper sorrow than Hungary. Not a house in Budapest was without a black flag, and everyone in the streets wore a black scrap of crepe. The king was deeply moved when he heard about the tears shed by the Hungarian people for their queen: "they may well weep, for they do not know what a warm friend they have lost in their Queen."[20] Quite the contrary. The Magyars knew very well, indeed, what they had lost with the tragic departure of their "guardian angel."

Empress Elisabeth was in possession of a fortune, and no one, least of all Franz Joseph, was aware of this. Each year from 1875 on, she had invested her annual allowance and pin monies, and with wise advisement on various investments, she accumulated a great deal of money. She held stocks and bonds in railways and shipping and acquired a number of saving accounts, one in the First Austrian Savings Bank, where she held an account under the alias of Hermengild Harazti. She also invested some money in the House of Rothschild in Switzerland. She bequeathed one-fifth of her private fortune to Marie Valerie, and an equal portion to Gisela; another fifth went to granddaughter Erzsi, who was still unmarried and had no dependents.

Valerie had often thought that her mother had not been very kind to her father. She often thought her mother simply neglected her wifely duties. Now she deeply regretted her earlier feelings. For now she, too, found dealing with Franz Joseph anything but easy. "The trial it is to me now to be in Papa's company is my punishment for my former harshness," she wrote in her diary, as an expression of remorse toward her mother.[21]

Upon being told of Sisi's death, Franz Joseph lowered his head into his hands and was silent for several minutes. At last he said in a husky voice, "*Mir bleibt doch gar nichts erspart*" (I am spared nothing in this world). He remained standing, his body stiff. Then he began to read his morning mail. His life would hardly change with her death; he simply resumed his daily duties and his regular activities. But certainly there was a void. Franz Joseph and Elisabeth hadn't been companions for years, but she was still around. Her presence was felt even though physically and emotionally she was far away. She could still be reached by letter at least, which always began "Edes Lelkem" (My darling heart). Now she was not here and she would never be.

The body of the empress was robed in white and laid in a triple coffin of polished oak with silver fittings, lined with white satin and later given a glass top. The inscription on the coffin had originally described her only as "Empress of Austria." This caused vehement protests from the Hungarians and the words "Queen of Bohemia" was added to the inscription. As the funeral train left Geneva and rolled through Innsbruck and Salzburg, all the houses were draped in mourning. Vienna itself was transformed; crepe and black banners hung from the flagpoles in the Ringstrasse and on every balcony.

Elisabeth had been imprisoned by the rules of others — society, the Austrian court, the Archduchess Sophie, and her husband, Franz Joseph. Many women — royal and nonroyal, then and even today, from all spectrums of society, rich and poor — have had to face social mores and attitudes that were effective barriers in limiting aspirations and lifestyles. Sisi's story should not be considered a sad one but one of inspiration. She refused to become a pawn and in her own way fought against being shaped and molded by the gender-traditionalism and the assigned spheres of the court and of society. She longed for some control and spent her life trying to achieve that control and freedoms she associated with her real and fictionalized heroes. She succeeded in some important ways — notably in her fight for Hungarian egalitarianism and in her commitment to an Austrian-Hungarian settlement on the basis of special rights and freedoms for Hungary. In smaller ways she succeeded by ignoring nonsensical court etiquette and achieving some control, albeit late, over her children's lives. Her legacy was to the common people and her charitable works on their behalf. Elisabeth's will stipulated that a large part of her jewel collection should be sold and the proceeds, then estimated at over £600,000, were to be distributed to various religious and charitable organizations. Franz Joseph remarked to Prince Leichtenstein, who was the couple's devoted equerry, "That a man could be found to attack such a woman, whose whole life was spent in doing good and who never injured any person, is to me incomprehensible."[22]

At last Elisabeth was at peace. She had returned to Vienna — forever. She now belonged to the world of Heine and Homer and to Shakespeare's Titania. Her desire for love, satisfaction, recognition, and freedom never materialized. Elisabeth always believed in the power of fate: "most things are settled by Providence."

Chapter Eleven

The Aging Emperor

Franz Joseph awoke to a beautiful morning at Bad Ischl and thought of the evening before — his Golden Jubilee celebration of the fiftieth year of his reign. It was 2 December 1898; he was sixty-eight years old. For several decades the people of Austria had experienced an external peace, a longer period of peace than any other Habsburg emperor had known. Few Austrian soldiers could even remember military wars, but the emperor could vividly recall them all.[1] Now there were ominous signs that these peaceful days might be coming to a close. Over the next twelve years, the political strife in both halves of the dual monarchy continued to swell and became quite intense, so much so that European public opinion wondered about the actual survival of Austria-Hungary.

As the years ticked forward as they always manage to do, Franz Joseph celebrated his eightieth birthday. Like so many other birthdays preceding this one, it was celebrated among the mountains of the Salzkammergut. Every year on 18 August the emperor's family gathered at Bad Ischl to observe his birthday. A rather large contingency — seventy-two members of the Habsburg clan — joined him that year at Bad Ischl. It was commonly agreed that Franz Joseph looked more like fifty than eighty, at least from afar. He still presented a commanding figure on horseback, sitting tall and erect in the saddle. While Franz Joseph had been in general good health all his life he now suffered from occasional attacks of bronchial asthma.

In April 1911 he fell seriously ill. He was visiting his daughter Marie Valerie at her home at Wallsee on the Middle Danube. It was Easter time but the weather refused to give way to spring-like conditions. It was chilly and rainy, the perfect weather to sap Franz Joseph's strength and prevent him from throwing off that persistent cough. Upon doctor's orders, he was to remain in bed. Even in his bedridden state, Franz Joseph asked to have official papers brought to him each morning. His physical condition was serious enough that the Archduke Franz Ferdinand, the heir apparent was notified.

When Franz Ferdinand was twelve, his cousin Duke Francis V of Modena died. In his will he named Franz Ferdinand his heir but added one condition: He should add the name Este to his own; Franz Ferdinand d'Este willingly complied. A man of strong loathing, he hated the Jews and the Serbs, and he distrusted the Hungarians and the Italians. He was cautious in foreign and military affairs, opposed to war with Serbia and in favor of a rapprochement with Russia, which had become by then Austria-Hungary's most dangerous enemy. Franz Ferdinand by most accounts was considered to be "egotistical, not refined in matters of culture, and had a bombastic temperament to boot."[2] In other words he clearly lacked the necessary charisma to win the hearts of the Viennese people or even the ruling aristocracy for that matter.

The royals were not enamored of Franz Ferdinand, not because of his character but because of the policies he intended to implement when he ascended to the throne. His ideas were to replace Austro-Hungarian dualism with "trialism," a triple monarchy in which the empire's Slavs would have an equal voice in government with the Germans and Magyars. His friendliness towards the southern Slavs caused Serbia to see him as a threat to their own expansion plans. "Gavrilo Princip, like the Great Serbian, or Yugoslav"-oriented Bosnian Serb nationalists in general, did not want to accept this solution. The nationalists sought to block the road of trialist reorganization of the monarchy and to join Serbia and the other South Slavic nations in an effort to realize their dream of true national independence. The nationalist ideology had thus conquered Central and Eastern Europe, and from the early twentieth century onward embarked on its triumphant march toward self-realization."[3] Franz Ferdinand also embraced the idea of replacing the Austro-Hungarian Empire with a federalism made up of sixteen states.

Franz Ferdinand also alienated many Hungarian nationalists who were opposed to his policy of universal male suffrage. Such a policy would undermine the domination of the Magyars in the Hungarian kingdom. The Magyars as well were suspicious of Franz Ferdinand's trialism and his idea for a third Croat-dominated Slav kingdom including Bosnia and Herzegovina. Non-Catholics were also against his patronage of the Catholic Schools Association.

For years Franz Joseph kept Franz Ferdinand out of any positions of responsibility. Then when the heir did start to assert himself in 1906, Franz Joseph only grudgingly relinquished some power but refused to cede anything of real substance. Moreover he never thought to transfer more power to the representative assemblies and governments of his empire and kingdom. Franz Joseph's reluctance to share power was, in part, because he still thought of himself as an emperor by divine grace, and still thought of his empire as, well — his. Some historians believed that "it was the persistence of this essentially authoritarian way of thinking which marked his whole career, and it was the persistence of this hierarchical top-down, imperial structure of authority, which was at the root of the Monarchy's problems in 1914."[4] Part of his reluctance to relinquish some power to Franz Ferdinand was also due to his dislike of Ferdinand's character and future policies.

The Habsburg court breathed a sigh of relief when Franz Joseph's health improved and he was in good enough shape to travel to Schwarzau, about forty miles from Vienna, to attend his nephew (and eventual successor) Archduke Charles' wedding. Nineteen-year-old Princess Zita of Bourbon-Parma was the bride. Early newsreels of the reception show Franz Joseph appearing to be in good spirits and engaging in an animated conversation with the bridegroom's mother.

In 1912 his asthma returned with vengeance. Once again he was under strict medical supervision from the court physician, Dr. Joseph von Kerzl, who insisted that he spend most of his time at Schönbrunn where the air was cleaner. For the better part of a year, the emperor was rarely seen in public. He carried out his official paper duties but his moments of contentment were spent in Katharina Schratt's presence.

Katharina was now approaching sixty and had been a widow for a few years, but her eyes were still lively, as was her demeanor around Franz Joseph. Due to the fact that both of them were free, rumors circulated that Franz Joseph and Katharina were secretly married. While none of the rumors were substantiated, they persist to the present day. Franz Joseph was still in love; in fact, according to Ketterl's memoirs, he often acted like a nervous adolescent. When the lonely emperor awaited visits from his old friend in pleasurable excitements, Ketterl wrote, "He restlessly would jump out of his chair to go to the bedroom and brush his hair or comb his side-whiskers."[5]

Frau Schratt continued to give him the material comforts the emperor still neglected, ranging from placing a warm rug beside his bed to ordering milder cigars when the doctor prohibited the stronger ones he was smoking.

When in better health, Franz Joseph would spend a few summer evenings at a private dinner party for two at No. 9 Gloriettegasse. Katharina would even see to it that one of the popular quartets was on hand to play familiar Strauss waltzes during their meal.

Katharina had been away from Vienna for a long time and Franz Joseph, in one of his dejected moods, wrote to her: "I am very tired, the weakness of my age increases. My mood is sad and bored. I am afraid I will bore you."[6] In 1912, physical issues reached such a point of concern that the emperor appointed Franz Ferdinand "General Inspector of All the Armed Forces." Making this appointment was tantamount to resignation. Officially as well as unofficially, the power was now being transferred to his successor.

In 1914 tension mounted between the Habsburg monarchy and Serbia, backed by Russia. That tension had been fed by a series of incidents going back to the beginning of Franz Joseph's reign. The Crimean War between Russia and Turkey had been motivated by the czar's urge to expand his power and possessions in the Balkans at the expense of the crumbling Turkish Empire. England and France came to the aid of Turkey. Not only did Austria fail to come to the aid of its benefactor Russia, it placed its troops along the Austro-Russian border and presented Russia with an ultimatum, forcing Russia to withdraw from the Balkans. Nicholas II was shocked by Franz Joseph's perfidy. Austria's betrayal set the stage for the catastrophic war, which eventually destroyed both empires.

In November 1912 Franz Joseph exclaimed, "I don't want war. I have always been unlucky in wars. We would win, but lose provinces."[7] Less than two years later, after the assassination of yet another close relative, his nephew, the self-styled "peace Emperor," was to declare war on Serbia, thus "starting a conflagration which was to destroy much of European civilization and the Habsburg Dynasty with it."[8]

Franz Joseph was planning the annual maneuvers to be held in Bosnia and Herzegovina, but in view of reports that agents of the Black Hand infested Sarajevo, he canceled his arrangements. It was now that Franz Ferdinand, always eager to oppose the emperor, came to a quick decision: "He could not overrule his uncle's word and order the maneuvers to take place, but he could laugh off the old man's worry."[9] Despite repeated warnings from the foreign office against visiting the hostile territory, Franz Ferdinand was determined to go there. He had married a Slav; the insurgent races could bear him no grudge, or so he thought. Headstrong and decidedly Germanic in his point of view, the Archduke was a poor psychologist.

He headed, with his wife, Sophie, for Sarajevo, a little country on the edge of Europe soon to come to the forefront of the political stage.

The archduke and the Duchess of Hohenberg had survived a bomb attack earlier that morning, but Ferdinand decided to continue. He longed to appear in the parade — his triumphal procession. While once fresh with eagerly smiling faces, after the bomb scare their confidence looked shattered and their faces looked drawn: "Count Harrach stood on the left-hand running board, on the side from which the bomb had been thrown. The Archduke's car was preceded by the lead car, which carried the chief of police and other officials, as they made their way to Sarajevo."[10]

In the city, there were six members of the Black Hand, an organization whose stated aim was to realize the national ideal, the unification of all Serbs. This organization preferred terrorist action to cultural activities. When the first assassination bomb attempt failed, five of the members fled the city, leaving only one — Gavrilo Princip, who "wanted to kill Ferdinand because he knew of his plan to unite Austria's Servo-Croat citizens and set them up on a basis of equality with the other national groups. Such a plan would have ended the dream of secession and alignment with Serbia, and might indeed have ended the Black Hand altogether."[11] Therefore Ferdinand's death, to Gavrilo, was a necessity of life.

"As the car reached the Latin Bridge it turned right to go up Franz Joseph Street. That was the originally scheduled itinerary. Nobody had bothered to inform the chauffeur of the lead car that the route had been changed."[12] Naturally the archduke's chauffeur followed the lead car. "Not that way," Potiorek frantically waved and shouted at the first car. Potiorek stopped the car so that he could shift into reverse. With the car stationary, Gavrilo was able to fire at his victims from less than five feet away. He took careful aim and fired twice. The first bullet hit Franz Ferdinand in the chest; the second hit Sophie in the abdomen. Gavrilo was pinned fast by bystanders and was nearly beaten to death by police. "Sopherl, Sopherl, don't die! Live for our children!" cried Franz Ferdinand, and then he died.[13] "Assassination in Sarajevo — Heir to the Throne Murdered with His Wife" ran the headlines on the title page of the *Illustrierte Kronen-Zeitung* of 30 June 1914.

When the news reached Vienna it caused no real grief among the Sunday strollers. They thought it was a most barbaric act committed by a most barbaric people, but their reaction was one of indifference to the death of Franz Ferdinand. After all, most Viennese had never even caught a glimpse of the man. German-Austrian parliamentarian Joseph Redlich wrote in his diary: "No mood of mourning pervades the city. Music continues to be played in the Prater and out here in Grinzing."[14] The Hofburg crowd secretly rejoiced, hiding their elation behind a proper melancholy mien. There appeared to be indifference in Vienna and that indifference was surpassed in Budapest, where little attempt was made to disguise the widespread relief at the death of an archduke notorious for having hated everything Magyar. The first reaction of the world to the double murder was shock and indignation rather than fear of war.

On hearing of the murders the emperor is said to have "slumped in the chair at his desk" before pacing the room in great agitation and saying, almost to himself, "Terrible, the Almighty is not to be challenged.... A higher power has re-established the order which I, alas, could not preserve."[15] (The familiar tale derives from what Count Paar, the sole witness of his master's grief, told Colonel von Margutti, his deputy, who wrote his account ten years later.) Franz Joseph viewed the assassination of his heir as divine retribution for Franz Ferdinand's defiance of his dynastic duties by marrying a mere noblewoman. It was for this reason, Margutti reported, the "Emperor could not restrain a feeling of relief."[16] The emperor's first response was thus far from being one of such outrage as to immediately call for war against Serbia.

Upon hearing the news, Marie Valerie went to her father and found him "amazingly fresh," as she wrote in her journal, though he was "shocked, with tears in his eyes ... when he spoke of the poor children." He had more confidence in the tact and skills of the new heir than in the murdered archduke. "For me it is a relief from a great worry," he admitted to his daughter, thinking of the fate of the dynasty. No one in the family circle foresaw that the event, which they mourned as a personal tragedy, would be for Europe a complete cataclysmic disaster.[17]

The emperor's poor health precluded his acting as host to any gathering of European sovereigns; thus the funeral ceremonies in the capital would be limited to a single day. On Franz Ferdinand's coffin rested the symbols of his rank: the hat of an archduke along with the crown of an imperial prince and the cap and saber of an Austrian general. On Sophie's coffin they placed a fan and a pair of white gloves, a snide reminder that she was once merely a lady-in-waiting. Franz Ferdinand would have been entitled to burial in the Habsburg Capuchin crypt along with the other royals but his wife could not be buried alongside him.

Franz Ferdinand had been aware of this burial protocol and in his will he specified that he wished to be buried in his castle in Artstetten on the shore of the Danube. The two were interred as he requested. On the day of the funeral there were "no tolling of bells, no bearers of candles, no procession, and no solemn incantations. Military honors to which any plain lieutenant would be entitled were refused. The insult was obvious. It was like a bad dream, foretelling a worse reality to come."[18] Baron Morsey, a member of Franz Ferdinand's staff, was incensed that the archduke and his wife had been given a "third class burial."

Not a shred of evidence was found that the Serbian government had arranged, abetted, or even known about the crime. Nevertheless, Austrian ministers agreed to present Serbia with demands that the Serbian government would have to reject, thus giving the monarchy an excuse for military intervention. The note assumed Serbia's responsibility for the murders and demanded what amounted to surrender of Serbian sovereignty to the monarchy. Austria claimed "the right to send her own officials to participate in the suppression of Irridentist activity, and to carry out a thorough investigation of all those who might have been implicated in the crime."[19] "*Die Note ist sehr hart*" [The note is very harsh], declared Franz Joseph on reading it.[20] Count Edward Paar, Franz Joseph's adjutant, reacted in disbelief when his master sighed, "Men of eighty-four years of age don't sign war proclamations."[21] But the Austrian-Hungarian nation was moving in that direction.

Istvan Tisza, prime minister of the Kingdom of Hungary noted, "I cannot share responsibility for the proposed military aggression against Serbia.... I must declare that in spite of my devotion to ... Your Majesty ... I could not share the responsibility for the exclusively and aggressively warlike solution."[22] Sir Edward Grey, Britain's foreign secretary, tried to get the monarchy to call off the war and offered mediation, promising that Franz Joseph's honor would be vindicated and his prestige enhanced.

Franz Joseph extended a listless hand to Germany. If the Austrians initiated the move to war in July 1914, the Germans were only too willing to back them up, for they already had been seeking just such an opportunity for a preemptive strike. The July crisis saw the Austrians as Germany's stooges, but willing stooges. On 6 July, Foreign Minister Count Berchtold duly learnt of a telegram from Berlin "over Serbia" and that Austria-Hungary could "always count" on German support as "a faithful ally and friend" and his German offer of an "a blank cheque" was confirmed by the Austro-Hungarian diplomat Alexander Graf von Hoyos.[23]

Foreign Minister Count Leopold von Berchtold told Franz Joseph that Serbian troops had already attacked Austrian-Hungarian Army units near Teme-Kubin. This was not true. It is also thought that he kept Sir Grey's reconciliation offer from the emperor. Thus Franz Joseph was misinformed about Serbia's alleged attack on imperial military units. History has accused Berchtold as being to a high degree responsible for the war. But it was not he who made the decision for war; it was Franz Joseph.

Perhaps Franz Joseph thought that the ultimatum to Serbia was merely a diplomatic bluff, because he was visibly shaken when he read Serbia's reply and realized the unacceptability of their reply. He took the paper, and, like a man infinitely weary, sat down at his desk to read the message. This time, at this moment of crisis, his hands trembled so that only with difficulty could he place his spectacles on his nose. Then he read, bent closely over the page. The Serbs said that they agreed to almost every point and for the rest "we count upon your chivalry." Serbia would not allow Austria to enter Serb territory to investigate the assassination. Franz Joseph remained silent. At last, having seemingly forgotten Margutti's presence, he said to himself, "Well, breaking off diplomatic relations does not necessarily mean war."[24] It was not a convincing soliloquy. The council of ministers of the monarchy reconvened and all but the Hungarian Tisza voted for "a resolution by force." While eighty-four years of age is not a time of life associated with bellicosity, two hours later, 9:23 to be precise, Franz Joseph issued the command for mobilization.

In the war, the Habsburg empire with a "population of 52,000,000 people lost 1,200,000 killed; 3,500,000 were wounded and 2,200,000 became prisoners of war, of whom an unspecified but large number never returned."[25] One must also consider the operations in theaters of war across Europe and Asia. In a manifesto issued to his peoples on 29 July 1914, Franz Joseph said, "It is My most fervent desire to dedicate the years which by the Grace of God are still left to Me to works of peace and to preserve My peoples from the heavy sacrifice of a war [65,038,810 total mobilized forces]. Divine Providence has decreed otherwise [8,528,831 killed]. The machinations of a hate-filled enemy force Me, after long years of peace, to reach for the sword to preserve the honor of My Monarchy [21,189,154 wounded], to defend its prestige and power position to secure its property.... I follow the path of duty"[26] [37,466,904 total casualties].

Because of its Slav heritage, Russia was a historic ally of Serbia. On 30 July Russia mobilized its armies, triggering a German declaration of war on the first of August. By August the great martial symphony had opened. Russia, Germany, France, England and a galaxy of smaller nations rushed in to embellish the score. It all happened like an avalanche. In this gigantic holocaust Habsburg went to its doom. Franz Joseph never ceased to wonder at the number of countries eager to destroy their wealth and manhood for no better reason than the carelessness of his own nephew in getting shot on the street corner of a Balkan town.

The implications of the assassination for Austrian prestige, and the opportunity it seemed to offer for "settling" the Serbian threat once and for all, led to the same monarch who had felt "relief" at his heir's demise going to war against Serbia to avenge the same man's murder. Experts, both military and psychological, have offered their opinions as to why Franz Joseph gave the orders to mobilize Austrian troops. All seem to agree that Franz Joseph went to war extremely reluctantly, and was often swept along by events and the "hawkishness" of his military and diplomatic advisers and German allies. While there were a great number of forces at work in the month which led up to the declaration of war on 28 July 1914, most of them were for war; but the man who signed the declaration was Franz Joseph and, for the last and most fatal time, he played a crucial role on the world stage.

One of the overwhelming reasons for war relates to the Habsburg tradition. Habsburgs, as with Franz Joseph, always put dynastic advantage first, often to the detriment of national understanding, if the latter worked against imperial power. Franz Joseph was thus given the dubious privilege of signing the death warrant of the dynastic empire that he had battled his whole life to preserve. He had agreed to war, as ever, to uphold the dignity and status of the dynasty. One concept immutable to Franz Joseph was Habsburg sanctity. As time elapsed, the pistol shot that had hit Franz Ferdinand attacked that sanctity: war was the only adequate answer. Franz Joseph's policies were policies of peace. But peace had its limits — limits of decency and self-respect, but particularly of concern for the continuation of the patrimonial legacy he had inherited. Similarly, another powerful reason for war was to preserve the great-power status of Austria.[27] It seems the major reason the emperor agreed to war was to preserve and uphold the dignity of the Habsburg dynasty and to preserve the power and prestige of the Austrian Empire. "Finally the incident at Sarajevo may have unloosed in Franz Joseph's hat a rancor long muffled. It may have been the one drop of blood too many. First his brother, then his son, then his wife, and now his nephew — they all had been snatched away by violence. The cumulative force of these tragedies may have shattered that prudence which was his stock trade."[28] That is a conjecture, but a reasonable one.

The consequences of war were understood by hardly anyone in Austrian ruling circles. They were only dimly aware of the global-level calculations with which the Germans were working, and even the implications of war for the monarchy were only vaguely determined. When war was proclaimed, one ironic result was that the man who had declared war, Franz Joseph, ceased to be the ruler of the monarchy. All power was concentrated in the Army High Command, Conrad von Hotzendorf. The emperor, approaching his eighty-fourth birthday, was deemed too ancient to take an active part in the direction of the war.

Instead he now spent his time virtually interned at Schönbrunn, basically living in his study, being fed information about the campaign by headquarters. He had time to contemplate major issues and in his punctilious way, and minor issues as well. Someone had removed the worn old carpet from Franz Joseph's study and replaced it with a new one. The old carpet was shabby and full of holes but he missed that carpet. He was used to the pattern, and when he had retreated to his den for heavy thinking the emperor paced up and down over the riddled nap, unconsciously keeping track of each familiar hole. The new rug was a nuisance. It interfered with meditation. The old rug was returned to its honored place.

The Gödöllő castle and the royal palace at Buda were boarded up and only the most necessary apartments were used at Schönbrunn. The glorious steeds of the Spanish Riding School, Habsburg's pride, were sold at auction. Franz Joseph's favorite white stallion, Florian, was led from royal stables and harnessed to a milk wagon. Franz Joseph remarked to Margutti, "Things are going badly with us, perhaps worse than we suspect. The starving people can't stand much more. It remains to be seen whether and how we shall get through the winter. I mean to end the war next spring whatever happens, I can't let my Empire go to hopeless ruin."[29] He did not stop it and made no attempts to stop it.

Almost to the very end, he was at his desk working. But Ketterl intervened and ordered him to bed. With orders for his servant to wake him at the usual hour, Franz Joseph, the last of the last line of German emperors beginning with Charlemagne in Rome and extending since over more that a thousand years, died. To his very last day on earth, Franz Joseph remained sovereign in the old sense, the monarch of the old school, which he felt himself to be.

A codicil was added to Franz Joseph's will in March 1889 in which he pledged the sum of five hundred thousand gulden, an extremely large sum of money, to the court actress Katharina Schratt, "to whom I am bound by deepest and purest of friendships and who has always been loyally and faithfully at my side and that of the Empress during the hardest moments of our life."[30]

The old Emperor was spared seeing with his own eyes the final turns in this tragedy called World War I. On 30 November 1916, his body lay in state in the Cathedral of St. Stephen. Emperor Charles and Empress Zita led his funeral cortege with their eldest son, Otto, preceding on foot to the Capuchin Church, where, for nearly three hundred years, the Habsburgs had found their last resting places. The funeral was one of the last great displays of imperial Habsburg pomp Vienna was to witness. Yet, in the midst of the catastrophe of the war such pomp had lost much of its meaning and hence its authority. Joseph Relich wrote, "The dynastic empire which had for centuries relied on such splendour; majesty and magnificence, the appearances of power, did not long survive him."[31]

The casket arrived at the iron gate of the Capuchin crypt. The Lord Chamberlain knocked three times with his golden staff, whereupon a voice within demanded:

> "Who knocks?"
> "His Apostolic Majesty, the Emperor of Austria."
> "Him I know not."
> Again three raps of the staff, again the voice:
> "Who knocks?"
> "The King of Hungary."
> "Him I know not."
> Once more the same gesture, the same demand:
> "Who knocks?"
> "Franz Joseph, a poor sinner."
> "Enter, then!"[32]

Chapter Twelve

Into History

Two years after the death of Franz Joseph, World War I, the greatest worldwide catastrophe to that time, ended and something unthinkable occurred — the final collapse of the four great dynasties: Romanov, Hohenzollern, Ottoman, and Habsburg. Each of these great and old dynasties disappeared from the stage of history.

The war years, 1914 to 1918, were particularly devastating to Russia. War casualties were high, with Russia losing hundreds of thousands of young men. Czar Nicholas II was the reigning Romanov monarch, who had married, in 1894, Princess Alice, daughter of the grand duke of a small duchy in Germany. Upon her baptism into the Russian Orthodox faith her name became Alexandra Feodorovna. Four daughters — Maria, Anastasia, Tatiana and Olga — and one son, Alexis, were born from this union. Alexis was a hemophiliac, a genetic disease carried through the mother's genes, generally to male offspring. He was frail and sick a great deal of the time, a constant worry to his mother.

Nicholas II did not deal with Russia's growing internal problems of poverty and poor living conditions for the lower classes, partly due to his ignorance and to his belief that his people adored him unconditionally. The problems of the lower-class populace, in particular the food shortages, precipitated the revolts in 1917. Nicholas II, like Franz Joseph, believed in his divine right to rule and being above the common proletariat and this infuriated dissidents, liberals, and minorities. The end of this dynasty began a decade before World War I with another war, "the first great war of the twentieth century," the Russo-Japanese War of 8 February 1904 to 5 September 1905.[1] The Russians sought a warm-water port on the Pacific Ocean for maritime trade as well as a port for its navy. The Japanese wanted to expand its empire into China and Korea. The war started as a result of these rival imperial ambitions between Russia and Japan over Manchuria and Korea.

According to authors Mark D. Steinberg and Vladimir M. Khrustalev, Nicholas II, throughout his reign, made decisions that not only discredited his regime but also provoked fury from the populace against his governance.[2] The masses blamed the loss of the Russo-Japanese War on the czar's misguided leadership as a result of totally disregarding his ministers' advice. Due to its loss, Russia had to give up all influence in the Far East. By the end of his reign, Tsar Nicholas II had provoked fury among the aristocracy, the bourgeoisie and the lower classes.

Then, too, the imperial family was not well liked, particularly Alexandra. She was blamed for Alexis' hemophilia and was further disliked for her friendship to — actually worship of— Gregori Rasputin. This man was considered demonic by the Russian people and his Satanic influence over the czarina was considered dangerous. Gregori Rasputin remains one of Russia's most controversial and mysterious figures. The "Mad Monk," as he was called, posed as a holy man and contributed to the destruction of the czar's political image and reputation through a series of political manipulations and scandals.

During the reign of Nicholas II, the Socialist Party was beginning to exert a more powerful influence over the masses. Subsequent events changed czarist Russia forever. In March 1917, Czar Nicholas had to sign away the Romanov Empire. By all accounts, his son, Alexis, was considered to be too sick and weak to fulfill the obligations of a czar and the czar's brother, Grand Duke Michael, thought the situation was too volatile and refused to take the throne. The October Revolution of 1917 established Russia as a communist state; the Bolsheviks took office, leading to drastic political changes. In a communist state, there was no tolerance or room for an imperial family.[3]

A few months later, the imperial family was put under house arrest at the Alexander Palace. The rebellion of the anticommunist White Movement was supposed to help release the royal family. Promises were made to the czar to take him and his family away and protect them from the revolutionaries. The czar and his family waited. For more than a year, they lived in the palace and subsequent locations, until the night of 17 July 1918. By order of Lenin, the family had been taken to Ekaterinburg in the foothills of the Urals. That night, under a barrage of machine-gun fire, all seven members of the Romanov family, along with their servants, were killed. (A rumor that Princess Anastasia had survived persisted for years.

In 1991, near Ekaterinburg, her remains were identified, thus ending those hopes.) Due to the war and to the czar's incompetence in his inability to lead, the Romanov dynasty, rulers of Russia for more that three hundred years and one of the most powerful and influential dynasties in Russia, ceased to exist.

The Hohenzollern dynasty began in southern Germany. The dynasty may have taken its name from the German word *zöller,* meaning "watchtower" or "castle," and in particular from the Swabian castle of Hohenzollern, the ancestral seat in the Black Forest.[4] This noble family, traceable to the eleventh century, ruled over Prussia, Germany, and Romania. As with the Habsburgs, this dynasty also believed in absolutism. Throughout its history it viewed the populace as subjects. Democracy was repressed, and obedience to the crown was considered to be the chief virtue of the people. Of the 20 rulers who reigned in Brandenburg and Prussia for five centuries, from the first elector to the last emperor-king, there were not more than eight who ruled with efficiency, industry and talent. The rest were weak and vain and squandered the money and success accumulated by their predecessors.

At the outbreak of World War I, the Hohenzollern leader, Kaiser Wilhelm II, grandson of Queen Victoria, was in power. Kaiser Wilhelm II ruled both the German Empire and the Kingdom of Prussia from June 15, 1888 to November 9, 1918. Like many of his predecessors, he was an ineffective war leader and, because of his bellicose policies, by war's end he was losing the control of his army. Within two years of becoming kaiser, he forced the resignation of one of Germany's greatest statesmen, Otto von Bismarck. Wilhelm wanted to preclude the emergence of another popular "Iron Chancellor" who would carry the lion's share of political power. A common belief among the German people was that by dismissing Bismarck that Wilhelm II had destroyed any chance of Germany's continuing with a stable and effective government.[5]

In early spring, Germany launched the "drive of 1918," which was a series of grand offensives it hoped would break the allied front and end the war with a victory, or at least a draw. The German plan was to win the war before the bulk of the newly arrived U.S. troops could be brought into action on the Western Front. The plan almost succeeded. But the German failure to break the Allied lines in these spring offensives was a prelude to the collapse of the Hohenzollern dynasty.

The last chancellor of the German empire was Maximilian, prior to the revolution and the creation of a German republic. In 1917, Maximilian was opposed to a resumption in unrestricted submarine warfare. Instigating that policy would prove to be disastrous and would eventually draw the neutral United States into the war against the Central Powers. In 1918, Prince Max, along with most Germans, was aware of the hopelessness of their situation.

The chancellor formed a coalition cabinet that included members of the Center, Progressive, and Socialist parties, the three major parties in the *Reichstag*. In late October 1918, social unrest led to mutiny among the sailors at Kiel, which spread and soon erupted into the German Revolution.[6] Prince Max hoped to save the monarchy and bolster Germany's situation by requesting that Kaiser Wilhelm II abdicate in favor of a regency with his twelve-year-old grandson, Prince Wilhelm. The kaiser refused. The clamoring for his abdication grew louder, especially after U.S. president Woodrow Wilson made it a prerequisite of peace negotiations.

With increasing pressure from his generals, in November, Kaiser Wilhelm II boarded the royal train and headed for Holland. To a most bewildered Dutch border guard, the kaiser handed him his sword. Chancellor Maximilian announced the abdication of Kaiser Wilhelm, King of Prussia and Emperor of Germany, on 9 November 1918. Several hours later Wilhelm surrendered the government to the Socialist leader Friedrich Ebert. The revolutionary period ended in August of 1919 when the Weimar Republic was formally established, thus bringing an end to the Hohenzollern monarch. Although the Treaty of Versailles provided that Wilhelm be tried for promoting the war, the Dutch government refused to extradite him, and he remained in retirement at Doorn.

The Hohenzollern dynasty, through its long years as leaders of Germany, often gave the country a stable government in unstable times. The fact that they did not adjust to the changing times, continued to believe in the power of monarch rule, and disliked democracy certainly led to the downfall of Hollenzollern Germany. Undoubtedly the most humiliating portion of the Treaty of Versailles for the defeated Germany was Article 231, commonly known as the "War Guilt Clause," which forced Germany to accept complete responsibility as initiator of World War I. As such, Germany was liable for all material damages.

Thus, as a direct consequence of war, Russia, Germany, Austro-Hungary, and Ottoman empires ceased to exist. The latter was a large multi-ethnic empire that dominated much of Europe and lasted from 1299 to 1922. Historically the Ottoman Empire is also referred to as the Turkish Empire or Turkey, founded by Turkish tribes under Osman Bey in north-western Anatolia in 1299. The height of its power occurred in the sixteen and seventeen centuries. One of its great leaders was Suleiman the Magnificent (1520–1566). He was the tenth and longest-reigning emperor, Sultan of the Ottoman Empire, from 1520 to his death in 1566. It was under his governance that the Ottoman Empire reached the height of its power. Modern-day countries comprising the empire included Vassal and Nominal territories of Turkey, Iraq, parts of western Iran, Israel, Lebanon, Syria, Saudi Arabia, Kuwait, Bahrain, Qatar, Egypt, parts of western Libya, and Sudan.

Suleiman, also known as the "lawgiver," built bridges, mosques, aqueducts, and fortresses, and vastly increased the expanse and wealth of the Ottoman Empire. Other constructions during his time included schools, city walls, and an aqueduct that surpassed any built in Rome. Suleiman was also responsible for a proliferation of art and literature that is greatly valued even today.

During World War I, based mainly on Germany's early victories, the Turkish ambassador Rifat Pasha chose to become an ally of the Central Powers. Turkey had joined the war on the side of the Central Powers under considerable German pressure. The Ottoman Empire had more to fear from a Russian-British victory than from a German-Austrian victory. The formal beginning occurred when the Ottomans declared war on Russia on 29 October 1914 and the formal ending occurred with the Treaty of Sevres on 10 August 1920. The fall of the Ottoman Empire was also attributed to the continuous tensions that erupted between its many different ethnic groups and to the leadership failure to successfully handle these frictions. The Ottoman Empire, once the leading Islamic state in cultural and geopolitical terms, had now vanished.[7]

The Austro-Hungarian high command, which had blundered into the war unprepared in 1914, did little better at its conclusion. The possessions of the Habsburg dynasty, acquired over the centuries by marriage or war, were divided, re-formed, expanded and contracted roughly along ethnic lines. Austria, Hungary, and Czechoslovakia all became independent states. Austria lost land to Italy, Czechoslovakia and Serbia. The Austrian province of Galicia was combined with the former German-Polish lands, and the Russian-Polish lands taken by Germany at the Treaty of Brest-Litovsk were combined as well to reestablish the Republic of Poland. The army was to be reduced to thirty thousand men. Austria was to pay reparations but went bankrupt before the rate could be set. Hungary lost land to Austria, Czechoslovakia, Romania and Serbia which reduced its size from 283,000 square kilometers to less than 93,000 square kilometers. The population was reduced from 18.2 million to 7.6 million. The army was to be reduced to 35,000 men.[8]

The last Habsburg emperor, Karl Franz Joseph Ludwig Hubert George Otto Marie von Habsburg-Lothringen, or Charles I of Austria and Charles IV of Hungary, was born on 17 August 1887 in Persenbeug Castle, Austria. Karl was a grandnephew of the man he succeeded, Emperor Franz Joseph I. Because of Archduke Franz Ferdinand's morganatic marriage barring his own children from rights of succession, Charles I was next in line to the throne when Franz Ferdinand died. He knew the danger World War I posed and that it was likely to prove to be the undoing of the Habsburg dynasty. Thus he quickly sought a means of negotiating a separate peace with the allies. Because he was regarded as weak, his attempts were unsuccessful. Eventually, he was forced into what largely amounted to economic and military union with Germany following a meeting with the German kaiser, Wilhelm II, at Spa on 11 May 1918.

Charles I's country and the Habsburg dynasty had both reached their tipping point and his efforts to save the sinking ship failed. When Germany was compelled to admit defeat, the Austro-Hungary Empire collapsed internally. Now there was no stopping the revolutions and revolts exploding around Vienna, Prague, and Budapest. At the moment of truth, this gentle man could not bring himself to suppress the revolts and revolutions: "Within two years of Franz Joseph's death the Dual Monarchy had become a cast-off relic of history. The good intentions of Emperor Charles — his proposals for federalist restructuring of his realm and, in particular, his desire for an early negotiated peace — were frustrated by the sheer weight of powerful interests massed against their attainment. Austria-Hungary was so closely integrated militarily with Germany that Vienna lost all independent diplomatic options."[9]

Habsburg properties were confiscated; insignia were torn down, and hardship existed for many families in Vienna, especially for those dependent on Habsburg state pensions. In November 1918 Emperor Charles signed a message at Schönbrunn to his peoples renouncing all participation in the affairs of state. The official end of the Habsburg Empire came on 11 November 1918 when Emperor Charles 1 (Karl Franz Joseph), King of Hungary, King of Bohemia and Croatia, and Galicia and Lodomeria made his famous proclamation: "Filled now as ever with unchangeable love for my people I will no longer set my person as a barrier to their free development.... The people have now taken over the government through its representatives."[10] He never abdicated, but retired with the empress and their children to the shooting-lodge of Eckartsau in Marchfeld to the northeast of the capital, thus ending six centuries of Habsburg power and rule in Europe. (On 3 October 2004 the tragic "last Emperor" Charles was beatified by Pope John Paul II for his valiant but unsuccessful attempts to end World War I.)

At the beginning of just about anything that's considered to be positive, there is a general state of excitement or enthusiasm. World War I for many Austrians brought about a feeling of change — of optimism. The mobilization of Austrian troops created a feeling of unity "as never before, thousands and hundreds of thousands felt what they should have felt in peace time, that they belonged together."[11] Many countries in Europe felt a surge of positive emotions at the beginning of World War I. Four years later that enthusiasm had vanished and was replaced by pessimistic feelings, or what Gertrude Stein told Ernest Hemingway, "*une generation perdue*,"[12] or "Lost Generation," because those who fought the war never really recovered from the experience. The period immediately following the war was one for mourning and one for erecting memorials in thousands of towns large and small throughout Europe and America.

A kind of existential spirit pervaded the soldiers who returned from war, many of whom were physical or mentally (or both) wounded. The feeling that they were doing something good for their country and they would be justly rewarded for their valor just didn't materialize. Writers of the lost generation captured much of that spirit — the emotionally barren hopelessness — in their literary works for they, too, considered themselves lost. The spirit embraced the work Ernest Hemingway, F. Scott Fitzgerald, John Dos Passos, e.e. cummings, Archibald MacLeish, and Hart Crane, among others.

Gertrude Stein captured it in her work *The Autobiography of Alice B. Toklas* (1933), actually Stein's own autobiography. Hemingway used it as an epigraph to *The Sun Also Rises* (1926), which was a naturalistic and shocking expression of postwar disillusionment. It was a novel that captured the attitudes of a hard-drinking, fast-living set of disillusioned young expatriates in postwar Paris. Dos Passos wrote the antiwar story *Three Soldiers*, which brought him considerable recognition. His novel *Manhattan Transfer* reveals the extent of his pessimism, as he indicated the hopeless futility of life in an American city. F. Scott Fitzgerald wrote about the jazz age, a time of drinking and frivolity meant to mask feelings of depression. Fitzgerald's Gatsby is the story of a somewhat refined and wealthy bootlegger whose morality is contrasted with the hypocritical attitude of most of his well-heeled acquaintances.

The Viennese also experienced these feelings, but even if Vienna failed to secure victory it did survive. The dissolution of the Habsburg dynasty represented a stage in the evolution of a new and highly promising era of cultural achievements. A cultural awakening began with people like Sigmund Freud, Gustav Mahler, Otto Wagner, Adolf Loos, George Lukacs, Karl Mannheim, Franz Kafka and Ludwig Wittgenstein. With the brilliance of their contributions, life could not have been entirely without merit. It is true that much of this "cultural sagacity" was directed against the society from which it sprang. Franz Kafka in his *Metamorphosis* was, indeed, a devastating critique of it. It is also true that a very large number of the leading cultural and intellectual figures were of a Jewish emancipatory background.[13]

A significant part of the infrastructure and organizations responsible for the high standard of living in contemporary Vienna were created after World War I. The amazing art nouveau architecture inspired by such giants as Otto Wagner, Josef Hoffmann, Joseph Maria Olbrich and Adolf Loos in Vienna are still on display today. New schools were built; there was even a new project that would have been most dear to Empress Elisabeth — the construction of the Steinhof insane asylum.

Rarely have so many artists and doctors and scientists flourished in the remaking of their city and society. Drs. Bruer and Freud would establish psychiatry and collaborate on a seminal work, *Studies in Hysteria*. For the insane, instead of boring holes in people's heads to relieve them of their demon spirits, Freud would create the humane "talking cure." Perhaps the most widely recognized Austrian scientist of this century, Freud's theory and therapy penetrated to the United States

While Vienna has always been known for its music since the days of Hayden, Mozart and Beethoven, a renewed burst of creativity occurred with composers and conductors such as Gustav Mahler, Johannes Brahms, Arnold Schonberg, Johann Strauss, Jr., Fritz Kreisler, Franz Lehar, Alban Berg, Anton Webernand and others. The philharmonic concerts of a world-renowned orchestra conducted under various maestros were unparalleled in continental Europe. In poetry and theatre, the works of Friedrich Nietzsche and Sigmund Freud inspired the works of Hugo von Hofmannsthal and Arthur Schnitzler.

Viennese artist Gustav Klimt, known for simplified realism with an ornamental style of the female body, was actually famous while he was alive rather than posthumously. In addition to *The Kiss*, he was also famous for his murals. At the Burgtheater he recreated the theater of antiquity in Taormina, Sicily. The stairwell wall is adorned with a depiction of the London Globe Theater and the final scene from Shakespeare's *Romeo and Juliet*. Egon Schiele, Koloman Moser, and Rudolf von Alt, to name just a few, were international sensations in their day and founders of the Austrian Secession movement that dominated artistic style and thought throughout Europe.

Fortunately, Franz Joseph's children were spared seeing their beloved Austria ripped apart because of the spectacle of Hitler's ascendancy over German lands. Valerie died in September 1924; her sister Gisela remained in Bavaria and died in Munich in July 1932. Katharina Schratt did live to see the ascendancy of Hitler. When he entered Vienna, with spectators giving stiff right-arm salutes hailing their chief, Katharina defiantly closed the blinds to her windows. She lived until 1940 and died at 86. Rudolf's wife, Stephanie, died in 1945 in western Hungary.

The Habsburgs gathered dynastic power and momentum from the early twelfth century until the end of World War I. The impact of the dynasty is evident in every country it ruled: "Its greatness, the originality, and the wide appeal abroad of the Habsburg empire's cultural accomplishments and of the wealth of ideas generated in the last century of its existence makes it conceivable that this cultural impact may last even longer than the six centuries of the Habsburg Dynasty's existence."[14] The legacy of the Habsburg dynasty is seen in its people, who are proud of their heritage and of the House of Habsburg. In the dynasty's twilight this was vividly characterized by Emperor Franz Joseph and Empress Elisabeth. Schönbrunn, with its fading splendor of the monarch, was witness to the Habsburg dynasty's end. But it is also a witness to its cultural message to the world in an ever widening sense that had now just begun.

Appendix A

Chronology

1830	Franz Joseph born on 18 August in Vienna.
1835	Death of Emperor Francis I of Austria: accession of Ferdinand I.
1837	Elisabeth born 24 December in Munich.
1848	Formation of separate Hungarian ministry on 17 March.
	Franz Joseph joins battle at Santa Lucia on 6 May; field marshal Josef Radetzky defeats Italy.
	Ferdinand abdicates; Franz Joseph's accession to the throne on 2 December.
	Hungary defeated with Russian help; Hungary surrenders to Russians at Vilagos, 13 August.
1852	Austrian statesman Felix of Schwarzenberg dies.
1853	Assassination attempt on Franz Joseph.
	Franz and Elisabeth become engaged on 18 August.
1853	Crimean War. Russia loses her preeminence in the Balkans; in many ways Austria is the biggest loser.
1854	Franz Joseph and Elisabeth wed on 24 April in Augustinerkirche, Vienna.
1855	Birth of Archduchess Sophie, 5 March.
1856	Birth of Archduchess Gisela, 15 July.
	Treaty of Paris, 30 May.
1857	City walls of Vienna razed, 20 December.
1858	Birth of Crown Prince Rudolf, 21 August.
1859	Franco-Austrian War, April–July.
	Death of Metternich, 11 June.
	Austria wages war against Sardinia and France.
	Austria loses Lombardy.

1862	Otto von Bismarck becomes Prussian prime minister, 29 September.
1864	Archduke Ferdinand Maximilian becomes Emperor of Mexico.
1865	Opening of Ringstrasse.
1866	War between Austria and Prussia. Defeat at Koniggratz, 3 July. Austria lost dominance over Prussia. Dissolution of the German Confederation. Loss of Venice to Italy.
1867	Franz Joseph crowned King of Hungary, Elisabeth Queen of Hungary. Maximilian executed in Mexico, 19 June. Dual monarchy of Austria-Hungary established. Hungary given full internal autonomy. Andrássy serves as imperial and royal foreign minister.
1870-71	German Empire created.
1872	Death of Archduchess Sophie, 28 May. Death of Emperor Ferdinand I. Franz Joseph is the principal heir.
1879	Conclusion of Dual Alliance between Germany and Austria.
1881	Marriage of Crown Prince Rudolf and Stephanie of Belgium.
1882	Triple Alliance: German, Austria and Italy, 20 May.
1886	Franz Joseph meets Katharina Schratt. Death of Ludwig II of Bavaria, 13 June.
1888	Wilhelm II succeeds to German throne.
1889	Death of Crown Prince Rudolf at Mayerling.
1898	Assassination of Empress Elisabeth in Geneva, 10 September.
1914	Assassination of Franz Ferdinand in Sarajevo, 28 June. Austro-Hungarian ultimatum issued to Serbia, 23 July. Austria declares war on Serbia, 28 July. Russian general mobilization, 30 July. German ultimatum to France and Russia, 31 July. German declaration of war on France, 3 August. British and French declaration of war on Austria-Hungary, 12 August.
1916	Death of Franz Joseph in Vienna, 21 November.

Appendix B

The following members of the Habsburg dynasty were rulers of the Holy Roman Empire:

> Rudolf I, ruled 1273–1291
> Albert I, ruled 1298–1308
> Albert II, ruled 1438–1439
> Frederick III, ruled 1440–1493
> Maximilian I, ruled 1493–1519
> Charles V, ruled 1519–1558
> Ferdinand I, ruled 1558–1564
> Maximilian II, ruled 1564–1576
> Rudolf II, ruled 1576–1612
> Matthias, ruled 1612–1619
> Ferdinand II, ruled 1619–1637
> Ferdinand III, ruled 1637–1657
> Leopold I, ruled 1658–1705
> Joseph I, ruled 1705–1711
> Charles VI, ruled 1711–1740
> Charles VII, ruled 1742–1745 (Habsburg-Wittelsbach)
> Joseph II, ruled 1765–1790 (Habsburg-Lorraine)
> Leopold II, ruled 1790–1792 (Habsburg-Lorraine)
> Francis II, ruled 1792–1806 (Habsburg-Lorraine)

The rule of the Habsburg dynasty was ended by World War I: The last significant emperor was Franz Joseph. Briefly the Habsburg Kaiser, Charles I (Germany: Karl I), ruled after Franz Joseph's death, until 1918.

Notes

Chapter One

1. Josef Redlich, *Emperor Francis Joseph of Austria: A Biography* (New York: Macmillan, 1929), p. 40.
2. Ibid., p. 43.
3. Ibid., p. 46.
4. Alan Sked, *The Decline and Fall of the Habsburg Empire 1815–1918* (White Plains, NY: Longman, 2001), p. 1.
5. Editors of Time-Life Books, *What Life Was Like at Empire's End: Austro-Hungarian Empire AD 1848–1918* (Alexandria, VA: Time-Life Books, 2000), p. 16.
6. *Franz* Joseph is called by his German name, not *Francis* Joseph. The German spelling of his surname *Joseph* and not *Josef* is adhered to as well. (The emperor himself spelled his name with a "ph.")
7. Hans Kohn, "Reflections on Austrian History," *Austrian History Yearbook* 1 (1965): pp. 4–22.
8. Anatol Murad, *Franz Joseph I of Austria and His Empire* (New York: Twayne, 1968), p. 9.
9. Redlich, p. 14.
10. Ibid., p. 9.
11. Lady Mary Wortley Montague, *Selected Letters* (New York: Penguin, 1997), p. 211.
12. David Cairns, ed., *The Memoirs of Hector Berlioz* (New York: Alfred A. Knopf, 1912), p. 392.
13. Harold C. Schonberg, *The Lives of Great Composers* (New York: W.W. Norton, 1997), p. 311.
14. Cliff Eisen and Simon P. Keefe, ed., *The Cambridge Mozart Encyclopedia* (New York: Cambridge University Press, 2006), p. 268.
15. Carl Eduard Vehse, *Memoirs of the Court, Aristocracy, and Diplomacy of Austria*, vol. 2, trans. Franz K. Demmler (London: Longman, Brown, Green & Longmans, 1856), p. 314.
16. Adolphe Theirs and D. Forbes Campbell, *History of the Consulate and the Empire of France Under Napoleon*, vol. 9–10 (London: Henry Colburn, 1845), p. 82.
17. Gustave Flaubert, *Correspondance, 1857–1863*, ed. Maurice Nadeau (Lausanne: Editions Rencontre, 1965), p. 63.

Chapter Two

1. James Harvey Robinson, *Readings in Modern European History: A Collection of Extracts from the Sources Chosen with the Purpose of Illustrating Some of the Chief Phases of the Last Two Hundred Years*, vol. 1 (Boston: Ginn & Company, 1908–09), p. 341.
2. John Lord, *Beacon Lights of History*, vol. 9 (FQ ebooks, 2010), pp. 30–132.
3. Ibid., pp. 30–132.
4. Charles Maurice Talleyrand-Perigord, *Memoirs of the Prince de Talleyrand*, vols. I–III, ed., Duc de Broglie. ed, trans. Rapheal de Beaufort (New York: G.P. Putnam, 1895), p. 4.
5. Klemens von Metternich, *Memoirs of Prince Metternich*, vol. II, trans. Gerald W. Smith. (New York: Howard Fertig, 1970), p. 258.
6. Ibid., p. 135
7. Ottila Regina Kohlberg, *The Policy*

of Prince Metternich at the Congress of Vienna (Charleston, SC: Nabu Press, 2010), p. 111.

8. Daniel Unowsky, *The Pomp and Politics of Patriotism: Imperial Celebrations in Habsburg* (Lafayette, IN: Perdue University Press, 2005), p. 78.

9. Gregory Fremont-Barnes, *Encyclopedia of the Age of Political Revolutions and New Ideologies, 1760–1815* (Westport, CT: Greenwood, 2007), p. 473.

10. Ibid.

11. Unowsky, p. 23.

12. Joan Haslip, *The Crown of Mexico: Maximilian and Empress Carlota* (New York: Avon, 1973), p. 17.

13. George Richard Marek, *The Eagles Die: Franz Joseph, Elisabeth, and Their Austria* (White Plains, NY: Harper & Row, 1974), p. 39.

14. Alan Sked, *The Decline and Fall of the Habsburg Empire 1815–1918* (White Plains, NY: Longman, 2001), p. 55.

15. The names of these two cities weren't combined until 1831.

16. Robert A. Kann, *A History of the Habsburg Empire 1526–1918* (Berkeley: University of California Press, 1974), p. 300.

17. Anatol Murad, *Franz Joseph I of Austria and His Empire* (New York: Twayne, 1968), p. 64.

18. Editors of Time-Life Books, *What Life Was Like at Empire's End: Austro-Hungarian Empire AD 1848–1918* (Alexandria, VA: Time-Life Books, 2000), p. 18.

19. Murad, p. 97.

20. Editors of Time-Life Books, p. 16.

21. Alan Palmer, *Twilight of the Habsburgs: The Life and Times of Emperor Francis Joseph* (New York: Atlantic Monthly Press, 1994), p. 47.

22. Sked, p. 93.

23. Murad, p. 39.

24. Ibid., p. 33.

25. Egon Caesar Corti, *Mensch und Herrscher: Wege und Schicksale Kaiser Franz Joseph I, zwischen Thronbesteigung und Berliner Kongress* (Graz: Verlag Styria, 1952), pp. 43–45.

26. Murad, p. 137.

27. Sked, p. 137.

28. Murad, p. 57.

29. Jonathan Steinberg, *Bismarck: A Life* (New York: University of Oxford Press, 2011), p. 29.

30. Ibid.

31. Ibid., p. 35.

32. Bismarck to Louis von Klitzing, 10 September 1843.

33. Otto Pflanze, *Bismarck and the Development of Germany: The Period of Unification 1815–1871* (Princeton: Princeton University Press, 1971), p. 177.

34. See H. Friedjung, *The Struggle for Supremacy in Germany, 1859–1866*, 10th ed. (New York: Russell & Russell, 1966).

35. Steinberg, p. 257.

36. Ibid., p. 3.

37. John C. G. Rohl, Trans. Sheila de Bellaigue. *Wilhelm II: The Kaiser's Personal Monarchy, 1888–1900* (New York: Cambridge University Press, 2004), p. 316.

38. Kann, p. 317.

Chapter Three

1. Anatol Murad, *Franz Joseph I of Austria and His Empire* (New York: Twayne, 1968), p. 96.

2. Egon Caesar Corti and Hans Sokol, *Franz Joseph* (Graz: Verlag Styria, 1960).

3. Brigitte Hamann, *The Reluctant Empress* (Berlin: Ullstein, 1998), p. 52.

4. Ibid.

5. Jasper Ridley, *Maximilian and Juárez* (New York: Ticknor & Fields, 1992).

6. George Richard Marek, *The Eagles Die: Franz Joseph, Elisabeth, and Their Austria* (New York: Harper & Row, 1974), p. 57.

7. Hamann, p. 52.

8. Alan Palmer, *Twilight of the Habsburgs: The Life and Times of Emperor Francis Joseph* (New York: Atlantic Monthly Press, 1994), p. 13.

9. Murad, p. 60.

10. Palmer, p. 15.

11. Marek, p. 59.

12. Ibid., p.103.

13. Palmer, p. x.

14. Ibid., p. xi.

15. Steven Beller, *Francis Joseph* (New York: Addison Wesley Longman, 1996), p. 100.

16. Alice Freifeld, *Nationalism and the Crowd in Liberated Hungary: 1848–1914* (Baltimore: Johns Hopkins University, 2000), p. 128.

17. Joseph Redlich, *Emperor Francis Joseph of Austria: A Biography* (New York: Macmillan, 1929), p. 60.

18. Jean Bérenger, *The History of the*

Habsburg Empire 1700–1918 (London: Longman, 1997), p. 226.
19. Hamann, p. 221.
20. Marek, p. 230.
21. Ibid.
22. Eugen Ketterl and Cissy Klastersky *The Emperor Franz Joseph I: An Intimate Study*, trans. M. Ostheide (Boston: Stratford, 1929).
23. Beller, p. 57.
24. Editors of Time-Life Books, *What Life Was Like at Empire's End: Austro-Hungarian Empire AD 1848–1918* (Alexandria, VA: Time-Life Books, 2000). p. 39.
25. Cissy Klastersky, *Der Alte Kaiser wie nur Einer ihn sah. Der wahrheitsgetreue Bericht seines Leibkammerdieners Eugen Ketterl* (Vienna: Gerold & Co., Universitäts-Buchhandlung, 1929), p. 163.
26. Robert A. Kann, *History of the Habsburg Empire 1526–1918* (Berkeley: University of California Press, 1974), p. 310.
27. Murad, p. 2.
28. Beller, p. 57.
29. Ibid., p. 58.
30. Ibid., p. 57.

Chapter Four

1. Bertita Harding, *Golden Fleece: The Story of Franz Joseph & Elisabeth of Austria* (New York: Bobbs-Merrill, 1937), p. 14.
2. Ibid., p. 13.
3. Ibid., p. 18.
4. Ibid., p. 19.
5. George Richard Marek, *The Eagles Die: Franz Joseph, Elisabeth, and Their Austria* (New York: Harper & Row, 1974), p. 96.
6. Sigrid-Maria Größing, *Sisi und ihre Familie* (Vienna: Ueberreuter Carl, 2005).
7. Brigitte Hamann, *The Reluctant Empress* (Berlin: Ullstein, 1998), p. 348.
8. Harding, p. 19.
9. Clara Tschudi and E. M. Cope, *Elizabeth, Empress of Austria and Queen of Hungary* (New York: E.P. Dutton, 1901), p. 13.
10. Ibid., p. 14.
11. Marek, p. 223.
12. Harding, p. 131.
13. Ibid., p. 96.
14. Hamann, p. 281.
15. Tschudi and Cope, p. 193.
16. Ibid., p. 191.
17. Hamann, p. 284.
18. Tschudi and Cope, p. 3.
19. Marek, p. 136,
20. Marie Louise von Wallersee-Larisch, *Kaiserin Elisabeth und ich* (Paderborn, Germany: Salzwasser Verlag, 1933), p. 74.
21. Wilfrid Blunt, *The Dream King: Ludwig II of Bavaria* (New York: Viking Press, 1970), p. 98.
22. Desmond Chapman-Huston, *Ludwig II: The Mad King of Bavaria* (New York: Dorset Press, 1990), p. 208.
23. Blunt, p. 24.
24. Ibid., p. 212.
25. Joan Haslip, *The Emperor and the Actress* (New York: The Dial Press, 1982), p. 42.
26. Marek, p. 197.

Chapter Five

1. Carlile Aylmer Macartney, *The Social Revolution in Austria* (Cambridge: Cambridge University Press, 1926), p. 301.
2. Bertita Harding, *Golden Fleece: The Story of Franz Joseph & Elisabeth of Austria* (New York: Bobbs-Merrill, 1937) p. 34.
3. George Richard Marek, *The Eagles Die: Franz Joseph, Elisabeth, and Their Austria* (New York: Harper & Row, 1974), p. 111.
4. Editors of Time-Life Books, *What Life Was Like at Empire's End: Austro-Hungarian Empire AD 1848–1918* (Alexandria, VA: Time-Life Books, 2000), p. 22.
5. Brigitte Hamann, *The Reluctant Empress* (Berlin: Ullstein, 1998), p. 13.
6. Harding, p. 27.
7. Marek, *The Eagles Die: Franz Joseph, Elisabeth, and Their Austria* (New York: Harper & Row, 1974), p. 99.
8. Hamann, pp. 13–14; Harding, p. 39.
9. Harding, p. 39.
10. Ibid.
11. Marek, pp. 99–100. Based on Wilhelm von Weckbecker *Memoirs*, 1929.
12. Hamann, pp. 10–11.
13. Harding, p. 36.
14. Marek, p. 101.
15. Ibid., pp. 101–102.
16. Harding, p. 43.
17. Anton Langer, *Dies Buch gehört der Kaiserin. Eine Volksstimme aus Österreich* (Vienna: Österreichischen Akademie der Wissenschaften, 1854), pp. 8–11.
18. Harding, p. 44.
19. Marek, p. 101.
20. Harding, pp. 49–50.

21. Ibid.
22. Ibid., p. 53.
23. Hamann, p. 38.
24. Ibid.
25. Harding, p. 60.
26. Ibid., p. 66.
27. Hamann, p. 44.
28. Ibid., p. 46.
29. Ibid.
30. Ibid., p. 220.
31. Harding, p. 69.
32. Max II Papers, Schönbrunn, 12 July 1849.
33. Palmer, p. 78.
34. Ibid.
35. Daryl Meakes, *Drunkcow Landmines* (West Conshohoken, PA: Infinity, 2004), p. 216.
36. Marek, p. 102.

Chapter Six

1. Bertita Harding, *Golden Fleece: The Story of Franz Joseph & Elisabeth of Austria* (New York: Bobbs-Merrill, 1937), p. 77.
2. Ibid., p. 80.
3. Briton Hadden and Henry R. Luce, *Time*, vol. 29, part 1, 1937, p. 86.
4. Brigitte Hamann, *The Reluctant Empress* (Berlin: Ullstein, 1998), p. 67.
5. Ibid.
6. Ibid., p. 68.
7. Harding, p. 241.
8. Hamann, p. 78.
9. George Richard Marek, *The Eagles Die: Franz Joseph, Elisabeth, and Their Austria* (New York: Harper & Row, 1974), p. 257.
10. Hamann, p. 120.
11. Clara Tschudi and E. M. Cope, *Elizabeth, Empress of Austria and Queen of Hungary* (New York: E.P. Dutton, 1901), p. 108.
12. Editors of Time-Life Books, *What Life Was Like at Empire's End: Austro-Hungarian Empire AD 1848–1918* (Alexandria, VA: Time-Life Books, 2000), p. 109.
13. Ibid., p. 110.
14. Harding, p. 238.
15. Alan Palmer, *Twilight of the Habsburgs: The Life and Times of Emperor Francis Joseph* (New York: Atlantic Monthly Press, 1994), p. 149.
16. Barry Deneberg, *The Princess Bride* (New York: Scholastic, 2004), p. 98.
17. Marek, p. 256.
18. Harding, p. 239.
19. J. P. Bled, *Franz Joseph*, trans. T. Bridgeman (Oxford: Blackwell, 1992), pp. 211–212.
20. Rudolf von Habsburg, *Majestät, ich warne Sie: Geheime und privat Schrifen*, ed. Brigitte Hamann (Vienna: Amaltheas, 1979), p. 10.
21. Editors of Time-Life Books, p. 44.
22. Marek, p. 262.
23. Ibid., p. 258.
24. Ibid., p. 257.
25. Ibid., p. 258.
26. Ibid., p. 261.
27. Ibid., p. 258.
28. Ibid., p. 256.
29. Ibid., p. 257.
30. Ibid., p. 258.
31. Ibid.
32. Ibid.
33. Clara Tschudi and E. M. Cope, *Elizabeth, Empress of Austria and Queen of Hungary* (New York: E.P. Dutton, 1901), p. 149.
34. Hamann, p. 331.
35. Ibid., p. 332.
36. Harding, p. 282.
37. *New York Times*, 1 August 1890.
38. Joan Haslip, *The Emperor and the Actress* (New York: The Dial Press, 1982), p. 97.
39. Hamann, p. 341.
40. Corti papers copied from Valerie's diary.
41. Friedjung papers, interview with M. Festetics, 23 March 1909.
42. Cited in John Lehmann and Richard Bassett, *Vienna: A Traveller's Companion* (London: Constable, 1988), p. 98.
43. Palmer, p. 249.
44. L.D. Hankoff and Bernice Einsidler, eds., *Suicide: Theory and Clinical Aspects* (Littleton, MA: PSG, 1979), p. 171.
45. Marek, p. 265.
46. Editors of Time-Life Books, p. 47.
47. Marek, p. 364.
48. Hamann, p. 348.
49. Haslip, p. 133.
50. Tschudi and Cope, p. 226.

Chapter Seven

1. Alan Palmer, *Twilight of the Habsburgs: The Life and Times of Emperor Francis Joseph* (New York: Atlantic Monthly Press, 1994), p. 267.
2. Ibid., p. 268.
3. Bertita Harding, *Golden Fleece: The*

Story of Franz Joseph & Elisabeth of Austria (New York: Bobbs-Merrill, 1937), p. 339.
　4. Joan Haslip, *The Emperor and the Actress* (New York: The Dial Press, 1982), p. 33.
　5. Brigitte Hamann, *The Reluctant Empress* (Berlin: Ullstein, 1998), p. 132.
　6. H. Eugene Lehman, *Lives of England's Monarchs* (Chapel Hill: University of North Carolina Press, 2004), Chapter 33: King George II (1727–1760), pp. 351–358.
　7. Hamann, p. 307.
　8. Palmer, p. 236.
　9. Haslip, p. 40.
　10. George Richard Marek, *The Eagles Die: Franz Joseph, Elisabeth, and Their Austria* (New York: Harper & Row, 1974), p. 218.
　11. Ibid., p. 211.
　12. Harding, p. 324.
　13. Marek, p. 218.
　14. Clara Tschudi and E. M. Cope, *Elizabeth, Empress of Austria and Queen of Hungary* (New York: E.P. Dutton, 1901), p. 45.
　15. Marek, p. 218.
　16. Ibid., p. 390.
　17. Tschudi and Cope, p. 44.
　18. Ibid., p. 45.
　19. Harding, p. 324.
　20. Palmer, p. 243.
　21. Hamann, p. 314.
　22. Marek, p. 213.
　23. Palmer, p. 243.
　24. Haslip, p. 69.
　25. Palmer, p. 243.
　26. Harding, p. 338.
　27. *New York Times*, 12 January 1918.
　28. Marek, p. 391.
　29. Ibid.
　30. *New York Times*, 12 January 1918.
　31. *The Catholic Herald*, 27 September 1935, p. 16.
　32. Haslip, p. 53.
　33. Lyndall Gordon, *Vindication: A Life of Mary Wollstonecraft* (New York: HarperCollins, 2005), p. 23.
　34. Marek, p. 195.
　35. Ibid., p. 111.

Chapter Eight

　1. Brigitte Hamann, *The Reluctant Empress* (Berlin: Ullstein, 1998), p. 145.
　2. Ibid., p. 146.
　3. Ibid., p. 147.
　4. Ibid., p. 166.

　5. Ida Miriam Bobula, *Origin of the Hungarian Nation* (Aster Park, FL: Danubian Press, 1966).
　6. Hamann, pp. 64–65.
　7. Karl Tschuppik, *The Empress of Austria* (London: Brentanos, 1930), p. 46.
　8. George Richard Marek, *The Eagles Die: Franz Joseph, Elisabeth, and Their Austria* (New York: Harper & Row, 1974), p. 143.
　9. Hamann, p. 148.
　10. Marek, p. 141.
　11. Clara Tschudi and E. M. Cope, *Elizabeth, Empress of Austria and Queen of Hungary* (New York: E.P. Dutton, 1901), p. 172.
　12. Marek, p. 141.
　13. Joan Haslip, *The Lonely Empress* (Cleveland: World, 1965), p. 188.
　14. Stephen Sisa, *The Spirit of Hungry: A Panorama of Hungarian History and Culture* (Toronto: The Rakoczi Foundation, 1995), p. 172.
　15. Ibid.
　16. Alan Sked, *The Decline and Fall of the Habsburg Empire 1815–1918* (White Plains, NY: Longman, 2001), p. 231.
　17. Marek, p. 149.
　18. Hamann, p. 174.
　19. Bertita Harding, *Golden Fleece: The Story of Franz Joseph & Elisabeth of Austria* (New York: Bobbs-Merrill, 1937), pp. 213–214.
　20. Hamann, p. 174.
　21. Sisa, p. 178.
　22. Harding, p. 213.
　23. Sisa, p. 171.
　24. Ibid., p. 172.
　25. Andrew Sinclair, *Death by Fame: A Life of Elisabeth Empress of Austria* (New York: St. Martin's Press, 1998), p. 63.
　26. Sisa, p. 177.
　27. Sked, p. 189.
　28. John Komlos, *The Habsburg Monarchy as a Customs Union, Economic Development in Austria-Hungary in the Nineteenth Century* (New York: Guilford, 1983), p. 218.
　29. David F. Good, *The Economic Rise of the Habsburg Empire, 1750–1914* (Berkeley: University of California Press, 1984).
　30. Sked, p. 191.

Chapter Nine

　1. George Richard Marek, *The Eagles Die: Franz Joseph, Elisabeth, and Their Aus-*

tria (New York: Harper & Row, 1974), p. 87.
  2. Steven Beller, *Francis Joseph* (New York: Addison Wesley Longman, 1996), p. 65
  3. Joan Haslip, *The Emperor and the Actress* (New York: The Dial Press, 1982), p. 249.
  4. Jonathan Steinberg, *Bismarck: A Life* (New York: University of Oxford Press, 2011), p. 144.
  5. J. P. Bled, *Franz Joseph*, trans. T. Bridgeman (Oxford: Blackwell, 1992).
  6. Robert A. Kann, *History of the Hapsburg Empire 1526–1918* (Berkeley: University of California Press, 1974), p. 519.
  7. Joseph Redlich, *Emperor Francis Joseph of Austria: A Biography* (New York: Macmillan, 1929).
  8. Edward Crankshaw, *The Fall of the House of Habsburg* (New York: Viking Penguin, 1963), p. 306.
  9. Steinberg, p. 71.
  10. Marek, p. 111.
  11. Clara Tschudi and E. M. Cope, *Elizabeth, Empress of Austria and Queen of Hungary* (New York: E.P. Dutton, 1901), p. 45.
  12. Ibid., p. 48.
  13. Ibid., p. 133.
  14. Brigitte Hamann, *The Reluctant Empress* (Berlin: Ullstein, 1998), p. 72.
  15. Ibid.
  16. Stephen Sisa, *The Spirit of Hungry: A Panorama of Hungarian History and Culture* (Toronto: The Rakoczi Foundation, 1995).
  17. Hamann, p. 72.
  18. Ibid., p. 117.
  19. Marek, p. 198.
  20. Marie Louise von Maerker-Branden and Elsa Wallersee-Larisch, *Secrets of a Royal House* (London: J. Long, 1936), p. 121.
  21. Hamann, p. 64.
  22. Tschudi and Cope, p. 200.
  23. Alan Palmer, *Twilight of the Habsburgs: The Life and Times of Emperor Francis Joseph* (New York: Atlantic Monthly Press, 1994), p. 121.
  24. Hamann, p. 106.
  25. Ibid., p. 101.
  26. Hamann, p. 58.
  27. Tschudi and Cope, p. 89.
  28. Hamann, p. 55.
  29. Tschudi and Cope, p. 205.
  30. Marek, p. 107.
  31. Ibid.
  32. Hamann, p. 53.
  33. Ibid.
  34. Marek, p. 100.
  35. Hamann, p. 95.
  36. Ibid., p. 62.
  37. Ibid., p. 58.

Chapter Ten

  1. Stephen Sisa, *The Spirit of Hungry: A Panorama of Hungarian History and Culture* (Toronto: The Rakoczi Foundation, 1995), p. 171.
  2. Clara Tschudi and E. M. Cope, *Elizabeth, Empress of Austria and Queen of Hungary* (New York: E.P. Dutton, 1901), p. 84.
  3. Brigitte Hamann, *The Reluctant Empress* (Berlin: Ullstein, 1998), p. 150.
  4. Edward Morgan Alborough De Burg, *Elisabeth, Empress of Austria: A Memoir* (London: Hutchinson & Company, 1899).
  5. Hamann, pp. 146–154.
  6. Ibid., p. 119.
  7. Tschudi and Cope, p. 170.
  8. De Burgh, p. 57.
  9. Anatol Murad, *Franz Joseph I of Austria and His Empire* (New York: Twayne, 1968) p. 111.
  10. George Richard Marek, *The Eagles Die: Franz Joseph, Elisabeth, and Their Austria* (New York: Harper & Row, 1974), p. 127.
  11. Hamann, p. 132.
  12. Ibid., p. 138.
  13. Albert Leon Guerard, *Five Masters of French Romance: Anatol France, Pierre Loti, Paul Bourget, Maurice Barres, Romain Roland* (New York: Charles Scribner's Sons, 1916), pp. 20–25.
  14. Marek, p. 191.
  15. Ibid.
  16. The much younger and more athletic Countess Irma Sztaray, also a Hungarian, finally replaced Marie Festetics. Accompanied by Irma, the empress spent her final years wandering though Europe and around the Mediterranean.
  17. Irma Countess Sztaray, *Aus den letzten Jahren der Kaiserin Elisabeth* (Wein: A. Holzhausen, 1909*)*, p. 203.
  18. Sisa, p. 174.
  19. De Burgh, p. 309.
  20. Stephen, Sisa, *The Spirit of Hungary: A Panorama of Hungarian History and Culture* (Ontario: The Rakoczi Foundation, 1995), p. 174.

21. Hamann, pp. 173–174.
22. De Burgh, p 323.

Chapter Eleven

1. Alan Palmer, *Twilight of the Habsburgs: The Life and Times of Emperor Francis Joseph* (New York: Atlantic Monthly Press, 1994), p. 300.
2. Gordon Brook-Shepherd, *Archduke of Sarajevo: The Romance and Tragedy of Franz Ferdinand of Austria* (New York: Little, Brown, 1984), p. 19.
3. Tibor Ivan Berend, *Decades in Crisis: Central and Eastern Europe Before World War I* (Berkeley: University of California Press, 1998), p. 61.
4. Alan Sked, *The Decline and Fall of the Habsburg Empire 1815–1918* (White Plains, NY: Longman, 2001), p. 180.
5. Eugen Ketterl and Cissy Klastersky, *The Emperor Francis Joseph I: An Intimate Study*, trans. M. Ostheide. (Boston: Stratford, 1929). Cited in Alan Palmer, *Twilight of the Habsburgs: The Life and Times of Emperor Francis Joseph* (New York: Atlantic Monthly Press, 1994), p. 317.
6. George Richard Marek, *The Eagles Die: Franz Joseph, Elisabeth, and Their Austria* (New York: Harper & Row, 1974), p. 415.
7. Palmer, p. 314.
8. Steven Beller, *Francis Joseph* (New York: Addison Wesley Longman, 1996), p. 157.
9. Bertita Harding, *Golden Fleece: The Story of Franz Joseph & Elisabeth of Austria*. (New York: Bobbs-Merrill, 1937), p. 342.
10. Merek, p. 433.
11. Ibid.
12. Ibid., 434.
13. Edward F. Willis, *Prince Lichnowsky, Ambassador of Peace: A Study of Prewar Diplomacy 1912–1914* (London: Kessinger, 2007), p. 232.
14. Joseph Redlich, *Emperor Francis Joseph of Austria: A Biography* (New York: Macmillan, 1929), p. 497.
15. Palmer, p. 324.
16. Albert Alexander Vinzenz Margutti, *The Emperor Francis Joseph & His Times* (Charleston, SC: Nabu Press, 2010), p. 139.
17. Palmer, p. 324.
18. Marek, p. 437.
19. Joan Haslip, *The Emperor and the Actress* (New York: The Dial Press, 1982), p. 266.
20. Harding, p. 343.
21. Beller, p. 213.
22. Anatol Murad, *Franz Joseph I of Austria and His Empire* (New York: Twayne, 1968), p. 210.
23. A. J. P. Taylor, *The Habsburg Monarchy, 1809–1918: A History of the Austrian Empire and Austria Hungary* (Chicago: University of Chicago Press, 1976), p. 3.
24. Marek, p. 449.
25. Robert A. Kann, *History of the Habsburg Empire 1526–1918* (Berkeley: University of California Press, 1974), p. 483.
26. Murad, p. 212.
27. Sked, p. 217.
28. Marek, p. 442.
29. Margutti, p. 362.
30. Palmer, pp. 277–278.
31. Redlich, p. 530.
32. Marek, p. 465.

Chapter Twelve

1. Piotr Olender, *Russo-Japanese Naval War, 1905*, vol. 1. (Sandomierz: Stratus, 2009–2010), p. 233.
2. Mark D. Steinberg and Vladimir M. Khrustalev, *The Fall of the Romanovs: Political Dreams and Personal Struggles in a time of Revolution* (New Haven: Yale University Press, 1995).
3. Hugh Chisholm, ed., *The Encyclopædia Britannica: A Dictionary of Arts, Sciences, Literature, and General Information* (reprint; Charleston, SC: Nabu Press, 2010), p. 113.
4. Carl Cavanagh Hodge, ed., *Encyclopedia of the Age of Imperialism, 1800–1914* (Westport, CT: Greenwood, 2007), p. 327.
5. Jonathan Steinberg, *Bismarck: A Life* (New York: University of Oxford Press, 2011).
6. Matthew Seligmann and Roderick R. McLean, *Germany from Reich to Republic, 1871–1918: Politics, Hierarchy and Elites* (New York: St. Martin's Press, 2000), p. 171.
7. Paul C. Helmreich, rev. of Roderic Davison, *From Paris to Sevres: The Partition of the Ottoman Empire at the Peace Conference of 1919-1920, Slavic Review*, 34, no. 1 (March 1975): pp. 186–187.
8. Richard C. Frucht, *Eastern Europe: An Introduction to the People, Lands, & Culture*, vol. 1 (Santa Barbara: ABC-CLIO, 2004), p. 24.
9. Alan Palmer, *Twilight of the Habsburgs: The Life and Times of Emperor Francis*

Joseph (New York: Atlantic Monthly Press, 1994), p. 345.

10. Carlile Aylmer Macartney, *The Social Revolution in Austria* (Cambridge: Cambridge University Press, 1926), p. 82.

11. William J. Duiker and Jackson J. Spielvogel, *The Essential World History: Since 1500* (Boston: Wadsworth, Cengage Learning, 2012), p. 569.

12. A. E. Hotchner, *Papa Hemingway: A Personal Memoir* (Cambridge, MA: Da Capo Press, 2004), p. 49.

13. Steven Beller, *Francis Joseph* (New York: Addison Wesley Longman, 1996), p. 175.

14. Robert A. Kann, *History of the Habsburg Empire 1526–1918* (Berkeley: University of California Press, 1974), p. 564.

References

Andrássy, Count Julius. *Bismarck, Andrássy and Their Successors*. New York: Houghton Mifflin, 1927.
Balfour, Michael. *The Kaiser and His Times*. New York: W. W. Norton, 1986.
Beales, Derek Edward Dawson. *Joseph II: Against the World, 1780–1790*, vol. 2. New York: Cambridge University Press, 2009.
Beller, Steven. *Francis Joseph*. New York: Addison Wesley Longman, 1996.
_____. *Vienna and the Jews 1867–1938: A Cultural History*. Cambridge: Cambridge University Press, 1989.
Berend, Tibor Ivan. *Decades in Crisis: Central and Eastern Europe Before World War I*. Berkeley: University of California Press, 1998.
Bérenger, Jean. *The History of the Habsburg Empire 1700–1918*. London: Longman, 1997.
Bled, J.P. *Franz Joseph*. Trans. T. Bridgeman Oxford: Blackwell, 1992.
Blunt, Wilfrid. *The Dream King: Ludwig II of Bavaria*. New York: Viking Press, 1970.
Bobula, Ida Miriam. *Origin of the Hungarian Nation*. Astor Park, FL: Danubian Press, 1966.
Branscombe, Peter, ed. *Heinrich Heine: Selected Verse*. New York: Penguin, 1993.
Bridge, F.R. *The Habsburg Monarchy Among the Great Powers: 1815–1918*. Oxford: Berg, 1991.
Brook-Shepherd, Gordon. *Archduke of Sarajevo: The Romance and Tragedy of Franz Ferdinand of Austria*. New York: Little, Brown, 1984.
_____. *The Austrians: A Thousand-Year Odyssey*. New York: Carroll & Graf, 1996.
Bulletin of the New York Academy of Medicine, 41, no. 2 (Feb. 1965).
Burg, Katerina von. *Elisabeth of Austria: A Life Misunderstood*. London: Windsor, 1991.
Butler, E.M. *Heinrich Heine: A Biography*. Westport, CT: Greenwood, 1970.
Cairns, David, ed. *The Memoirs of Hector Berlioz*. New York: Alfred A. Knopf, 1912.
Carroll, Leslie. *Royal Affairs: A Lusty Romp Through the Extramarital Adventures That Rocked the British Monarchy*. New York: Penguin, 2008.
Cartland, Barbara. *The Private Life of Elizabeth, Empress of Austria*. London: Pyramid Press, 1959.
The Catholic Herald, 27 September 1935.
Channon, Henry. *The Ludwigs of Bavaria*. Leipzig: Pyramid Press, 1934.
Chapman-Huston, Desmond. *Ludwig II: The Mad King of Bavaria*. New York: Dorset Press, 1990.

Chisholm, Hugh, ed. *The Encyclopædia Britannica: A Dictionary of Arts, Sciences, Literature, and General Information.* Reprint. Charleston, SC: Nabu Press, 2010.
Clark, Christopher. *Kaiser Wilhelm II.* London: Pearson Education Limited, 2000.
Cooper, D. *Talleyrand.* New York: Grove Press, 1932.
Cornwall, Mark. *Last Years of Austria-Hungary: A Multi-National Experiment in Early Twentieth-Century Europe.* 2nd ed. Exeter: University of Exeter Press, 2002.
_____. *The Undermining of Austria-Hungary: The Battle for Hearts and Minds.* New York: St. Martin's Press, 2000.
Corti, Egon Caesar. *Elizabeth, Empress of Austria.* New Haven, CT: Yale University Press, 1936.
_____. *Mensch und Herrscher: Wege und Schicksale Kaiser Franz Joseph I, zwischen Thronbesteigung und Berliner Kongress.* Graz: Verlag Styria, 1952.
_____, and Hans Sokol. *Franz Joseph.* Graz: Verlag Styria, 1960.
Crankshaw, Edward. *The Fall of the House of Habsburg.* New York: Viking Penguin, 1963.
Cunliffe-Owen, Marguerite. *Keystone of Empire: Francis Joseph of Austria.* New York: Harper & Row, 1903.
De Burgh, Edward Morgan Alborough. *Elizabeth, Empress of Austria: A Memoir.* London: Hutchinson, 1899.
Deneberg, Barry. *The Princess Bride.* New York: Scholastic, 2004.
Duiker, William J., and Jackson J. Spielvogel. *The Essential World History: Since 1500* Boston: Wadsworth, Cengage Learning, 2012.
Editors of Time-Life Books. *What Life Was Like at Empire's End: Austro-Hungarian Empire AD 1848-1918.* Alexandria, VA: Time-Life Books, 2000.
Eisen, Cliff, and Simon P. Keefe, eds. *The Cambridge Mozart Encyclopedia.* New York: Cambridge University Press, 2006.
Erickson, Raymond. *Shubert's Vienna.* New Haven: Yale University Press, 1997.
Evans, R.J.W. *The Making of the Habsburg Monarchy, 1550-1700: The Interpretation.* Oxford: Clarendon, 1979.
Ewen, David. *Wine, Women And Waltz: A Romantic Biography of Johann Strauss, Son And Father.* London: Kessinger, 2008.
Freifeld, Alice. *Nationalism and the Crowd in Liberated Hungary: 1848-1914.* Baltimore: Johns Hopkins University, 2000.
Fremont-Barnes, Gregory. *Encyclopedia of the Age of Political Revolutions and New Ideologies, 1760-1815.* Westport, CT: Greenwood, 2007.
Frucht, Richard C. *Eastern Europe: An Introduction to the People, Lands, & Culture,* vol. 1. Santa Barbara, CA: ABC-CLIO, 2004.
Gahl, Hans. *Johannes Brahms.* New York: Seven House, 1963.
Giffard, Philippe Valentin. *Otto of Bavaria: Maximilian II of Bavaria, Marie of Prussia, Ludwig II.* London: Tort, 2012.
Good, David F. *The Economic Rise of the Habsburg Empire, 1750-1914.* Berkeley: University of California Press, 1984.
Gordon, Lyndall. *Vindication: A Life of Mary Wollstonecraft.* New York: HarperCollins, 2005.
Größing, Sigrid-Maria. *Sisi und ihre Familie.* Vienna: Ueberreuter Carl, 2005.
Guerard, Albert Leon. *Five Masters of French Romance: Anatol France, Pierre Loti, Paul Bourget, Maurice Barres, Romain Roland.* New York: Charles Scribner's Sons, 1916.
Habsburg, Rudolf von. *Majestät, ich warne Sie: Geheime und privat Schrifen.* Ed. Brigitte Hamann. Vienna: Amaltheas, 1979.

Hadden, Briton, and Henry R. Luce, *Time*, vol. 29, part 1, 1937.
Hamann, Brigitte. *The Reluctant Empress*. Berlin: Ullstein, 1998.
Harding, Bertita. *Golden Fleece: The Story of Franz Joseph & Elisabeth of Austria*. New York: Bobbs-Merrill, 1937.
Hartig, Franz Paula. *Genesis or Details of the Late Austrian Revolution*. Charleston, SC: Nabu Press, 2010.
Haslip, Joan. *The Crown of Mexico: Maximilian and Empress Carlota*. New York: Avon, 1973.
_____. *The Emperor and the Actress*. New York: The Dial Press, 1982.
_____. *The Lonely Empress*. Cleveland: World, 1965.
Helmireich, Paul C. Rev. of Roderic Davison, *From Paris to Sevres: The Partition of the Ottoman Empire at the Peace Conference of 1919–1920. Slavic Review*, 34. no. 1, March 1975.
Hingley, Ronald. *The Tsars: 1533–1917*. New York: Macmillan, 1968.
Hobsbawm, Eric. *The Age of Empire: 1875–1914*. New York: Random House, 1987.
Hodge, Carl Cavanagh, ed. *Encyclopedia of the Age of Imperialism, 1800–1914*. Westport, CT: Greenwood, 2007.
Horne, Alistair. *How Far from Austerlitz: Napoleon 1805–1815*. New York: St. Martin's Press. 1996.
Hotchner, A. E. *Papa Hemingway: A Personal Memoir*. Cambridge, MA: Da Capo Press, 2004.
Ingrao, Charles W. *The Habsburg Monarchy, 1618–1815*. New York: Cambridge University Press, 2000.
Jacob, H.E. *Johann Strauss — Father and Son — A Century of Light Music*. New York: Greystone Press, 1939.
Johnston, William M. *The Austrian Mind: An Intellectual and Social History*. Berkeley: University of California Press, 1972.
Kann, Robert A. *The Habsburg Empire 1526–1918*. Berkeley: University of California Press, 1974.
Ketterl, Eugen, and Cissy Klastersky. *The Emperor Francis Joseph I: An Intimate Study*. Trans. M. Ostheide. Boston: Stratford, 1929.
Klastersky, Cissy. *Der Alte Kaiser wie nur Einer ihn sah. Der wahrheitsgetreue Bericht seines Leibkammerdieners Eugen Ketterl*. Wien: Gerold & Co., Universitäts-Buchhandlung, 1929.
King, David. *How The Conquerors of Napoleon Made Love, War, and Peace at the Congress of Vienna*. New York: Random House, 2008.
Kohlberg, Ottila Regina. *The Policy of Prince Metternich at the Congress of Vienna*. Charleston, SC: Nabu Press, 2010.
Kohn, Hans. "Reflections on Austrian History." *Austrian History Yearbook* 1 (1965): pp 4–22.
Komlos, John. *The Habsburg Monarchy as a Customs Union, Economic Development in Austria-Hungary in the Nineteenth Century*. New York: Guilford, 1983.
Kugler, Georg. *Elisabeth, Empress of Austria — Queen of Hungary*. Graz: Bonechi Verlag Styria, 1999.
Langer, Anton. *Dies Buch gehört der Kaiserin. Eine Volksstimme aus Österreich*. Vienna: Österreichischen Akademie der Wissenschaften, 1854.
Lehman, H. Eugene. *Lives of England's Monarchs*. Chapel Hill: University of North Caroline Press, 2004.
Levetus, A.S. *Imperial Vienna*. London: John Lane, 1905.
Lord, John. *Beacon Lights of History*, vol. 9. FQ ebooks, 2010.

Ludwig, Emil, and Ethel Colburn Mayne. *Wilhelm Hohenzollern, the Last of the Kaisers.* New York: G.P. Putnam's Sons, 1927.
MacArtney, Carlile Aylmer. *The Habsburg Empire 1790–1918.* New York: Macmillan, 1969.
_____. *The Social Revolution in Austria.* Cambridge: Cambridge University Press, 1926.
MacIntosh, Christopher. *The Swan King: Ludwig II.* New York: Palgrave Macmillan, 2003.
Marek, George Richard. *The Eagles Die: Franz Joseph, Elisabeth, and Their Austria.* New York: Harper & Row, 1974.
Margutti, Albert Alexander Vinzenz. *The Emperor Francis Joseph & His Times.* Charleston, SC: Nabu Press, 2010.
_____. *The Emperor Franz Joseph and His Times.* New York: G. H. Doran, 1922.
Meakes, Daryl. *Drunkcow Landmines.* West Conshohoken, PA: Infinity, 2004.
Metternich, Klemens von. *Memoirs of Prince Metternich,* vol. II. Trans. Gerald W. Smith. New York: Howard Fertig, 1970.
Montagu, Lady Mary Wortley. *Selected Letters.* New York: Penguin, 1997.
Murad, Anatol. *Franz Joseph I of Austria and His Empire.* New York: Twayne, 1968.
The New York Times. January 12, 1918.
Nicolson, Harold Sir. *The Congress of Vienna: A Study in Allied Unity: 1812–1822.* New York: Harcourt, Brace, 1946.
Olender, Piotr. *Russo-Japanese Naval War, 1905,* vol. 1. Sandomierz: Stratus, 2009–2010.
Page, Brigette H. *Elisabeth: Kaiserin wider Willen.* Munchen: Serie Piper, 1982.
Pflanze, Otto. *Bismarck and the Development of Germany: The Period of Unification 1815–1871.* Princeton: Princeton University Press, 1971.
Rath, R. John. *The Viennese Revolution of 1848.* Austin: University of Texas Press, 1957.
Redlich, Joseph. *Emperor Francis Joseph of Austria: A Biography.* New York: Macmillan, 1929.
Ridley, Jasper. *Maximilian and Juárez.* New York: Ticknor & Fields, 1992.
Robinson, James Harvey. *Readings in Modern European History: A Collection of Extracts from the Sources Chosen with the Purpose of Illustrating Some of the Chief Phases of the Last Two Hundred Years,* vol. 1. Boston: Ginn & Company, 1908–09.
Rohl, John C. G. *Wilhelm II: The Kaiser's Personal Monarchy, 1888–1900.* Trans. Sheila de Bellaigue. New York: Cambridge University Press, 2004.
Rothenberg, Gunther. *The Army of Francis Joseph.* West Lafayette, IN: Perdue University Press, 1976.
Sadie, Stanley, *Mozart: The Early Years 1756–1781.* New York: W.W. Norton, 2006.
Schonberg, Harold C. *The Lives of Great Composers.* New York: W.W. Norton, 1997.
Schreiber, Hermann. *Life Story of Painter Hans Makart.* Zurich: Diana-Verlag, 1990.
Seligmann, Matthew, and Roderick R. McLean. *Germany from Reich to Republic: 1871–1918: Politics, Hierarchy and Elites.* New York: St. Martin's Press, 2000.
Shaw, Karl. *Royal Babylon: The Alarming History of European Royalty.* New York: Random House, 1999.
Sinclair, Andrew. *Death by Fame: A Life of Elisabeth Empress of Austria.* New York: St. Martin's Press, 1998.
Sisa, Stephen. *The Spirit of Hungry: A Panorama of Hungarian History and Culture.* Toronto: The Rakoczi Foundation, 1995.
Sked, Alan. *The Decline and Fall of the Habsburg Empire 1815–1918.* White Plains, NY: Longman, 2001.
Steinberg, Jonathan. *Bismarck: A Life.* New York: University of Oxford Press, 2011.
Steinberg, Mark D, and Vladimir M. Khrustalev. *The Fall of the Romanovs: Political*

Dreams and Personal Struggles in a Time of Revolution. New Haven: Yale University Press, 1995.
Sztaray, Irma Countess. *Aus den letzten Jahren der Kaiserin Elisabeth*. Wein: A. Holzhausen. 1909.
Talleyrand-Perigord, Charles Maurice. *Memoirs of the Prince de Talleyrand*, vols. I-III. Ed. Duc de Broglie. Trans. Rapheal de Beaufort. New York: G.P. Putnam, 1895.
Tanner, M. *The Last Descendant of Aeneas: The Habsburgs and the Mythic*. New Haven: Yale University Press, 1993.
Taylor, A. J. P. *The Habsburg Monarchy, 1809–1918: A History of the Austrian Empire and Austria Hungary*. Chicago: University of Chicago Press, 1976.
Taylor, Edmond. *The Fall of Dynasties: The Collapse of the Old Order 1905–1922*. Charleston, SC: Nabu Press, 2011.
Theirs, Adolphe, and D. Forbes Campbell *History of the Consulate and the Empire of France under Napoleon*, vol. 9–10. London: Henry Colburn, 1845. University of California Libraries, 1845.
Tschudi, Clara, and E. M. Cope. *Elizabeth, Empress of Austria and Queen of Hungary*. New York: E.P. Dutton, 1901.
Tschuppik, Karl. *The Empress of Austria*. London: Brentanos, 1930.
Unowsky, Daniel. *The Pomp & Politics of Patriotism: Imperial Celebrations in Habsburg*. West Lafayette, IN: Perdue University Press, 2005.
Unterreiner, Katrin. *Sisi—Myths and Truths*. Zurich: Bucher, 2010.
Valiani, Leo. *The End of Austria-Hungary*. London: Martin Secker & Warburg, 1973.
Van der Kiste, John. *Emperor Francis Joseph: Life, Death and the Fall of the Habsburg Empire*. Stroud: Sutton, 2005.
Vehse, Carl Eduard. *Memoirs of the Court, Aristocracy, and Diplomacy of Austria*, vol. 2. Trans. Franz K. Demmler. London: Longman, Brown, Green & Longmans, 1856.
von Maerker-Branden, Marie Louise, and Elsa Wallersee-Larisch. *Secrets of a Royal House*. London: J. Long, 1936.
von Wallersee-Larisch, Marie Louis. *Kaiserin Elisabeth und ich*. Paderborn, Germany: Salzwasser Verlag, 1933.
Wank, Solomon. "The Habsburg Empire." *After Empire. Multiethnic Societies and Nation Building. The Soviet Union and the Russian, Ottoman, and Habsburg Empires*. Eds. Karen Barkey and Mark von Hagen. Boulder, CO: Westview Press, 1997.
Webster, C. K. *The Congress of Vienna*. London: University of Oxford Press, 1973.
Wheatcroft, A. *The Habsburgs*. New York: Penguin, 1999.
Willis, Edward F. *Prince Lichnowsky, Ambassador of Peace: A Study of Prewar Diplomacy 1912–1914*. London: Kessinger, 2007.

Index

Age of Enlightenment 25
Alexander I (Czar) 27
Andrássy, Gyula 97, 119–121, 123–124, 126, 143, 176
anorexia nervosa 146
Austro-Hungarian Compromise of 1848 120
Austro-Hungarian Compromise of 1867 37, 97, 117, 126
Austro-Prussian War 36, 83

Bad Ischl 45, 53, 58, 67, 70, 71, 74, 102, 145, 155
Battle of Austerlitz 16
Battle of Santa Lucia 31, 175
Battle of Waterloo 22, 51
Biedermeier 51
Bismarck, Otto von (Chancellor) 2, 34–37, 168, 176
Black Hand 158–159
bulimia 146–147

Charlemagne (Emperor) 3, 5, 21, 164
Charles II (King) 15
Charles V (Emperor) 11
Charles VI (Emperor) 17
Charles VII Albert (Emperor) 12
Chotkova, Sophie Chotek von (Archduchess) 100, 102, 115, 159–160
Concordat of 1855 54
Confederation of the Rhine 22
Congress of Vienna 20, 24–27, 129
Crimean War 76, 129, 139, 158, 175

Danish War of 1864 36
Deák, Ferenc 119–121
Diet of Worms 24
d'Orléans, Henri (Duke) 150

Ebert, Friedrich (President) 169
Elizabeth (Queen) 7

Eugene (Prince de Ligne) 26
Eugénie (Empress) 144

Falk, Max 118, 119
Felix of Schwarzenberg (Prince) 33, 34, 48
Ferdinand I (Emperor) 8, 10, 14, 21, 28–32, 34, 47, 50, 175
Ferdinand II (Archduke/Emperor) 14, 83, 93
Ferdinand Maximilian (Archduke) 41, 42, 45, 176
Francis I (Emperor) 7, 22, 24, 28, 40, 41, 44, 54, 68, 175
Francis II (Emperor) 21, 22
Francis Stephen (Emperor) 68
Franz Ferdinand (Emperor) 10, 31, 99, 100, 156–158, 160–161, 171, 176
Franz Karl (Archduke) 31, 40, 42
Frederick I (Burgrave) 7
Frederick Wilhelm IV (King) 34
French Revolution 18, 21, 25, 29
Friedrich Wilhelm III (King) 27

German Confederation 22, 26, 27, 34, 36, 176
German Revolution 169
Gisela (Archduchess) 84, 85, 92, 95, 136, 153, 174–175
Grunne, Karl 34

Heine, Heinrich 2
Holy Alliance 27
Holy Roman Empire 9, 10, 12, 21
House of Habsburg-Lorraine 15
House of Rothschild 153
House of Wittelsbach 40, 57

imperialism 1, 2

Joseph II (Emperor) 14, 15, 31, 48, 54

191

Karl Ludwig (Archduke) 42, 45, 70, 90, 99, 111
Karl Theodor (Duke) 62
Ketterl, Eugen 52, 53, 114, 157, 164
Kossuth, Franz 111
Kossuth, Lajos (Regent-President) 32, 55, 124

Larisch, Marie (Countess) 63
Libenyi, Johann 55
liberalism 1, 9, 18
"Lieutenant Red Legs" 48
Louis XVI (King) 23, 25, 68
Louis XVIII (King) 23-25
Louise of Coburg (Princess) 85
Lucheni, Luigi 150-151
Ludovika (Princess) see Marie Ludovika (Princess)
Ludwig II (Crown Prince) 41, 59, 62-66, 69, 90, 176
Ludwig Viktor (Archduke) 42

Makart, Hans 17, 18
Maria Theresa (Empress) 14, 15, 49, 68, 69, 77, 84, 101, 124, 126
Marie Antoinette (Queen) 25
Marie Ludovika (Princess) 40, 58, 69-74, 80
Marie Valerie (Archduchess) 61, 62, 88, 90, 92-95, 97, 136, 139-140, 142-143, 147, 153, 155, 160
Maximilian (Prince) 168-169
Maximilian II (King) 64
Maximilian Joseph (Duke) 40, 56-57, 59, 62, 64, 73-74
Mayerling 94, 97, 99, 101
Metternich, Klemens von (Prince) 2, 6, 22-24, 26-30, 32-33, 43, 45, 175
Metternich, Melanie von (Princess) 6
Montagu, Lady Mary Wortley 11

Napoleon III (Emperor) 42
Napoleon Bonaparte (Emperor) 2, 15-17, 21, 23-28, 51, 116
Napoleonic Wars 23, 26
nationalism 1, 9, 18, 19
neurasthenia 138
Nicholas I (Czar) 33, 74, 130
Nicholas II (Czar) 158, 166-167
North German Confederation 22

Osman I (Sultan) 7
Osmanlt Hanedant 7
Ottoman Empire 7, 74, 129, 170

Palmer, Alan 47, 100
Princip, Gavrilo 156, 159

Revolutions of 1848 8-10, 18, 29-32, 37, 38, 55, 78, 83, 116
Roman Catholic Church 12, 41
Roosevelt, Theodore (President) 53
Rothschild, Julie (Baroness) 150
Rothschild, Mayer Amschel 7
Rudolf (Crown Prince) 10, 85-91, 94-98, 108, 136, 141, 148-149, 174-176
Rudolph I (King) 10
Russian Revolution 7, 167
Russo-Japanese War 166-167

Sarajevo 158-159, 163, 176
Schönbrunn Palace 3, 9, 14-17, 39, 43, 45, 51, 52, 75, 77, 81, 101, 144-145, 150, 157, 164, 171, 174
Schratt, Katharina 47, 102-112, 152, 157-158, 164, 174
Sked, Alan 8, 123
Smythers, Ruth 79, 81
Sophie (Archduchess) 5, 6, 8, 9, 11, 29-31, 39, 41, 43, 44, 46, 47, 55, 56, 69-73, 75-77, 80, 82-86, 88, 117, 126, 130, 135-137, 140, 142, 153
Sophie Charlotte (Duchess) 63, 64
Stephanie (Princess) 89-91, 94-95, 174, 176

Talleyrand, Charles Maurice de (Foreign Minister) 24-26, 28
Treaty of Paris (1814) 23
Treaty of Paris (1815) 24
Treaty of Paris (1856) 175
Treaty of Versailles 20, 169
Treaty of Vienna 17
Tschuppik, Karl 119

Valeria 127
Vetsera, Maria (Baroness) 92, 94, 96, 97
Victoria (Queen) 47, 55, 168
Vienna Exposition (1873) 84
Viribus Unitis 2

Wagner, Richard 63-65
Wiemar Republic 169
Wilhelm I (King) 34, 35, 37
Wilhelm II (Kaiser) 7, 37, 50, 169, 171, 176
Wilhelm Karl (Prince) 58
Wilson, Woodrow (President) 169
World War I 7, 32, 84, 128, 130, 165, 166, 168-174, 177
World War II 108

www.ingramcontent.com/pod-product-compliance
Lightning Source LLC
Chambersburg PA
CBHW020837020526
44114CB00040B/1240